International Business Finance

International Business Finance introduces students to the fundamental workings of business and finance in the global economy. The text brings clarity and focus to the complexities of the field, and demonstrates the key linkages between the foreign exchange markets and world money markets.

Core topics examined include:

- corporate aspects of international finance, with special attention given to contractual and operational hedging techniques
- the mechanics of the foreign exchange markets
- the building blocks of international finance
- the optimal portfolio in an international setting.

International Business Finance also contains:

- up-to-date statistics from across the globe
- relevant international case studies
- problem sets and solutions
- links to an online PowerPoint presentation at http://www.routledge.com/textbooks/9780415701532/.

International Business Finance is an engaging and stimulating text for students in undergraduate and MBA courses in International Finance and a key resource for lecturers.

Michael B. Connolly is Professor of Economics at the University of Miami, USA and Professor of Finance at Hunan University, China.

International Business Finance

Michael B. Connolly

Routledge
Taylor & Francis Group

NEW YORK AND LONDON

First published 2007
by Routledge
270 Madison Ave, New York NY 10016

Simultaneously published in the UK
by Routledge
2 Park Square, Milton Park, Abingdon, Oxon OX14 4RN

Routledge is an imprint of the Taylor & Francis Group, an informa business

© 2007 Michael B. Connolly

Typeset in Perpetua and Bell Gothic by
Florence Production Ltd, Stoodleigh, Devon
Printed and bound in Great Britain by
TJ International Ltd, Padstow, Cornwall

British Library Cataloguing in Publication Data
A catalogue record for this book is available from the British Library

Library of Congress Cataloging in Publication Data
Connolly, Michael B. (Michael Bahaamonde), 1941–
    International business finance / Michael B. Connolly.
        p. cm.
    Includes bibliographical references and index.
    1. International finance.   2. International business
    enterprises—Finance.   I. Title.
    HG3881.C668 2006
    332′.042—dc22   2006014542

ISBN10: 0–415–70152–X (hbk)
ISBN10: 0–415–70153–8 (pbk)
ISBN10: 0–203–79932–1 (ebk)

ISBN13: 978–0–415–70152–5 (hbk)
ISBN13: 978–0–415–70153–2 (pbk)
ISBN13: 978–0–203–79932–1 (ebk)

This volume is dedicated to my family—
Annick, Michelle, Ken, Catherine, and Tristan

Contents

Figures

Tables

Preface

This volume seeks to provide a basic working knowledge of international business finance. Corporate aspects of international finance are analyzed, especially hedging techniques. It also aims to help readers understand how managers of international corporations do or should behave and examines the mechanics of the foreign exchange market, reviewing spot, forwards, futures, and options—the main tools used to hedge exchange rate risk. The book also constructs the building blocks of international finance: (1) interest rate parity, (2) purchasing power parity, and (3) the international Fisher equation. It then turns to international management issues, international financial scams, and the Sarbanes-Oxley Act of 2002, which attempts to address them. Finally, the book lays out the optimal portfolio model in an international setting based upon an investor's degree of risk aversion and the reward–risk ratio.

For those new to international finance, I strongly recommend a reference book for terminology: John Downes and Jordan Elliot Goodman, *Dictionary of Finance and Investment Terms*, seventh edition, Barron's Financial Guides, Barron's Educational Series, 2006.

I have kept explanations to a minimum. More important is the understanding of the concepts rather than their derivations or lengthy elaboration. Over the years, I have developed these materials for my MBA and Executive MBA students in international finance at the University of Miami, and have been honored by several prizes for excellence in teaching at Miami. My students in international finance at Duke University kindly provided suggestions on the final version of the manuscript.

Originally from Longford, Ireland, I started work as a newspaper boy in Phoenix, Arizona, where I learned the concept of credit risk when collecting accounts receivable. Each delivery boy was his own independent operator, buying newspapers from the *Phoenix Gazette* and selling them to subscribers—something not understood by the subscriber on my route who had an especially high rate of default. At UC Berkeley as an undergraduate, I worked in restaurants and the library. At the University of Chicago, I benefited from a scholarship to the Ph.D. program in economics where I had the great fortune of having Nobel Laureate Robert Mundell as my Ph.D. thesis advisor. Upon graduation, I held teaching positions at Harvard University, at the University of Florida, in South Carolina, and at Columbia University. I now teach and advise on international business at the University of Miami and at Hunan University, Changsha, China. I also do economic impact reports for projects such as Rivertown, a condominium complex in Miami, the Miami Performing Arts Center, the School of Medicine of the University of Miami, and The Miami Partnership, a civic center revitalization project. The latter applies net present value calculations—the time value of money, using the cost of borrowing of Miami-Dade County. As a consultant to UBS Warburg, I had the opportunity to work with Michael Gavin, Managing Director, on the underwriting of sovereign debt in emerging markets in 2002 and 2003. It has also been a privilege to teach courses in Cameroon and the Ivory Coast, Africa, in Paris at the Université de Paris-Dauphine, at the Université d'Auvergne, France, in Mexico at ITAM, Mexico City, in Costa Rica, Peru, and at IDEM, Uruguay, in Latin America. As a consultant, I participated in World Bank finance and trade missions to Mongolia, Uzbekistan, Ecuador, Peru, Cameroon, Kenya, Malawi, and Sénégal.

In recent years, I have been teaching finance and trade at Hunan University, China, as well as doing joint research with colleagues there. It is exciting to take part in China's movement toward free markets and the development of financial markets for risk management, hedging, and trading. Futures markets in petroleum were only opened in March 2005, and there are still neither deliverable forwards in the yuan nor in foreign exchange, such as the US dollar. In 2006, foreign banks and companies may have full ownership of local operations. Capital transfers still require approval of SAFE, the State Administered Foreign Exchange System, which approved the failed $18.5 billion CNOOC Ltd offer for UNOCAL. The Chinese government is encouraging direct foreign investment and acquisitions, making available the foreign exchange necessary for these investments.

My colleague in the finance department at the University of Miami, Tie Su, made especially helpful comments and suggestions that significantly improved the exposition. Discussions with Adam Swartz of the University of Mississippi clarified my thinking on a number of topics. My greatest debt of gratitude is to Robert Z. Aliber of the Graduate School of Business, University of Chicago, and to Ed Tower, Duke University, who made significant, detailed suggestions on the content and focus of the volume. Robert Langham, the Economics and Finance Editor of Taylor and Francis Books plc, London, shepherded the project through its various stages, suggesting additional coverage. Emma Rasiel, Duke University, helped out on bid–ask spread-corrected interest rate parity, and on margin requirements. Alexandre Moltchanov provided able research assistance.

The plan of the book is as follows:

Chapter 1 introduces the topic of international finance by highlighting its main characteristics, in particular currency risk and conversion.

Chapter 2 begins with the history of international finance and monies, stressing the importance of money as a medium of exchange, a store of value, and a unit of account. Bills of exchange are identified as the source of the first financial securities in foreign currency and the origin of the stock exchanges.

Chapter 3 concerns the exchange rate. The foreign exchange market is analyzed, including spot, future, forward, options, and swap markets in foreign exchange. The basic building block for forecasting future exchange rates—interest rate parity—is illustrated as a no-profit arbitrage condition. The bid–ask spread—the difference between the ask and the bid price of foreign exchange dealers— represents the currency dealers' profits, in addition to any commission paid, and as a transaction cost in currency conversion for the firm. Unanticipated foreign exchange risk involves the risk that a subsequent spot rate will deviate from its current forward level. Forwards and foreign exchange swaps are analyzed and laid out as a particularly useful way of hedging long-term and operational commitments in foreign exchange.

Chapter 4 deals with the hedging of foreign exchange risk by the firm. To hedge or not is the first issue addressed, then hedging techniques. If a firm or an individual has a "long" position in say euros, foreign exchange risk is said to be hedged or guarded against by acquiring an equal and opposite "short" position in euros. A simple hedge of a million euros of accounts receivable in 90 days could involve the sale of one million euros forward for delivery in 90 days. The firm would no longer be subject to foreign exchange risk: neither unanticipated gains if the euro rises relative to the forward price in dollars or pounds, nor unanticipated losses if the euro declines relative to the forward rate. Chapter 4 also covers contractual hedges: futures, forwards, money market hedges, and options, as well as operational, accounting, and transactional hedging by the international business.

Chapter 5 deals with international financial management issues that confront the multinational firm: transfer pricing, working capital management, international taxation, offshore banking, and international mergers and acquisitions. In addition, the currency conversion of free-cash flows in an international business plan is covered in detail.

Chapter 6 covers financial scams and swindles, including pyramid schemes, insider trading, accounting malfeasance, and other scams that have surged worldwide in recent years. Partly, the problem seems to be old-fashioned greed, but another culprit seems to be the linking of bonus and options compensation with reported earnings, not necessarily actual earnings.

Problem sets are also provided at the end of Chapters 3, 4, and 5 to give the reader confidence in problem-solving with numerical and conceptual analysis, and answers to these sets and an index close the book.

When I was a graduate student at the University of Chicago, the Black-Scholes model for the valuation of options was not yet published, Robert Merton had not done his seminal work in continuous finance, and John Hull had not yet completed his classic reference on forwards and futures. I did benefit from Robert Mundell's courses in international money and open-economy macroeconomics while at Chicago. At Harvard, I published in international finance with Stephen Ross of MIT, who went on to establish his mark in agency and options theory. Finally, I am pleased to acknowledge financial support from Project 985, Hunan University, for this project. I hope you enjoy this little volume. My students do and I had fun writing it.

Michael Connolly
School of Business Administration,
University of Miami, Florida

College of Finance, Hunan University,
Changsha, People's Republic of China

Editor, *The Journal of Economic Policy Reform*

Abbreviations

ADR	American depositary receipt
AMEX	American Stock Exchange
APA	advanced pricing agreement
BFC	British Finance Centre
BIS	Bank for International Settlements
BSCH	Banco Santander Central Hispano
CAD	covered arbitrage differential
CAOC	China Aviation Oil Corporation
CAOHC	China Aviation Oil Holding Company
CHIPS	Clearing House Interbank Payments System
CSFB	Crédit Suisse First Boston
DJIA	Dow Jones Industrial Average
EDGAR	Electronic Data Gathering and Retrieval
FASB	Financial Accounting Standards Board
FATF	Financial Action Task Force
FCPA	Foreign Corrupt Practices Act
FED	Federal Reserve System
Footsie	Financial Times Stock Exchange
FOREX	foreign exchange
FSC	foreign sales corporation
GAAP	generally accepted accounting practice
GATT	General Agreement on Tariffs and Trade
GKOs	*Gosydarstvennye Kratkosrochnye Obligatsii*
HLI	highly leveraged institution
IAS	international accounting standard
IBC	international business corporation
IFOC	international financial offshore center
IMF	International Monetary Fund
IPO	initial public offer
IRR	internal rate of return

IRS	Internal Revenue Service
L/C	letter of credit
LSE	London Stock Exchange
LTCM	Long Term Capital Management
MEI	marginal efficiency of investment
MIGA	Multilateral Investment Guarantee Association
NASDAQ	National Association of Securities Dealers Automated Quotations
NCCTs	Non-Cooperative Countries and Territories
NDF	non-deliverable future
NPV	net present value
NYSE	New York Stock Exchange
OECD	Organization for Economic Cooperation and Development
OFC	offshore financial center
OTC	over-the-counter
PPP	purchasing power parity
RER	real effective exchange rate index
RIC	Reuters Instrument Code
S&P	Standard & Poor's
SASAC	State Asset Supervision and Administration Commission
SEC	Securities and Exchange Commission
SIMEX	Singapore International Monetary Exchange
SOES	Small Order Execution System
SOX	Sarbanes-Oxley Act
SSE	Shanghai Stock Exchange
SWIFT	Society for Worldwide Interbank Financial Telecommunications
T-bill	Treasury bill
UAL	United Airlines Corporation
UNCAC	UN Convention Against Corruption
USD	US dollars
WACC	weighted average cost of capital
WTO	World Trade Organization

Chapter 1

Introduction to international finance

FEATURES OF INTERNATIONAL FINANCE

In what sense does international finance differ from finance? In fact, there are many.

Currencies

The key distinction between international finance and finance is the exchange rate issue. Issues of valuation, uncertainty about the future exchange rate, and its convertibility and transactions costs, lead to market segmentation. Consider the important decision to make a foreign acquisition. To value the foreign firm, it is customary to work up an income statement forecasting free-cash flow over the next five years, then compute a terminal resale value of the acquisition. When the forecast is in terms of a foreign currency, say the euro, the forward cash flows must then be converted to the home currency, say the dollar or the pound. This task is easy enough using forward rates for the euro up to two years and interest rate parity to forecast the exchange rate for years three to five. The corresponding conversion of free-cash flows is now in dollars for each year, ready to be discounted by the firm's weighted average cost of capital in dollars. If the net present value is positive and higher than alternative investments, the firm may decide to undertake the acquisition. In doing so, the firm is faced with foreign exchange risk due to unexpected deviations from forecasted exchange rates. This exchange risk takes different forms: transactions risk associated with a specific transaction in foreign exchange; operational risk associated with ongoing operations in the foreign currency; and translation risk associated with the accounting requirements of FASB 52 (Financial Accounting Standards Board). In addition, reporting requirements are in local currency to the Internal Revenue Service or Inland Revenue. In order to hedge exchange risk, there are contractual, operational, and financial hedges, but these add to the costs of risk management of the firm. If done selectively, hedging incurs costs, but may increase the net present value of the firm by lowering borrowing costs and risks of financial distress.

1

Accounting rules

Another important consideration is the issue of different accounting rules and practices. In the United States, the generally accepted accounting practice (the GAAP) is used and sanctioned by the FASB. Overseas, the standard practice is the international accounting standard (IAS), which depends more on concept and principle than on practice. Ford Motor Co., for example, initially bid $6.9 billion for the acquisition of the insolvent and bankrupt Daewoo Motor Corp. of Korea, but withdrew its bid when its accountants and analysts converted Daewoo's books to the GAAP. The conversion revealed larger debt and commitments made by the Korean chaebol. Among the accounting irregularities reported were:

- A shell company in London, British Finance Centre (BFC), which conducted bogus import–export transactions to transfer $2.6 billion and divert an additional $1.5 billion from car exports to the London slush fund for "lobbying" in Korea and elsewhere. According to *Business Week*, a former Daewoo executive is quoted as saying: "Chairman Kim carried with him bundles of money to lobby for projects in emerging markets" (February 19, 2001: 51).
- To book profits at a failed Ukrainian plant, Daewoo Motor tore down fully assembled cars, and shipped them to the Ukraine plant for reassembly and sale.
- Daewoo Heavy Industry sold assets to Daewoo Motor at inflated prices, thus booking a profit in 1997. It actually posted a loss of $670 million that year.
- Daewoo Electronics borrowed nearly $1 billion from financial institutions by concealing that losses had wiped out shareholders' equity.

Kim Woo Choong, the founder of Korea's Daewoo Group, was a fugitive from justice from charges of fraud and embezzlement for five years, but returned to Seoul, Korea in June 2005 to face the charges. Kim Tae Gou, former Daewoo Motor chairman, and six other top officers of the Daewoo Group are currently under arrest (*Business Week*, 2001).

In general, reporting and disclosure requirements are higher in the United States, England, and continental Europe than elsewhere, particularly when compared to emerging markets. European accounting traditions are solidly grounded conceptually.

Stakeholders

A related issue is more philosophical; the US firm typically owes its allegiance to its owners, the shareholders. In Europe and elsewhere the firm may have different constituents or stakeholders: the shareholders, management, the government, its unions, and its customers. In the case of Daewoo Motor, militant unions were seeking back pay with no layoffs, making its acquisition by Ford more troublesome. Airbus is a majority government consortium that has not needed to rely upon shareholder monitoring and financing, although it issued an IPO in 2002 under the name EADS for financing the 600-passenger jumbo jet A380, which flew in prototype in the summer of 2005. It is not clear that EADS would be able to finance the jumbo jet without implicit guarantees by the governments and research and development subsidies.

Legal framework

A number of countries observe Napoleonic rather than Common Law, deriving from the Napoleonic codes that govern business law there. Spain also implanted the Napoleonic codes in most of Latin America. In Islamic countries, interest is prohibited by the Koran, so financial institutions must arrange for profit-sharing with its depositors-owners. As an amendment to the US Securities Act of 1934, the Foreign Corrupt Practices Act of 1977 (FCPA 1977) prohibits making payments to foreign officials for the purpose of securing contracts or licenses, influencing decisions, evading regulations and law, and obtaining business, retaining business, or directing business to any person. If a director, officer, or shareholder of the firm either knows or should know that a payment is being made as a bribe or kickback to favorably influence a decision, it is illegal and subject to civil penalties up to $100,000 and imprisonment for not more than five years, or both. There is an exception for routine governmental action "to expedite or to secure the performance of a routine governmental action by a foreign official." This is known as "grease money," which is not prohibited unless it is so by the local laws. If a grease payment is not large and is made to expedite governmental action to grant a license to operate a bank that is granted to everyone qualifying for a bank license, there may be no problem. If the payments are made simply to expedite the request, they are not illegal under FCPA 1977. If the official has some discretion, and few applicants are approved, the payment would be illegal. The Organization for Economic Cooperation and Development (OECD) established in February 1999 a Convention Against Bribery of Foreign Public Officials in International Business. The Convention makes it a crime to offer, promise, or give a bribe to a foreign public official in order to obtain or retain international business deals. In addition, The UN Convention Against Corruption (UNCAC) is an international treaty that has been signed by 113 countries since its launching in December 2003.

In Paraguay, there is a professional known as a "dispachador de aduana" (customs dispatcher), who is hired to make grease payments to customs inspectors on a routine basis. The use of a customs dispatcher to clear goods through customs would be permitted, but not to secure a unique license to import a certain good. In an anonymous interview, a customs dispatcher is quoted as saying: "To clear a shipment through Paraguayan customs, there are 15 hands in the customs office stretched out for money to facilitate the clearance procedures."

Institutional framework

There is no question that corruption exists everywhere to some degree. Klepto-cracies misappropriate profits and wealth, thereby discouraging enterprise and thrift. Instead, bribery and malfeasance are rewarded. It matters little to have laws against corruption, when it is institutionalized in practice. To combat brib-ery, on November 21, 1997, OECD member countries and five non-member countries, Argentina, Brazil, Bulgaria, Chile, and the Slovak Republic, adopted a Convention on Combating Bribery of Foreign Public Officials in International Business Transactions. The Convention was signed in Paris on December 17, 1997. However, Peter Eigen, Chairman of Transparency International, puts it this way:

> The scale of bribe-paying by international corporations in the developing coun-tries of the world is massive. Actions by the majority of governments of the leading industrial countries to curb international corruption are modest. The results include growing poverty in poor countries, persistent undermining of the institutions of democracy, and mounting distortions in fair international commerce.
>
> (www.transparency.org, January 20, 2001)

The current rage at the International Monetary Fund (IMF), if one is to believe their publication *Finance & Development*: "Taking the offensive against corruption" (IMF, 2000), is the fight against governmental and state enterprise corruption. The IMF's "crusade" is not credible as their history has been one of lending to corrupt governments worldwide, provided they qualify for a loan and agree to IMF conditionality. For example, much of the last standby loan to Russia before their sovereign default is rumored to have been deposited by Russian officials in an offshore bank in Jersey, the Channel Island, which honors banking secrecy and has no income taxes.

"The IMF should learn a lesson from the past five years," the former official, Boris Fyodor, said, referring to the IMF. "The IMF was pretending that it was seeing a lot of reforms in Russia. Russia was pretending to conduct reforms. The Western taxpayer was paying for it" (Gordon, 1998). However:

> The IMF was surprised by last year's discovery that the central bank was linked to an offshore investment company in the Channel Island of Jersey and that

the [Russian central] bank had misreported its asset levels to the fund. The offshore company, Fimaco, was acquired by a subsidiary of the central bank during Gerashchenko's previous tenure as central bank chief, although the Fimaco operations that have drawn the most attention to date fell during the 1994–98 period when he did not head the central bank. [Then US Secretary of the Treasury, Larry] Summers continued his public warnings to Russia on Sunday, repeating the line he took at the opening of a congressional inquiry last week into corruption, money-laundering and the still-unsubstantiated charges that IMF funds had been illegally diverted.

(Sanger, 1999)

Language

Language can be an important obstacle or, alternatively, an advantage in conducting business abroad. Banco Santander Central Hispano of Madrid is now the largest bank in Latin America. It is closely followed by Bilbao Viscaya of Barcelona in size of assets. No doubt the language, cultural similarities, and the use of Napoleonic Law explain in part the comparative advantage of Spanish banks in Latin America. Also, their long banking tradition serves them well in emerging markets.

Taxation

International taxation varies from country to country, ranging from zero corporate income taxes and zero personal income tax in some tax havens to 35 percent in the United States, 36.6 percent in France, 37.5 percent in Japan, and up to 45 percent in Germany. The highest corporate income tax reported by Pricewaterhouse in *Corporate taxes: a worldwide summary* (1999) is Kuwait at 55 percent of taxable income. In the United States, long term capital gains may be taxed at 15 percent, but in France they are taxed at a 26 percent rate. When profits of a US company are repatriated, they are converted into dollars and the US corporate tax rate of up to 35 percent is applied. If the foreign tax rate is lower, say 20 percent, the company receives a tax credit of 20 percent paid to the foreign government, and then pays the remaining 15 percent to the US Treasury. If it pays 55 percent corporate taxes, it will get a full offset up to 35 percent—its marginal tax rate on US earnings—as well as tax credits, possibly deferred or for other branches, on the additional 20 percent.

In some cases, companies are able to transfer profits out of the United States to shell corporations in tax havens to escape taxes by transfer pricing. This is not in principle a legal practice if done solely for the purpose of evading taxes. In other instances, such as with a Foreign Sales Corporation, companies may legally do so under US law. The portion of income exempted varies from 34 percent with arm's length pricing to 74 percent with an advanced pricing agreement.

5

However, tax rates are not applied if the earnings are not repatriated, in which case they remain untaxed. The World Trade Organization (WTO) has ruled that the foreign sales corporation (FSC) law of the United States violates Article VI, *Anti-dumping and countervailing duties*, since the law exempts export earnings of US corporations from corporate taxes, thereby constituting an export subsidy.

Regulatory framework

In the United States, the US Securities and Exchange Commission (SEC) regulates the major exchanges and securities dealers:

> The primary mission of the US Securities and Exchange Commission is to protect investors and maintain the integrity of the securities markets . . . The laws and rules that govern the securities industry in the United States derive from a simple and straightforward concept: all investors, whether large institutions or private individuals, should have access to certain basic facts about an investment prior to buying it. To achieve this, the SEC requires public companies to disclose meaningful financial and other information to the public, which provides a common pool of knowledge for all investors to use to judge for themselves if a company's securities are a good investment. The SEC also oversees other key participants in the securities world . . . Typical infractions include insider trading, accounting fraud, and providing false or misleading information about securities and the companies that issue them . . . The SEC offers the public . . . the EDGAR database of disclosure documents that public companies are required to file with the Commission.
>
> (www.sec.gov, April 30, 2001)

While overseas exchanges, firms, and securities dealers are also subject to scrutiny, in emerging markets many of these are recent and the same disclosure and transparency requirements do not apply. Interestingly, the SEC was created during the great depression (1929–37), precipitated by the October 1929 stock market crash, in which half of the $50 billion in new securities offered during the 1920s became worthless. Purchases on margin represented over 10 percent of the market.

The main purposes of the security and exchange law of 1933 can be reduced to two common-sense notions:

- Companies publicly offering securities for investment dollars must tell the public the truth about their businesses, the securities they are selling, and the risks involved in investing.
- People who sell and trade securities—brokers, dealers, and exchanges—must treat investors fairly and honestly, putting investors' interests first.

(www.sec.gov, April 30, 2001)

Here is a lexicon for some of the common filings by publicly traded companies. These are some of the more common entries from the EDGAR (Electronic Data Gathering and Retrieval) database of corporate filings:

10K	The official version of a company's annual report, with a comprehensive overview of the business.
10Q	An abridged version of the 10K, filed quarterly for the first three quarters of a company's fiscal year.
8K	If anything significant happens that should be reported before the next 10K or 10Q rolls around, the company files one of these.
12B–25	Request for a deadline extension to file a required report, like a 10K or 10Q. When the late report is ultimately filed, NT is appended to the report's name.
S1	Basic registration form for new securities, most often initial or secondary public offerings. Variants with higher numbers are used for registrations connected with mergers, employee stock plans and real estate investment trusts (REITs).
F6	Foreign companies use similar forms beginning with F; for example, F6 for American Depository Receipts.
Proxy statement	Information and ballot materials for shareholder votes, including election of directors and approval of mergers and acquisitions when required.
Forms 3, 4, and 5	Directors, officers and owners of more than 10 percent of a company's stock report their initial purchases on Form 3 and subsequent purchases or sales on Form 4; they file an annual statement of their holdings on Form 5.

(*New York Times*, June 21, 1998, www.edgar.gov)

A modern example of regulatory problems in emerging markets is the recent case of the Bombay Stock Exchange in India:

The Securities and Exchange Board of India said that starting July 2, it will prohibit carry-forward trading, the practice of buying stocks on margin and then rolling over the contract, rather than settling it. Carry-forwards increase market liquidity, but also volatility . . . India's regulators have been under considerable pressure to act since questionable margin trading earlier this year triggered a major stock-manipulation scandal. This caused the Bombay market to drop almost 30% in six weeks. In March, regulators ordered three brokerage groups to freeze brokerage activities, saying they were involved in share-price manipulation. A prominent Bombay broker also was arrested in relation to the scandal. In March, the SEBI banned some other forms of leveraged trading.

(Bailay, 2001)

7

Due to the reporting and disclosure requirements of the SEC, many international firms wishing to tap the US equity markets sponsor American Depository Receipts rather than directly listing on the US exchanges. Insider trading is to be disclosed under the fair disclosure provisions of the SEC. Disclosure is not always the case, however, as seen in the Mexican takeover of CompUSA. Grupo Sanborns SA, a company controlled by Mexican billionaire Carlos Slim Helu, made a public offer for the shares outstanding of Dallas computer retailer CompUSA Inc. Four days after Mr Slim publicly disclosed to the US Securities and Exchange Commission a 14.1 percent stake in CompUSA the Sanborns board member, Claudio Gonzalez, began buying shares of CompUSA. According to an SEC filing by Mr Slim, over the next two months, Mr Gonzalez bought 100,000 CompUSA shares with his personal funds at an average price of $6.74 a share. On January 24, 2000, Sanborns made a tender offer for CompUSA's shares outstanding at $10.10 apiece. The deal was completed. However:

> A US district Court in New York froze $6 million in assets belonging to eight Mexicans and four offshore companies pending an SEC investigation into possible insider trading involving CompUSA shares. Among those named in the SEC probe is a partner in a top Mexican law firm who advised Mr. Slim on the deal. Alejandro Duclaud and members of his family allegedly made almost $4 million trading shares while Sanborns was negotiating its takeover of CompUSA.
>
> (Fritsch, 2001)

In China:

> A flood of lawsuits is engulfing China's securities industry, as increasingly litigious stockholders bring into focus some of the markets' problems . . . The lawsuits target different parts of China's securities industry, but they share a common thread: Investors are fed up with what they see as a system tilted sharply in favor of government companies and powerful market speculators. The allegations, which range from misuse of shareholder funds to widespread share-price manipulation, have been largely ignored since China set up stock exchanges a decade ago.
>
> (Leggett, 2001)

POLITICAL RISK

Political risk refers to economic exposure to unanticipated changes in governmental policy that affect the earnings and value of your affiliate or subsidiary. Unanticipated nationalization would be an extreme example. The growing global membership in the WTO/GATT (General Agreement on Tariffs and Trade) has significantly reduced political risk as a signatory nation must adhere to Article III of the GATT, *National treatment on internal taxation and regulation* (see Chapter 5, pp. 121–2). "National treatment" requires that a country adhering to the GATT apply the same internal taxes and regulations to foreign firms as it does to national firms. Consequently, a government cannot levy a 25 percent corporate income tax on national firms and a 35 percent rate on foreign firms. Of course, in practice informal taxes may be solicited as "fees" from corrupt officials. China, a recent signatory of the GATT/WTO, and Russia, not a member, are sometimes accused of discriminating against foreign investors in favor of domestic investors. Thus, discrimination against foreign firms, while explicitly prohibited by the GATT, may take place. Even nationalization is possible when a populist government unexpectedly comes to power. The foreign oil companies in Venezuela are facing implicit nationalization through governmental decrees, as was the case under Alan Garcia in Peru from 1985 to 1990, where they were explicitly nationalized. A subsidiary of the World Bank, the Multilateral Investment Guarantee Agency (MIGA), provides insurance against investment risk in emerging markets.

INTELLECTUAL PROPERTY RIGHTS

Software code, Madonna's latest song, Microsoft's latest Windows operating system, Rolex watches, and Lacoste shirts are counterfeited worldwide on a regular basis. In some instances, the copying and manufacture of pharmaceuticals is perfectly legal. The Business Software Alliance publishes a blacklist of countries that pirate the most. Acceding to the WTO requires the signatory country to respect international patents, trademarks, and brands. In Latin America, Brazil seems to be the greatest culprit. In Asia, China is taking steps to enforce intellectual property rights, especially since it became a member of the GATT/WTO on December 11, 2001. Another step the Chinese are taking is the encouragement of the use of open software operating systems, such as Linux, on governmental and educational computers.

CONCLUSION

International finance involves currency conversion and foreign exchange risk issues. In addition, international taxation, the legal framework, and regulation are different across countries. Most countries have acceded to the GATT/WTO, so are required to extend national treatment to foreign banks and financial institutions, including insurance companies. Capital market integration equalizes the risk-adjusted rates of return worldwide, thereby increasing global rates of return and economic growth. Corruption remains a crucial issue in global markets: it is a brake on economic growth and foreign direct investment.

9

REFERENCES AND FURTHER READING

Bailay, Rasul (2001) "A ban on forward trading roils Bombay share market," *The Wall Street Journal*, May 16: A19.

Business Week (2001) "Kim's fall from grace: inside Daewoo's fraud scandal," February 19, 2001: 50–1.

Fritsch, Peter (2001) "Sanborns official bought CompUSA stake before buyout," *The Wall Street Journal*, May 18: A17.

Gordon, Michael R. (1998) "I.M.F. urged by Russia not to give more aid," *The New York Times*, October 1.

International Monetary Fund (IMF) (2000) "Taking the offensive against corruption," *Finance & Development*, June.

Leggett, Karby (2001) "Lawsuits flood China's securities industry: shareholders allege rife manipulation," *The Wall Street Journal*, May 30: C1.

PriceWaterhouse (1999) *Corporate taxes: a worldwide summary*, New York: PriceWaterhouse.

Sanger, David E. (1999) "Russia hotly protests audits demanded by I.M.F. for loans," *The New York Times*, September 27.

Chapter 2

The history of money and finance

INTRODUCTION

Money serves three important roles in an economy. It is a unit of account, a medium of exchange, and a store of value. As a medium of exchange, money avoids barter of one good for another. Barter, where individuals trade goods, requires a double coincidence of wants. You have a bicycle, but want an i-Pod, and someone you run into in the market has an i-Pod and wants a bicycle. When you meet by coincidence, you will exchange the goods. This is called barter, countertrade, or bilateral clearing: trade without a medium of exchange.

In the absence of a stable medium of exchange, countertrade flourishes, bringing oranges from Brazil in exchange for cotton from Uzbekistan or wheat from Kazakhstan. Indeed, Minnesota's Cargill in the United States is one of the largest firms engaging in countertrade worldwide. In the newly independent states, the rouble was unstable, losing value at over 20 percent a month, so that half of the trades made in the early and mid-1990s involved bilateral clearing and barter. It is still done, but using a medium of exchange—a hard currency—is far more efficient. A double coincidence of wants is not necessary. If you want an i-Pod, you take cash to the store and buy it. If you want a bicycle, you can pay cash—or, nowadays, use a debit card or a revolving credit card, which involves finance.

Money facilitates exchange. It also provides a unit of account—a yardstick by which we measure the value of goods, assets, and foreign currencies. When there is high inflation money loses its effectiveness both as a yardstick of value and as a medium of exchange. The seller is uncertain about the real amount that will be paid upon delivery since high inflation usually means unstable inflation rates. When a contract calls for payment in 30 days, yet there is 20 percent inflation in the month, the seller receives 20 percent less in real value. If the rate of inflation accelerates unexpectedly to 40 percent, the seller receives 40 percent less, but, if it slows to 10 percent, the receipt is only 10 percent less. High inflation sometimes moves economies to indexing for inflation. This reduces the resistance to inflation and makes stopping it more difficult. As a store of value, money is replaced by interest-yielding assets, foreign currency, or durables that rise in value along with inflation.

When the peso rapidly falls in value in Latin America, individuals substitute a more stable currency, which they hold as a store of value, a medium of exchange, and a stable unit of account. Informal dollarization takes place, as in Argentina and Peru. When the home currency becomes worthless as a medium of exchange, countries occasionally abolish it and formally adopt another currency as their own, as in Ecuador, which officially dollarized in 2000.

PREREQUISITES OF GOOD MONEY

A hard currency, such as gold or silver, costs resources to make. The resource cost ensures that too much money will not be produced, thereby checking inflation. The difference between a coin's value as money and the cost to mint it is called "seigniorage" or "mint profits." For example, a penny has 1 cent as its value as money, yet it costs over a penny to produce it. The cost of materials, zinc and copper, is 0.8 cents, while the manufacturing cost is 0.6 cents. The mint costs are thus 1.4 cents. Consequently, seigniorage is negative, −0.4 cents on a penny. However, consider a $100 bill. To make it difficult to counterfeit, its design requires high-quality linen with specks, and many colored inks and watermarks, yet the marginal cost of an extra $100 banknote is only about 12 cents. However, its value as money is $100. Seigniorage or mint profits are therefore $99.88. It is no wonder that it is the banknote that attracts the most counterfeiters. By law, only the realm can strike coinage. That is, a sovereign country enjoys the monopoly issue of the national currency. It consequently enjoys the seigniorage profits associated with the issue of currency.

To avoid inflation, the charters of central banks usually establish the independence of the central bank from the Treasury. That way, the Treasury cannot simply order the central bank to purchase its bonds in exchange for the issue of new money, that is the issue of new seigniorage, to finance its deficits.

As a medium of exchange, a good money must be divisible, even down to a penny. This allows a near continuum of prices to be settled upon rather than discrete price increments or the exchange of money plus some candy or gum, as has been the case in Italy in bygone days. It is a nickels or dimes problem. A $10 bill is divisible into 2 fives, a 5 into 10 ones, and a 1 into 20 nickels, 10 dimes, 4 quarters, or 100 pennies. This divisibility criterion is important in facilitating transactions. Cigarettes have been used in exchange in prisoner of war camps, as well as coupons that signify money. The UK shilling being worth 12 pence and 20 shillings being equal to £1 made for an awkward division and became obsolete with decimalization on February 15, 1971.

Fiat money—paper money not exchangeable for a commodity, such as silver— came about to save on the mint costs of mining gold and silver. It is also easier to change denominations and carry around paper money rather than heavy coin. The first paper money was issued in China during the eleventh century, around 1023. Seigniorage is greater with paper money than with coin. In some countries, such as Argentina in early 2001, protestors wore signs saying "No mas papel pintado" or "No more painted paper" to voice their opposition to the over-issue of money, the confiscation and freezing of bank accounts, and the ensuing inflation. It is always a temptation for government to finance its deficit by the printing press, thus making money less useful as a medium of exchange. The broader the currency zone of a money, and the fewer the transactions costs of conversion, the more useful it is. The use of the US dollar in the 50 US states and the euro in 12 European countries makes the moneyness of these currencies greater. Stable monetary policy is the key to having a currency substituted for those that depreciate rapidly in value. Price stability in a currency increases the zones that the particular money is used in.

MONEY AND EXCHANGE RATES

Great central banks, such as the Bank of England and the Banque de France, had gold windows where they bought and sold gold at a fixed currency price in the nineteenth century. In doing so, their currency rates were fixed. For example, if the Bank of England sets £10 per ounce of gold as the buy/sell rate and the Banque de France 100 francs, the equilibrium exchange rate is set at 100 francs per £10 or 10 francs a £1.

Arbitrage in gold kept the exchange rates within a narrow band of gold points. Let's say the exchange rate falls to 9.5 francs a £1. A gold arbitrageur purchases £10 for 95 francs, and presents the £10 to the Bank of England gold window in exchange for an ounce of gold. The arbitrageur then insures and ships the gold to the Banque de France, selling it for 100 francs, pocketing 5 francs less insurance and shipping as profits. This gold arbitrage kept the exchange rates within narrow margins known as "gold points"—the points at which profitable gold arbitrage took place. Consequently, countries that were on the gold standard had fixed exchange rates between themselves.

Similarly, countries in Asia were on the silver standard so that their currencies were pegged to one another and had corresponding "silver points." However, since there was usually no fixed relationship between the price of gold and silver, China, a silver standard country, floated its exchange rate with respect to the gold standard currencies. The silver depreciation kept Chinese exports up during the Great Depression in the West until 1934, when the United States passed the Silver Purchase Act to monetize silver at a significantly higher price. The implicit Chinese revaluation of 25 percent destroyed their export- and import-competing industries, sending them into a major recession that caused famine in the countryside (see Milton Friedman, 1992).

13

THE HISTORY OF MONIES

The first money originated in China during the Chou Dynasty, from the twelfth to the thirteenth century BC. It was in the form of shells connected by string and copper objects shaped in the form of grain. Bronze and copper coins in the shapes of small spades, chisels, hoes, and knives were later used in place of the articles themselves as a hard-bodied money. Some call these "quasi-coins," but it is legitimate to regard them as the first coinage. The copper coin called Yibi coin (ant nose) was made circa 500 BC, and the copper coin called Guinian coin (ghost face) was minted circa 400 to 300 BC. Both the Yibi coin and Guinian coin had shapes that resembled shells, the earliest currency in China. Both had marks indicating their use as coins. Glyn Davies (1994) believes that Chinese spade, hoe, and knife money preceded Lydian coinage of 600 to 575 BC but refers to them as "quasi-coins" despite clear markings. Jiaozi, the first paper money in the world, was issued in 1023 by the Soong Dynasty. Later dynasties issued paper money, but most were over-reliant on seigniorage—the printing press—to finance their expenditures. Hyperinflation resulted. Even the government at one point would not accept paper money in payment of taxes. Round copper and bronze coins replaced paper, but lost their worth due to ease of production and widespread counterfeiting. One-ounce silver ingots called "taels"—meaning 1 ounce—supplanted paper and copper money since silver was a better asset not subject to ease of coining. It was also a good international medium of exchange, used in trade payments. The Spanish peso contained 0.821791 troy ounce (25.561 grams) of pure silver and was also used as domestic money in China, having been minted in the New World in Mexico and Peru, then used in commerce—the so-called "pieces of eight." " 'Pieces of eight' were manufactured in the Americas and transported in bulk back to Spain to pay for wars . . ."—and commerce:

> The Manila Galleon transported Mexican silver to Manila, where it would be exchanged for Chinese goods, since silver was the only foreign commodity China would take. In oriental trade, Spanish dollars were often stamped with Chinese characters known as "chop marks" which indicate that that particular coin had been assayed by a well-known merchant and determined genuine.
>
> (www.wikipedia.com)

The use of taels reduced significantly the risk of inflation in terms of the silver price of goods because silver was widely hoarded as a store of wealth. The weight of a piece of silver determined its value as money, so it had the desired divisibility property. Indeed, the Spanish silver dollars were known as "pieces of eight" because they were frequently cut into eight pieces, allowing the use of smaller denominations of coin. Furthermore, silver was held in the form of jewelry, thereby reducing its supply as a medium of exchange. Under the silver standard,

China experienced 300 years of price stability (Huang, 1974). Paper money was used again from 1875 to 1908 during the Qing Dynasty, the last feudal dynasty in China. It was colorful and ornate, and was difficult to counterfeit, resembling modern banknotes.

The earliest known European coins appeared in Lydia (now Asia Minor, part of Turkey), c. 600 to 575 BC. These early coins were made of electrum, a precious alloy of gold and silver that "consists of about 54 percent gold, 44 percent silver, 2 percent copper, and trace amounts of iron and lead (http://rg.ancients.info/lion/article.html). The electrum coins were used to finance transactions between city states based on their weight. Greek coinage swiftly followed. The first bronze coins did not appear in Europe until the fifth century BC.

Alexander the Great introduced uniform coinage to all the territories he conquered. He confiscated the gold and silver treasuries in these countries and minted coins from them. At this time the Romans were developing their own metal monies. The Romans reduced the metal content of their coins, making them lighter, but maintaining the same face value. The government saved precious metals in this way to meet its debts by making greater seigniorage profits—the difference between value as money and mint costs.

The silver penny was first introduced around AD 760 in Britain. Following the Norman invasion in 1066, William the Conqueror continued to mint the Saxon pennies. He introduced the "sterling silver" standard. Silver was the coin of England from the time of the Norman invasion until 1920. The gold sovereign appeared c. 1500. It was called a sovereign because it bore the picture of Henry VII on the royal throne. It was minted until the outbreak of World War I.

The Chinese invented paper money in the AD 900s. The money remembled the French "Assignats," which were not uniform and were issued on an ad hoc basis. The Soong dynasty printed uniform paper currency, the Jiaozi, in 1023. In 1661, the first European banknote appeared in Sweden. Before the end of the seventeenth century, banknotes were being printed and issued in England. London goldsmiths originated the banknote when they began to act as bankers. People deposited gold with them for safe keeping, and the goldsmiths would give them a receipt. The words "or bearer" were added after the name of the depositor in 1670. This meant that the goldsmith would deliver metallic money to the person who presented the note for redemption, so the note was used as money.

When the first pilgrims arrived in America, they found the Indians using strings of shell beads, or "wampum" as money. The colonists traded goods with the Indians, but also adopted wampum as money. The Spanish dollar coming from Mexico was held as a store of value and used as a medium of exchange for large transactions. The colonists met their everyday needs by paying with sugar and tobacco—commodity monies.

The American colonists requested a supply of coins from Britain, but the British Treasury declined. Thus, they set up the first mint in Boston, producing shillings,

15

sixpences, and threepenny pieces in 1652. Each state issued its own money, both paper and coin, until the Civil War of 1861–5, when both the greenback and the confederate dollars were newly printed to finance the war efforts of the North and the South respectively. At the end of the war, the confederate currency was worthless and the greenback dollar evolved into the modern currency used in the United States. It still has a green back. The Federal Reserve system was created in 1913, splitting seigniorage between the 12 districts.

The latest prominent currency is the euro, created by the Maastricht Treaty, whereby Western European countries increased integration of their economies by adopting a common currency. On January 1, 1999 the exchange rates of the existing currencies were irrevocably set and the euro banknote and coin were introduced as legal currency on January 1, 2002. Euro area member states began implementing a common monetary policy. The 12 existing currencies of the participating member states were converted to euros and withdrawn from circulation on January 1, 2002.

FOREIGN EXCHANGE HISTORY

Foreign trade was initially conducted by barter, with the currency of the importing country acting as the medium of exchange. Foreign merchants accepted payment in local currency and spent the proceeds on the purchase of local goods. Foreign exchange emerged when uniform metallic coins bearing the marks and seal of a banker or merchant came into being. Having gold, silver, and copper as the units of account facilitated valuation and conversion, but did have some counterfeiting, as modern monies do.

Bills of exchange made their appearance in Babylonia and Assyria centuries before the invention of marked coinage in Lydia. The bill of exchange is used primarily in international trade, and is a written order by one person to pay another a specific sum on a specific date some time in the future. Since carrying large amounts of coins was risky, bills of exchange were used in order to facilitate currency and trade transactions.

The text of some bills of exchange indicates that payment was made in locations other than those of issue. The bill of exchange allowed trade to take place without the use of coinage—a precursor of the modern letter of credit (L/C). Furthermore, the bills were traded as financial instruments in trade fairs. They were discounted and converted into foreign units of account. These trade fairs were the precursors of modern stock and foreign exchanges.

The first semblance of foreign exchange consisted of meeting places in commercial centers. The discrepancies in the relative values of metals were exploited by foreign merchants when choosing their means of payment. This is a precursor of Gresham's Law—merchants use the lower-valued money in exchange, and hoard the higher-valued one. It also confirms the "law of one price" through arbitrage.

The role played by money-changers greatly increased in importance during the centuries of Roman debasement of the coinage. During the Middle Ages and the Renaissance, the bill of exchange could be used to disguise payments of interest in foreign exchange. Since they were discounted, their yield to maturity represented an interest payment. These disguised loans were referred to as "fictitious exchange," whereas conventional bill exchanges were referred to as "real exchange."

The convention was to quote foreign exchange rates in terms of bills payable at settlement. The pound was quoted in terms of foreign currencies. An important feature of the foreign exchange market was an interest-bearing loan disguised as a foreign exchange transaction. Merchants and financiers were able to make loans that evaded usury laws by using a sequence of two bill transactions—a precursor of today's foreign exchange swap.

An important sixteenth-century development was the appearance of a system of "betting" on future exchange rates: a non-deliverable forward market. The betters made forecasts on future exchange. The difference between the realized rates and the forecasted rate determined who won the bet and how much the loser would pay the winner. This form of forward exchange still exists today in the form of non-deliverable futures (NDFs) in the Chinese yuan (formally renminbi— "the people's currency") in Singapore and Hong Kong.

As Rudiger Dornbusch (1987) noted, Spanish writers of the sixteenth century discovered the basics of the purchasing power parity (PPP) theory. They noticed the relationship between the prices of goods exported from Spain to the New World. By the time they reached their destination, the prices of these goods were higher, owing to the costs and risks involved in transport. The purchasing power parities represented the differences between the prices of these goods in Spain and those in Mexico and Peru, adjusting for the costs of transport.

In the nineteenth century, Paris and London became the leading markets, dealers being in contact throughout business hours. Forward currencies were widely traded.

During the US colonial period, no business in dollars was transacted in London, so that trade with Britain was financed exclusively in sterling. A large proportion of the transactions in sterling bills was done in New Orleans, where bills drawn by cotton traders were sold. The 1944 Bretton Woods system of pegged but adjustable exchange rates triggered foreign exchange intervention in spot markets, but also occasionally in forward markets.

Central banks often suffer great losses due to forward intervention—when currency they have bought forward "high" eventually goes "low." This happened to Thailand, initiating the South-East Asia crisis of the 1990s. The era of fixed exchange rates came to an end in 1971–3, in particular when Richard Nixon closed the gold window in 1971 and Britain floated the pound in 1973. With the euro's launch in 2002, fixed rates have returned for many countries in the form of a common currency.

17

The London FOREX market

By the early 1920s, London was considered to be the world's leading foreign exchange (FOREX) center (Atkin, 2005). Floating exchange rates began in the early 1970s, and global markets were being integrated. The resulting need of multinational businesses to hedge their currency exposures caused the rapid growth of FOREX trading in the 1980s and 1990s. London is still by far the largest FOREX market today in terms of daily turnover. In 2004, daily turnover net of double-counting on the London FOREX market was a staggering $753 billion in currency spots, swaps, forwards, and options. This represented 31 percent of FOREX transactions, compared to 19 percent in the United States, and 8 percent in Japan (Bank for International Settlements, 2005: table E4).

BANKS AND BANKING

In 3,000 BC, the temples in Babylon are reported to have accepted deposits of money and made loans. In the Greek states of the fifth and fourth centuries BC the temples, the city authorities, and private individuals engaged in banking (Jones, 1973). In the twelfth century banking started again in some Italian cities after the fall of the Roman Empire. Risky lending by banks led to a demand for a bank that would transfer funds for its customers, but not make loans. The first "giro" or transfer banks came into being. These started in the great Italian trading cities: Florence, Siena, and Venice. German cities followed, but Amsterdam and London eventually became the most important financial centers.

The first modern bank was the Bank of Amsterdam, founded in 1609. Amsterdam was quickly followed by other major cities. The Bank of Hamburg was formed in 1619 and the Bank of Sweden in 1656. Sweden issued the first European paper banknotes in 1661.

Until 1640 the Tower of London provided merchants with a reliable deposit service. Other banking services, money transmission, and accounting, were provided by "scriveners," essentially accountants. The development of "goldsmith bankers" came about when the goldsmiths persuaded the scriveners to deposit money with them in return for a small interest payment. The main purpose was apparently to have an opportunity to pick over the coins (Atkin, 2005).

Charles I seized the assets deposited in the Tower in 1640, when refused a goldsmith loan of £300,000. The Tower was no longer a safe depository. The goldsmiths became commercial bankers, providing loans of revolving cash balances.

The Bank of England was founded in 1694 as a commercial bank by William Paterson with the right to issue notes up to the amount of its capital, initially £1.2 million. It was nationalized by Parliament in 1946. The shareholders received compensation and the Bank of England thereafter ceased its private business, becoming the banker of the government and, since 1997, taking responsibility for

18

monetary policy. Prudential oversight of the British commercial banking system was simultaneously transferred to the Securities and Investments Board.

The Federal Reserve System

The First Bank of the United States was established in 1791, but collapsed in 1811. The Second Bank of the United States was established in 1816 and survived only until 1836.

Thereafter, until 1862, only state-chartered banks existed. They issued notes against gold and silver and were regulated by the states in which they were chartered. The National Banking Act of 1863, in the middle of the US Civil War, created a system of national banks with higher standards than state banks. It also created a national currency—the greenback dollar. National banks were required to accept each other's notes at par. The government imposed a tax on state banks, forcing most to become national banks. Also, the use of checking accounts grew: by the turn of the century, 90 percent of narrow money—currency outside banks plus demand deposits—was in the form of checking accounts.

In 1907, a banking panic in the United States, accompanied by runs on deposits that were bankrupting banks, led to arguments for the establishment of a US central bank with an elastic currency to provide liquidity to commercial banks in the event of crises. The Federal Reserve Act established the Federal Reserve System (the FED) in 1913 with 12 districts. The Federal Reserve Banks provide liquidity, clear transactions, and control the money supply.

The FED was established primarily as a reserve institution—a lender of last resort to prevent bank runs and liquidity crises. The FED has developed into a supervisory institution for member banks and savings and loan associations that pay premia to the Federal Deposit Insurance Corporation, established in 1933, and the Federal Savings and Loan Insurance Corporation, established later. It is also responsible for US monetary policy: open market operations, discount rate determination, and the reserve requirements of commercial banks. The FED also serves as a clearing house for the transfer of monies by check and draft between banks within the United States and abroad.

THE INTERNATIONAL MONETARY INSTITUTIONS

The International Monetary Fund (IMF) was established in 1944 at the Bretton Woods Conference in New Hampshire. Its purpose was to establish orderly exchange rate arrangements based on a par value system, to eliminate exchange controls, especially for current account transactions, and to provide temporary short-term balance of payments assistance via loans to member countries that are short of foreign exchange reserves. It provided for a pegged exchange rate system with central bank intervention required in the foreign exchange market when the rate approached narrow margins around the official, par value. Rather than imposing exchange controls, it was considered better to make balance of payments adjustment loans that impose macro-economic policy conditions on the sovereign country that agrees to the conditions. If it agrees to the IMF's loan conditions, the finance minister and the governor of the central bank sign a memorandum of understanding with the IMF. The loan is typically disbursed in several "tranches," or slices, and satisfaction of the loan conditions is monitored between disbursements. Extended stand-by-loans can have a maturity up to 36 months and are essentially lines-of-credit that the country can draw from should it wish to or need to do so. There have been several criticisms leveled recently at the role of the IMF in the international financial system. Just before the Russian default, a multi-billion dollar disbursement was made. The IMF country economist called it a FIEF (foreign investor relief facility), since the dollars were sold for 6 roubles shortly before the Russian default and floating of the exchange rate to 18 roubles a dollar. A substantial portion of the IMF loan was also rumored to have been diverted by government officials into their private accounts in the Channel Island of Jersey (see Blustein, 2001). The argument is that the IMF creates "moral hazard," encouraging investors to invest in risky, high-return jurisdictions knowing that the IMF will bail them out. In a crisis, the IMF will lend foreign reserves to the central bank, which then dumps them in the foreign exchange market at discount prices before the ultimate depreciation takes place. Similarly, in the case of Argentina's currency board crisis of 2001—due to excessive foreign debt, provincial deficits, and spending before a Presidential campaign—the IMF is rumored to have known that Argentina was going to default, but was pressured by the US Treasury to make the loan anyway. In response to criticism, the IMF established an "Independent Internal Evaluation" unit—an oxymoron.

The World Bank, a sister institution of the IMF, created in 1944 at the Bretton Woods Conference, initially made long-term development loans for projects, such as dams, airports, rubber and concrete production, and water systems. It got involved in structural adjustment loans (SALs) in the 1990s in tandem with the IMF requiring structural adjustments to economic policy. This could mean privatization of state enterprises, lifting price and exchange controls, and improving monetary and fiscal policies, for instance. Some of its large-scale loans for dams in particular were criticized by environmentalists and human rights activists because of damage to the environment by immediate flooding of the dam, and the wholesale removal of villagers in the way of the projects. In modern times, World Bank officials are a bit more sensitive to the environment, as the IMF is to corruption, so they go in for micro-lending. Many economists think IMF and World Bank loans do more harm than good to the residents of the countries that receive them. Ultimately, the loans are the taxpayer's liability. Critics argue that the multilateral institutions have not successfully prevented the wholesale theft of loans by officials in corrupt environments.

The Bank for International Settlements

The Bank for International Settlements (BIS) is often referred to as the bank of central banks. It was established on May 17, 1930 at the Hague Convention. As such, it is the oldest international monetary organization. It does not do business with private individuals or corporations; only with central banks and international institutions. The head office is in Basel, Switzerland. In its role of fostering international monetary cooperation, the General Manager of the BIS has seen the need to address issues of the growth of offshore financial centers (OFCs), highly leveraged institutions (HLIs), large and complex financial institutions (LCFIs), deposit insurance, and the spread of money laundering and accounting scandals.

In his statement to the Financial Stability Forum (FSF), A. Crockett—then General Manager—specifically mentions Long Term Capital Management (LTCM), a Connecticut hedge fund, as an example of the near-collapse of an HLI. He also singles out Enron as an accounting scandal. These are the issues that need to be addressed by the international monetary institutions, in his view. Additionally, OFCs need to "facilitate efforts to strengthen supervisory, information sharing and cooperation practices in OFCs, which have taken on increased urgency following 11 September and the global efforts to combat terrorism financing" (Crockett, 2001).

THE HISTORY OF THE STOCK EXCHANGES

Adam Smith warned in 1776 about mismanagement of companies that issue shares to finance their operations, the primary role of the stock exchanges. He raises the principal–agent problem, where the shareholders are the principals or owners and the managers are the agents:

> The directors of such [joint stock] companies, however, being the managers rather of other people's money than of their own, it cannot well be expected that they should watch over it with the same anxious vigilance with which the partners in a private copartnery frequently watch over their own. Like the stewards of a rich man, they are apt to consider attention to small matters as not for their master's honour, and very easily give themselves a dispensation from having it. Negligence and profusion, therefore, must always prevail, more or less, in the management of the affairs of such a company.
>
> (1776: 107)

Yet, large corporations with many owners are able to limit the liability of the owners to the value of the shares they hold. The shareholder can enter a venture by buying shares, and exit it by selling them. The manager acts as the shareholders' agent. Under agency law, a corporation is a single entity, a "person" that

21

may sue or be sued without its members being held liable. It is chartered by the state in which it is located. A corporation is a business in which large numbers of people are organized in a single venture. Corporations can list and sell their shares on a number of exchanges. This is known as equity finance versus debt finance. Many of these exchanges use the "open-outcry" form of trading where the trader has to shout his or her order continuously until they are out of breath. If a trader stops shouting, the order is assumed no longer in effect. Since many are shouting at the same time, a system of hand signals has come about that effectively convey the order to the pit manager. While some argue that the presence of specialists and market makers on the floor aids in the conveyance of information, others welcome the transparency of the electronic exchanges that are taking business away from the open-outcry exchanges. Indeed, the New York Stock Exchange (NYSE) has acquired Archipelago, a state of the art electronic trading system.

Some of the main stock exchanges are:

- *The New York Stock Exchange*, which was established May 17, 1792 on Wall Street. Traders met at the old wooden wall, no longer in existence, but giving its name to the street. The Dow Jones Industrial Average (DJIA) started out with 12 stocks in October 1928. Only General Electric remains of the original 12. The S&P 500 Index covers the 500 most widely held companies.
- *The NASDAQ*, which is an acronym for National Association of Securities Dealers Automated Quotations. An online stock exchange, it began operations in 1971.
- *The American Stock Exchange (AMEX)*, which is a subsidiary of the National Association of Securities Dealers. The AMEX index is a composite index of the 739 stocks listed.
- *The London Stock Exchange*, which was established in 1773, formerly Jonathan's Coffee House where traders met. Trading has since moved off the floor with the introduction of the Stock Exchange Automated Quotations (SEAQ) system. The Footsie 100 Index is the *Financial Times* Stock Exchange Index of the 100 largest companies listed on the London Stock Exchange.
- *The Tokyo Stock Exchange*, which was established on May 15, 1878. Japan's Nikkei 225 Index is an average of stock market prices similar to the DJIA.
- *The Paris Bourse*, which was established by the order of the Royal Council in 1724. In 1986, the futures exchange—Le MATIF—was established. On September 22, 2000, the Amsterdam, Brussels, and Paris bourses merged to create Euronext. The CAC 40 Index is the acronym for

"Compagnie des Agents de Change 40 Index"—40 French companies listed on the Paris Stock Exchange.

- *The Shanghai Stock Exchange (SSE)*, which was founded in 1904, mainly dealing in rubber shares. The Japanese occupation brought an end to its operations. The modern SSE was founded in 1990 but suffers from transparency, disclosure, and monitoring issues that have put it into a serious slump from which it is just now recovering. The Shanghai Composite Index is a composite of hard-currency B shares sold to foreigners and yuan-denominated A shares sold to the Chinese.
- *The Frankfurt Stock Exchange*, which dates from the ninth century, when trade fairs were authorized. In 1585 it was organized as a bourse to fix exchange rates and by 1894 had became a formal stock exchange. Its main index, the DAX, consists of the 30 largest issues traded on the exchange.

The performances of the international stock markets indices are related. In fact, this is one aspect of the increased globalization of international trade and finance. The correlations between some of the major world stock indices are shown in Table 2.1.

The results in Table 2.1 suggest the globalization of the international financial markets. Since we are dealing with the monthly real rates of return adjusted for inflation, the positive and significant correlations suggest that arbitrage is keeping the real rates of return in line. Also, many real shocks are worldwide. The same phenomenon can be seen with the Moscow Times Index, the US S&P 500, and the UK Footsie 100 in Table 2.2.

Interestingly, the same cannot be said about the Nikkei 225 of Tokyo, nor the Bombay Stock Exchange Sensex Index, whose real returns display no significant positive correlation whatsoever with the S&P 500, nor the Footsie 100. The Czech PX50 index reported in Table 2.3, on the other hand, is weakly correlated to the Footsie 100 and strongly correlated to the S&P 500 index.

CONCLUSION

Money serves as a medium of exchange, a unit of account, and a store of value. Different monies must be converted into the same unit of account by the exchange rate in order to compare prices and rates of return. This currency conversion gives rise to foreign exchange risk in investing and operating internationally. The foreign exchange markets have arisen to deal with spot and forward transactions in different monies, as well as currency options to either hedge or speculate. The largest FOREX market remains London, accounting for 31 percent of daily turnover in the foreign exchanges. The exchange costs on the FOREX market are mainly the difference between the ask and the bid price of foreign currency—

23

Table 2.1 Correlations between the monthly real rates of return on major world stock indices[§]

Country	UK	US	Brazil	Canada	Chile	Germany	Mexico
UK	1	0.804**	0.465**	0.660**	0.201*	0.792**	0.514**
US	0.804**	1	0.549**	0.792**	0.170	0.765**	0.616**
Brazil	0.465**	0.549**	1	0.539**	0.307**	0.425**	0.509**
Canada	0.660**	0.792**	0.539**	1	0.301**	0.655**	0.665**
Chile	0.201*	0.170	0.307**	0.301**	1	0.245*	0.197*
Germany	0.792**	0.765**	0.425**	0.655**	0.245*	1	0.518**
Mexico	0.514**	0.616**	0.509**	0.665**	0.197*	0.518**	1

Notes:
§ 109 monthly observations of real rates of return on a major country index during the period April 1995–April 2004. The S&P 500 is used for the United States, the Footsie 100 for the UK, the Bovespa for Brazil, the TSE 300 for Canada, the IGPA for Chile, the DAX 30 for Germany, and the IPC for Mexico.
*   Correlation is significant at the 0.05 level (2-tailed).
** Correlation is significant at the 0.01 level (2-tailed).

Table 2.2 Correlations between the monthly real rates of return on the Moscow Times Index, the S&P 500, and the Footsie 100*

Index	Moscow Times	Footsie 100	S&P 500
Moscow Times	1	0.503**	0.505**
Footsie 100	0.503**	1	0.862**
S&P 500	0.505**	0.862**	1

Notes:
* 63 monthly observations of the real rates of return on the Moscow Times Index for the period February 1999–April 2004.
** Correlation is significant at the 0.01 level (2-tailed).

Table 2.3 Correlations between the monthly real rates of return on the Czech PX50 Index, the S&P 500, and the Footsie 100*

Index	PX50	Footsie 100	S&P 500
PX50	1	0.214	0.305**
Footsie 100	0.214	1	0.824**
S&P 500	0.305**	0.824**	1

Notes:
* 81 monthly observations of the real rates of return on the PX50 Index for the period August 1997–April 2004.
** Correlation is significant at the 0.01 level (2-tailed).

the bid–ask spread—as well as any commission associated with the conversion. These costs are not insignificant, amounting to approximately $1 billion daily. The world financial market is becoming increasingly integrated. The adoption of the euro as the same currency by 12 countries has removed exchange rate risk and conversion costs from the financial landscape of Europe. Greater openness in trade has brought with it greater openness in finance, since current account deficits must be financed, and surpluses provide foreign lending. The decade of the 1990s brought all of Latin America into the WTO/GATT, and in 2001 China became a signatory as well. There have been great foreign direct investment flows that follow trade, as well as portfolio investments. On the other hand, China still has not liberalized the capital account to permit foreign portfolio diversification, though larger direct foreign investments and acquisitions have been approved. There is increasing financial integration in the world financial markets, making for a more efficient distribution of worldwide finance.

REFERENCES AND FURTHER READING

Atkin, John (2005) *The foreign exchange market of London: development since 1900*, London and New York: Routledge.

Bahng, Seungwook (2003) "The response of the Indian stock market to the movement of Asia's emerging markets: from isolation toward integration," *Global Economic Review* 32(2): 43–58.

Bank for International Settlements (2005) *Trienniel central bank survey: foreign exchange and derivatives activity in 2004*, Basel: BIS, table E4, p. 56.

Blustein, Paul (2002) *The chastening: inside the crisis that rocked the global financial system and humbled the IMF*, New York: Public Affairs Books.

Chown, John F. (1994) *A history of money: from AD 800*, London and New York: Routledge.

Crockett, A. (2001) "Statement to the Financial Stability Forum," Ottawa, November 17.

Davies, Glyn (1994) *A history of money: from ancient times to the present day*, Cardiff: University of Wales Press.

Dornbusch, Rudiger (1987) "Purchasing Power Parity," in J. Eatwell, M. Milgate and P. Newman (eds), *The New Palgrave: a Dictionary of Economics*, Vol. 3, New York: Macmillan: 1075–84.

Einzig, Paul (1970) *The history of foreign exchange*, New York: Macmillan.

Friedman, Milton (1992) "FDR, Silver and China," in *Money mischief: episodes in monetary history*, Orlando, FL and San Diego, CA: Harcourt Brace & Company.

http://rg.ancients.info/lion/article/html (2006) "A case for the world's first coin: the Lydia Lion."

Huang, Ray (1974) *Fiscal administration during the Ming Dynasty*, London: Cambridge University Press.

Jones, J. P. (1973) *The money story*, New York: Drake Publishers.

Poitras, Geoffrey (2000) *The early history of financial economics, 1478–1776: from commercial arithmetic to life annuities and joint stocks*, Cheltenham and Northampton: Edward Elgar.

Racine, M. D. and Lucy F. Ackert (2000) "Time varying volatility in Canadian and US stock index and index futures: a multivariate analysis," *Journal of Financial Research* 23(2): 129–43.

Smith, Adam (1776) *An inquiry into the wealth of nations* (ed. Edwin Cannan, 1904, 5th edn), London: Methuen & Co.

Spahn, Heinz-Peter (2001) *From gold to euro: on monetary theory and the history of currency systems*, Berlin and New York: Springer.

Westermann, Frank (2002) "Stochastic trends and cycles in national stock market indices: evidence from the US and UK and Switzerland," *Swiss Journal of Economics and Statistics* 138(3): 317–28.

World Bank (2006) *Doing business in 2006: creating jobs*, Washington D.C.

www.wikipedia.org

Chapter 3

The foreign exchange market

INTRODUCTION

According to the Bank for International Settlements (BIS), average daily turnover in the foreign exchange market in 2004 was $1.9 trillion in foreign exchange markets—spot transactions, outright forwards, swaps and options—one of the largest financial markets in existence, if not the largest. The transactions costs involved are easily over a billion dollars a day, counting the bid–ask spread and commissions.

This chapter outlines floating and fixing the exchange rate in the spot market, forward and futures markets, and the options market in foreign exchange. As always, it is supply and demand that determines the equilibrium in each market, but arbitrage plays an important role in setting an equilibrium price in both the spot and futures markets. Broadly understood, arbitrage is buying low in one market and selling high in another, thereby bringing prices into equilibrium. No further profitable arbitrage is possible.

A FLOATING EXCHANGE RATE SYSTEM

With a floating exchange rate, supply and demand in the foreign exchange market determine the equilibrium exchange rate. When the central bank neither purchases nor sells foreign exchange, it is said to be a freely floating exchange rate system. The equilibrium rate is approximately the mid-point of bid and the ask rate: that is ((bid + ask)/2). The bid is what a bank pays for a unit of foreign exchange, the ask is the price at which it sells the same unit of foreign exchange. Individual firms and persons will pay the ask rate, which is slightly higher, and they will receive the slightly lower bid rate. The bank earns the bid–ask spread.

In Figure 3.1, at a spot price of S, the supply and demand for foreign exchange are reconciled, so S is the equilibrium exchange rate in terms of pesos per dollar. This is known as a European quote—foreign currency unit per USD (US dollar). When a currency is quoted as USD per unit of foreign currency, it is known as an American quotation. The equilibrium quantity bought (and) sold is Q.

Pesos per dollar

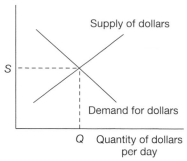

Figure 3.1 *A floating exchange rate*

Central banks occasionally intervene in the foreign exchange market by increasing or decreasing the supply of foreign exchange. With intervention, the float is said to be a "managed float." Foreign exchange dealers quote customers a bid and an ask (or offer) rate for foreign exchange. A dealer purchases at the bid rate and sells at the offer rate. The bid–ask spread (the difference between the ask and the bid rates) represents profits to the foreign exchange dealer.

Day trading in foreign exchange is not likely to be profitable. For one thing, the speculator pays fees per trade and, for another, buys at the ask and sells at the bid when trading foreign exchange. Consider a simultaneous purchase and sale of foreign exchange by a day trader: the trader buys high at the ask and simultaneously sells low at the bid, paying the exchange spread plus any commission on the trade. Table 3.1 indicates the bid–ask spread from a Reuters FOREX display.

Rabobank, London bids 1.2184 for the euro, and asks 1.2187. It is a market maker, standing ready either to buy or sell euros. Let's assume that, at the bid

Table 3.1 *Outright spot foreign exchange quotations*

RIC	Bid	Ask	Contributor	Time
EUR	1.2184	1.2187	Rabobank	LON 13:19
JPY	111.345	111.348	Barclays	GFX 13:19
GBP	1.7669	1.7675	Barclays	GFX 13:19
CHF	1.2860	1.2890	Rabobank	LON 13:19

Source: Reuters, July 13, 2005.

Note: RIC indicates Reuters Instrument Code.

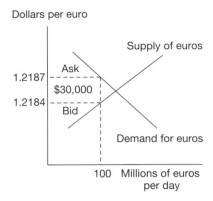

Dollars per euro

Figure 3.2 *The bid–ask spread*

and ask prices, Rabobank trades 100 million euros. It buys 100 million euros at 1.2184 and sells them at 1.2187. Its bid–ask spread is 1.2187–1.2184 = 0.0003, which is three basis points or "pips" in terms of foreign exchange. On the 100 million euros traded, Rabobank's profits in terms of dollars are 0.0003 × 100,000,000 = $30,000. This is represented graphically in Figure 3.2.

In terms of a spreadsheet, we can calculate the margins that Rabobank enjoys (see Table 3.2).

Table 3.2 *Rabobank's profits from the bid–ask spread*

RIC	Bid	Ask	Ask–Bid	Volume traded	Profits
EUR	1.2184	1.2187	$0.0003	€100,000,000	$30,000

Source: Computed from SaxoBank spot quotations, July 13, 2005.

American and European quotations

A FOREX quotation may be in American terms—USD per unit of foreign currency, or in European terms—units of foreign currency per dollar. In Table 3.1, the convention is to quote the pound and the euro in American terms, but the yen and the Swiss franc in European terms. The conversion is simple since 1/bid in one quotation equals the ask in the other. Similarly, 1/ask equals the bid when changing the style of quotation. The simple rule is that the ask must always exceed the bid after conversion. Table 3.3 displays the same quotations

29

of July 13, 2005 in American and European styles. For the yen, the American style quotation is awkward since it requires six decimal places to distinguish the bid from the ask.

A FIXED EXCHANGE RATE SYSTEM

A fixed exchange rate system usually has a ceiling and a floor ("intervention points"). The central bank purchases foreign exchange at the floor and sells it at the ceiling to maintain the exchange rate within a narrow band. When the supply of dollars is greater than the demand for dollars at the floor price, the central bank purchases dollars at the floor price and adds them to its foreign exchange reserves. To facilitate international adjustment, the central bank that purchases dollars with, say, pesos lets the domestic peso money supply rise. Occasionally, central banks "sterilize" or "neutralize" the monetary effects of FOREX purchases by simultaneously selling domestic currency bonds to take back the increase in the supply of pesos (see Hanke, 2002). This neutralizes adjustment and the surplus or deficit continues until policy or a shock changes the circumstances.

In Figure 3.3, the supply of dollars equals the demand for dollars inside the band, so central bank intervention is not necessary. Within the band, the exchange rate floats, solely determined by supply and demand, for instance, at the price 1.00 peso per dollar. At 1.01 pesos per dollar, the supply exceeds the demand. Consequently, the price falls to 1.00. At 0.99, there is an excess demand for dollars, so the peso price of the dollar rises to 1.00, the equilibrium. With a fixed exchange rate that has a ceiling and a floor the central bank purchases foreign exchange at the floor and sells it at the ceiling to maintain the exchange rate within a band.

Table 3.3 American versus European quotations

| RIC | American quotations | | European quotations | |
	Bid	Ask	Bid	Ask
EUR	1.2184	1.2187	0.8205	0.8207
JPY	0.009426	0.009434	106	106.09
GBP	1.7669	1.7675	0.5658	0.5660
CHF	0.563349	0.563507	1.7746	1.7751

Source: SaxoBank, July 13, 2005.

Pesos per dollar

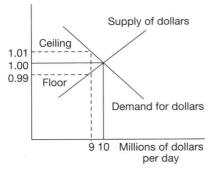

Figure 3.3 *A fixed exchange rate*

A central bank purchase of dollars

When the supply of dollars is greater than the demand for dollars at the floor price, the central bank purchases dollars at the floor price and adds them to its foreign exchange reserves. For example, in Figure 3.4 the supply of dollars exceeds the demand for dollars at a floor price of 0.99 pesos per dollar. This triggers central bank intervention (that is, purchases of 3 million dollars by the central bank) at 0.99 pesos per dollar. The equilibrium exchange rate is thus 0.99 pesos per dollar, including the central bank's demand for dollars. Normally, the 3 million dollars are added to central bank reserves. However, the central bank could sterilize the immediate impact on the domestic money supply by selling $0.99 \times \$3,000,000$ pesos in domestic bonds on the open market.

Notice that a central bank's ability to purchase foreign reserves is unlimited since it can always print or supply more domestic money. This is not the case when it comes to selling foreign reserves to support the home currency. It cannot print foreign currency.

Pesos per dollar

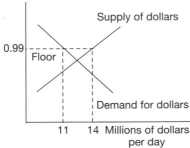

Figure 3.4 *Intervention at the floor*

31

A central bank sale of dollars

When the demand for dollars is greater than the supply of dollars at the ceiling price, the central bank draws from its reserves of dollars and sells them at the ceiling price. In Figure 3.5, the demand for dollars exceeds the supply of dollars at a price of 1.01 pesos per dollar, so the price increases to 1.01, triggering a sale of dollars by the central bank at the ceiling rate. The sale of reserves just equilibrates supply and demand at a price of 1.01 pesos per dollar. Neutralization would entail a purchase of domestic bonds equal to 1.01 × 3,000,000 pesos. However, the loss of dollars would continue and ultimately lead to an exchange rate crisis if neutralization continues.

A central bank's holdings of foreign reserves are limited. Consequently, it may sell reserves until it has sold all its reserves and exhausted its ability to borrow reserves to support its currency, if it chooses to do so. At that point, it must float (or worse yet, impose exchange controls, in which case the parallel market rate floats) its exchange rate. At that point, speculators who had "bet against the bank" make their profits. Most empirical studies show that, by taking a position opposite to central bank intervention, small systematic profits can be made (Taylor, 1982). The reason for this is that central banks often "lean against the wind", that is, resist changes in the fundamental equilibrium rate.

A managed floating exchange rate system allows the exchange rate to float according to the laws of supply and demand, but there are discretionary sales and/or purchases of foreign exchange to maintain the equilibrium exchange rate within small margins.

The effect of maintaining a fixed exchange rate on the money supply

When the demand for money declines, say due to a crisis in confidence in the home currency, the central bank must sell foreign exchange reserves, thereby

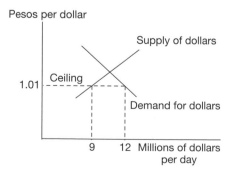

Figure 3.5 *Intervention at the ceiling*

reducing the supply of home currency. The effect on the domestic money supply is direct: when the central bank sells foreign exchange reserves, it simultaneously buys domestic currency. Consequently, domestic currency in the banking system declines. Sales of foreign exchange reserves automatically reduce the domestic money supply.

Similarly, when a central bank purchases foreign exchange and adds to reserves, it simultaneously sells domestic currency to the banking system. Consequently, the domestic money supply rises automatically.

Naturally, the ability of a central bank to maintain a fixed exchange rate depends on its holdings of foreign reserves. From the point of view of the balance sheet of the central bank in Figure 3.6, we have a simplified T-account.

On the asset side, foreign reserves are net foreign assets held by the central bank, and domestic credit represents loans made by the central bank, usually to the Treasury. On the liability side, the bank issues domestic currency to the public and it takes in deposits of commercial banks as required reserves. Commercial banks are also allowed to count cash on hand ("vault cash") as part of their reserves.

A decline in the demand for money is reflected by a decline in the demand for base money. By selling its foreign reserves at the spot rate, the central bank accommodates the decline in the demand for money by buying the excess domestic supply. Otherwise, the central bank could contract domestic credit to reduce base money supply. This is due to the asset identity: foreign reserves plus domestic credit equal base money. Notice that, if the demand for money were constant, base money is constant. Any attempt by the central bank to expand domestic credit (say to finance a fiscal deficit) under a fixed exchange rate regime would come at the expense of a loss in foreign reserves. The central bank would have to repurchase the excess supply of money on the foreign exchange market. This is the so-called "monetary anchor" role of a fixed exchange rate. In principal, a fixed exchange rate prevents the central bank from financing the fiscal and quasi-fiscal deficit. An independent expansion of the money supply by the central bank triggers excess demand in the foreign exchange market, requiring a sale of foreign exchange reserves to maintain the fixed exchange rate.

Assets	Liabilities
Foreign reserves	Currency held by the public
Domestic credit	Commercial bank reserves

Base money	Base money

Figure 3.6 The balance sheet of a central bank

The central bank thus expands credit and hence the money base, but contracts the base by the same amount when it sells foreign exchange reserves. Consequently, a fixed exchange rate serves as a monetary anchor on expansionary monetary policy.

Neutralization policy

When a central bank has an expansionary monetary policy (say to finance the fiscal deficit via the printing press), it continuously loses reserves until they are exhausted, usually by a sudden speculative attack or a run against remaining central bank reserves. At that point, the exchange rate must float since no further support of the exchange rate is possible—foreign exchange reserves are no longer available. Often, the central bank sees no alternative but to expand domestic credit as the financier of last resort of the Treasury's deficit. Monetary policy becomes dependent on the deficit of the Treasury. Thus foreign exchange reserves are spent until they run out.

Under neutralization or sterilization policy a central bank sells a million dollars of foreign currency and simultaneously buys with the proceeds a million dollars worth of Treasury debt. In doing so, it neutralizes the natural fall in the money supply triggered by the sale of foreign exchange.

THE EURO: IRREVOCABLY FIXED EXCHANGE RATES

Robert A. Mundell, Professor at Columbia University and 1999 Nobel Prize Laureate in Economics, noted in his "A theory of optimum currency areas" (1961) that the older economists of the nineteenth century were internationalists and generally favored a world currency. Thus John Stuart Mill wrote: "So much of barbarism, however, still remains in the transactions of most civilised nations, that almost all independent countries choose to assert their nationality by having, to their own inconvenience and that of their neighbors, a peculiar currency of their own" (1894: 176). John Stuart Mill clearly had in mind transactions costs involved in having separate monies—not only the bid–ask spread and commissions in foreign exchange, but also problems of exchange controls and currency risk that impede trade, investment, and factor mobility. Rigidly fixed exchange rates under a gold standard provided a nearly universal money for most of the nineteenth century, although Asia was mainly on a silver standard.

As Mundell put it succinctly: "Money, in its role of medium of exchange is less useful if there are many currencies; although the costs of conversion are always present, they loom exceptionally large under inconvertibility or flexible exchange rates" (1961). In 1973, he proposed "A plan for a European currency" and has become known as the "father of the euro." His plan extolled the benefits of a common currency: reserve pooling, less costly and more transparent financial intermediation, and policy coordination. The larger the zone of a common currency, the greater are its advantages.

The launching of the euro

On January 1, 2002 the euro banknote and coin were launched. The 12 member states launching the euro were Belgium, Germany, Greece, Spain, France, Ireland, Italy, Luxembourg, the Netherlands, Austria, Portugal, and Finland. At inception, the euro was worth $1.18, sank to $0.85, and then rose to a peak of $1.35, before stabilizing somewhat at $1.25. From a purchasing power point of view, it is still overvalued. Costs of conversion are disappearing. The bid–ask spread has gone to zero for banknotes and coins, and wire transfers are less expensive. In addition, exchange rate uncertainty under separate European currencies had led to an active market in London in foreign exchange options, futures, forwards, and swaps in cross-currency trading in Europe. With the adoption of a single currency, FOREX risk management is no longer necessary in the euro zone. Exchange rate volatility is zero, so options are worthless. European interest rates have converged since currency risk in the euro zone is eliminated.

As a result of currency integration, capital markets are enjoying lower interest rates virtually everywhere in Europe thanks to market integration and liquidity effects.

Further benefits of currency unification

In addition to the reduced cost of capital due to market integration and liquidity effects, transactions costs should, in theory, disappear in currency conversion and payments transfer within the euro zone. Prior to the US Civil War in the Confederated States (1861–5), each state had a separate currency, so each levied seigniorage on its residents. With the outbreak of the Civil War, the North issued the greenback dollar to finance its increased military expenditures, and the South printed the confederate dollar to finance theirs. With the ultimate victory of the North, the confederate dollar became worthless, and the greenback dollar evolved into the US dollar of today.

No one would deny the benefits from currency and trade integration of the 50 United States. Capital market integration and liquidity effects have led to a low cost of capital, high investment, and rapid growth in the United States. The US Constitution prohibits taxes on trade among the states, and a banknote issued in New York is legal tender in California. Similarly, a note issued in San Francisco is accepted in New York. This is now the case in Europe with the euro. Seigniorage

35

is spread among the member countries by the issue of slightly different banknotes and coins. All are acceptable as the medium of exchange in the member countries.

Convergence issues

Convergence in budget deficits to less than 3 percent of GDP, national debt less than 60 percent of GDP, and a common monetary policy are prerequisites established by the Maastricht Treaty for adherence to the euro zone. National macroeconomic policy is subjected to the monetary anchor of a common currency. European sovereign debt is denominated in euros. Germany had problems integrating the former Eastern Germany, and France has entitlements to minimum guaranteed incomes, generous unemployment insurance, early retirement of a huge civil servant force, and nearly free health benefits, so that both have run deficits exceeding the 3 percent benchmark. There is little chance, however, that an individual country, such as Italy, would forgo the benefits of the common currency zone to be able to run a higher deficit and finance it with seigniorage through the printing press.

THE CHINESE YUAN

The following piece makes the case for China maintaining a fixed exchange rate for stability and growth in the Chinese economy, despite much clamor for yuan revaluation of up to 35 percent. We take the position that a large appreciation would cause a major recession in China, much as the ever-appreciating yen caused recession, a housing and stock market slump, and a liquidity trap in Japan where interest rates approached zero.

THE SWIFT AND CHIPS INTERNATIONAL CLEARING SYSTEMS

In 1977, national interbank clearing systems were linked internationally through the SWIFT clearing system: an acronym for the Society for Worldwide Interbank Financial Telecommunications. The system has over 1,000 members for whom it provides secure electronic transfer of monies and communication of messages internationally. Each member bank has an electronic identification and some handshaking goes on through the international computer centers for identification. When the bank ID is confirmed, transactions and communications can take place swiftly and securely since the computer system is a dedicated one.

CHINA SYNDROME

In the 1980s and early '90s, Japan bashing was the favorite pastime in Washington. Japan's sin: its large "contribution" to a growing US trade deficit. To solve this "problem," the US demanded that Japan either strengthen the yen or face trade sanctions. Japan reluctantly complied. In Tokyo, "voluntary" export quotas and an ever-appreciating yen policy became orders of the day. But that one-two policy punch missed its target. Both the US trade deficit and Japan's surplus continued to grow. The "strong" yen wasn't benign, however. It created a monster of a problem in Japan—a deflationary slump. Today, the US trade deficit is almost double what it was five years ago. This time around China is the fingered culprit; it accounts for almost 25% of the deficit. To deal with China, Washington has dusted off the same defective game plan used to bash Japan. Senators Charles Schumer (D., N.Y.) and Lindsey Graham (R., S.C.) have led the mercantilist charge on Capitol Hill. They claim that China manipulates its currency, the yuan. As a result, the yuan is undervalued and Chinese exports are subsidized. To correct for China's alleged unfair trade advantage, Senators Schumer and Graham have sponsored currency revaluation legislation and the Senate has agreed to give it an up or down vote by July. If it becomes law, the Chinese would be given six months to negotiate a yuan reval-uation with the US. Absent a satisfactory revaluation, all China's exports to the US would be slapped with a 27.5% tariff—a rate equal to the alleged yuan undervaluation. Not to be outdone, members of the House have also laid the US trade deficit at the yuan's doorstep. Congressmen Duncan Hunter (R., Calif.) and Tim Ryan (D., Ohio) have introduced the China Currency Act. It defines "exchange rate manipulation" as a "prohibited export subsidy" which, if deemed harmful, could—under Article VI of the General Agreement on Tariffs and Trade—trigger an antidumping or countervailing duty to offset the "subsidy." Furthermore, if currency manipulation injured the US defense industry, the importation of Chinese defense products would be prohibited.

The clamor for a yuan revaluation is loud. At one time or another, everyone from President Bush to the G-7 has had a hand in the noisemaking. But the yuan quick fix might just be neat, plausible and wrong. Let's investigate:

- Does China manipulate its currency? It is not possible to give a categorical response to this question because "currency manipulation" is simply not an operational concept that can be used for economic analysis. The US Treasury admitted as much in a March 2005 report that attempted to clarify the statutory meaning of currency manipulation for the Committees on Appropriations.

- Is the yuan undervalued vis-à-vis the dollar? No. The nominal yuan/dollar rate has been set in stone at 8.28 since June 1995. Adjusting for inflation in China and the US, the real value of the yuan has depreciated by only 2.4% during the last decade. And today the yuan is in equilibrium in the sense that China's inflation rate has converged to the US rate. Not surprisingly, the IMF's most recent Country Report on China concluded that "it is difficult to find persuasive evidence that the renminbi [yuan] is substantially undervalued."

- Would a yuan revaluation reduce the US trade deficit? Not much, if at all. After a yuan revaluation, the US demand for foreign goods would simply be shifted from China to other countries.

- Would the House and Senate bills comport with international agreements and US obligations? No. The yuan revaluation required by the Schumer-Graham bill would violate China's rights and sovereignty. Under the IMF Articles of Agreement (Article IV, sec. 2(b)), a member country is free to choose its own currency regime, including a fixed exchange rate. The bill's revaluation mandate would also throw a wrench into what has been an incredibly successful economic performance. Over the last decade, China avoided the great Asian financial maelstrom of 1997–98 and has realized stable prices and an annual growth rate of over 9%. The yuan's fixed exchange rate against the dollar has provided the linchpin for that outstanding record.

According to Nobelist Robert Mundell, who is honorary president (along with Xu Jialu, vice chairman of the Standing Committee of the People's Congress) of Beijing's Mundell International University of Entrepreneurship, a substantial yuan revaluation would cut foreign direct investment, cut China's growth rate, delay convertibility, increase bad loans, increase unemployment, cause deflation distress in rural areas, destabilize Southeast Asia, reward speculators, set in motion more revaluation pressures, weaken the external role of the yuan and undermine China's compliance with World Trade Organization rules. In consequence, a forced revaluation would violate Article IV, sec. 1(i) of the IMF Articles of Agreement, which states that a member shall "endeavor to direct its economic and financial policies toward the objective of fostering orderly economic growth with reasonable price stability." If China failed to revalue the yuan, the across the board 27.5% tariff triggered by Schumer-Graham would violate China's Most Favored Nation status under Article I of the GATT. Both the tariff and import prohibition features of the Hunter-Ryan China Currency Act would also violate the MFN treatment of China and would be ruled illegal by the WTO.

- Would it be in China's interest to revalue and get the US politicos off its back? No. The effect of a yuan revaluation—deflation and recession—would even be more damaging to China than trade sanctions. We estimate that a 25% yuan revaluation against the dollar would result in a deflation of at least 15%. China would be forced to relive the terrible economic conditions induced by the 1930s yuan revaluation. In 1934, the US Silver Purchase Act monetized silver. This effectively revalued the yuan by 24% because China was on the silver standard. The price of the yuan against the dollar went from 33 cents at the end of 1933 to 41 cents in 1935. As Milton Friedman concluded in his classic study *Money Mischief*: "Because silver was China's money, the rise in the price of silver had produced a major deflation, which in turn had led to severely troubled economic conditions." It's time for the US to stop rushing to judgment based on false premises. Antagonizing the world's most populous country—and doing so by illegal means to boot—is both irrational and dangerous."

Source: Steve H. Hanke and Michael Connolly, *The Wall Street Journal*, May 9, 2005: A22. Reprinted with permission of *The Wall Street Journal* © 2005. *Artwork by David G. Klein © 2005.*

The CHIPS (Clearing House Interbank Payments System) clearing system in the United States handles tens of thousands of transactions and transfers many billions of dollars internationally per day. Member banks make electronic payments in CHIP dollars during the day and at the end of the day the master system nets out the sums to be paid, then transfers only the net amount of real money. This system is connected to the SWIFT system and is run by dedicated computers and member banks having strict code identification. Verification, confirmation, and authentification of transactions is also carried out by the CHIPS system.

THEORIES OF THE LONG-RUN MOVEMENT OF EXCHANGE RATES

During World War I, a Swedish economist, Gustav Cassell (1918) corresponded with John Maynard Keynes, then editor of the *Economic Journal*. His position was that movements in exchange rates reflected movements in their relative purchasing power. He plotted monthly changes in prices in different countries and compared those to the movements in exchange rates during the same time period. Countries with higher inflation suffered currency depreciations. He dubbed his theory the "purchasing power parity" (PPP) doctrine of the exchange rate. The PPP theory fits well with the wartime facts of high inflation and currency depreciation in the belligerent nations.

Purchasing power parity

If a commodity can be purchased in one place and sold in another without any transport costs, tariffs, or transactions costs, its price should be the same in both markets. This is the law of one price. It is an arbitrage relationship: arbitrageurs buying low and selling high will equalize commodity prices. That is:

$$P_{us} = SP_j,\qquad\qquad(3.1)$$

where the price of the product in yen is multiplied by the spot dollar price of the yen to yield the same price in the United States.

Absolute purchasing power parity

By the same token, if all goods are costlessly arbitraged, the spot exchange rate can be deduced from the ratio of any identical commodity price in each currency, or:

$$S = \frac{P_{us}}{P_j}.\qquad\qquad(3.2)$$

This strong version of PPP is known as "absolute PPP," where the prices correspond to consumer price indices of similar commodities in each country. The spot exchange rate can be inferred from commodity prices in different markets. This is the reasoning embodied in *The Economist*'s Big Mac hamburger standard.

Arbitraging Big Macs

Let's follow *The Economist*'s suggestion and buy Big Macs low in yuan and sell them high in USD. As the article suggests, the costs of arbitrage are high. First,

40

FAST FOOD AND STRONG CURRENCIES

Italians like their coffee strong and their currencies weak. That, at least, is the conclusion one can draw from their latest round of grumbles about Europe's single currency. But are the Italians right to moan? Is the euro overvalued? Our annual Big Mac index suggests they have a case: the euro is overvalued by 17% against the dollar. How come? The euro is worth about $1.22 on the foreign-exchange markets. A Big Mac costs €2.92, on average, in the euro zone and $3.06 in the United States. The rate needed to equalize the burger's price in the two regions is just $1.05. To patrons of McDonald's, at least, the single currency is overpriced. The Big Mac index, which we have compiled since 1986, is based on the notion that a currency's price should reflect its purchasing power. According to the late, great economist Rudiger Dornbusch, this idea can be traced back to the Salamanca school in 16th-century Spain. Since then, he wrote, the doctrine of purchasing-power parity (PPP) has been variously seen as a "truism, an empirical regularity or a grossly misleading simplification." Economists lost some faith in PPP as a guide to exchange rates in the 1970s, after the world's currencies abandoned their anchors to the dollar. By the end of the decade, exchange rates seemed to be drifting without chart or compass. Later studies showed that a currency's purchasing power does assert itself over the long run. But it might take three to five years for a misaligned exchange rate to move even halfway back into line. Our index shows that burger prices can certainly fall out of line with each other. If he could keep the burgers fresh, an ingenious arbitrageur could buy Big Macs for the equivalent of $1.27 in China, whose yuan is the most undervalued currency in our table [see Table 3.4], and sell them for $5.05 in Switzerland, whose franc is the most overvalued currency. The impracticality of such a trade highlights some of the flaws in the PPP idea. Trade barriers, transport costs and differences in taxes drive a wedge between prices in different countries. More important, the $5.05 charged for a Swiss Big Mac helps to pay for the retail space in which it is served, and for the labour that serves it. Neither of these two crucial ingredients can be easily traded across borders. David Parsley, of Vanderbilt University, and Shang-Jin Wei, of the International Monetary Fund, estimate that non-traded inputs, such as labour, rent and electricity, account for between 55% and 64% of the price of a Big Mac. The two economists disassemble the Big Mac into its separate ingredients. They find that the parts of the burger that are traded internationally converge towards purchasing-power parity quite quickly. Any disparity in onion prices will be halved in less than nine months, for example. But the non-traded bits converge much more slowly: a wage gap between countries has a "half-life" of almost 29 months. Seen in this light, our index provides little comfort to Italian critics of the single currency. If the euro buys less burger than it should, perhaps inflexible wages, not a strong currency, are to blame.

© *The Economist* Newspaper Limited, London, June 11, 2005.

Table 3.4 The hamburger standard

	Big Mac price in dollars*	Implied PPP† of the dollar	Under (−)/ over (+) valuation against the dollar, %		Big Mac price in dollars*	Implied PPP† of the dollar	Under (−)/ over (+) valuation against the dollar, %
United States‡	3.06	−	−	Aruba	2.77	1.62	−10
Argentina	1.64	1.55	−46	Bulgaria	1.88	0.98	−39
Australia	2.50	1.06	−18	Colombia	2.79	2,124	−9
Brazil	2.39	1.93	−22	Costa Rica	2.38	369	−22
Britain	3.44	1.63§	+12	Croatia	2.50	4.87	−18
Canada	2.63	1.07	−14	Dominican Rep	2.12	19.6	−31
Chile	2.53	490	−17	Estonia	2.31	9.64	−24
China	1.27	3.43	−59	Fiji	2.50	1.39	−18
Czech Republic	2.30	18.4	−25	Georgia	2.00	1.19	−34
				Guatemala	2.20	5.47	−28
Denmark	4.58	9.07	+50	Honduras	1.91	11.7	−38
Egypt	1.55	2.94	−49	Iceland	6.67	143	+118
Euro area	3.58**	1.05††	+17	Jamaica	2.70	53.9	−12
Hong Kong	1.54	3.92	−50	Jordan	3.66	0.85	+19
Hungary	2.60	173	−15	Latvia	1.92	0.36	−37
Indonesia	1.53	4,771	−50	Lebanon	2.85	1,405	−7
Japan	2.34	81.7	−23	Lithuania	2.31	2.12	−24
Malaysia	1.38	1.72	−55	Macau	1.40	3.66	−54
Mexico	2.58	9.15	−16	Macedonia	1.90	31	−38
New Zealand	3.17	1.45	+4	Moldova	1.84	7.52	−40
Peru	2.76	2.94	−10	Morocco	2.73	8.02	−11
Philippines	1.47	26.1	−52	Nicaragua	2.11	11.3	−31
Poland	1.96	2.12	−36	Norway	6.06	12.7	+98
Russia	1.48	13.7	−52	Pakistan	2.18	42.5	−29
Singapore	2.17	1.18	−29	Paraguay	1.44	2,941	−53
South Africa	2.10	4.56	−31	Qatar	0.68	0.81	−78
South Korea	2.49	817	−19	Saudi Arabia	2.40	2.94	−22
Sweden	4.17	10.1	+36	Serbia & Montenegro	2.08	45.8	−32
Switzerland	5.05	2.06	+65				
Taiwan	2.41	24.5	−21	Slovakia	2.09	21.6	−32
Thailand	1.48	19.6	−52	Slovenia	2.56	163	−16
Turkey	2.92	1.31	−5	Sri Lanka	1.75	57.2	−43
Venezuela	2.13	1,830	−30	Ukraine	1.43	2.37	−53
				UAE	2.45	2.94	−20
				Uruguay	1.82	14.4	−40

Sources: McDonald's; *The Economist.*
Notes:
*At current exchange rates. †Purchasing-power parity. ‡Average of New York, Chicago, San Francisco, and Atlanta. §Dollars per pound. **Weighted average of member countries. ††Dollars per euro.

we have to buy yuan to purchase a Big Mac in Shanghai. We pay the ask price of the yuan to the bank. Second, with our yuan, we buy the Big Mac in China. Third, we pay insurance and freight charges to ship the Big Mac to New York. Fourth, we pay any US customs duties on prepared foods. Finally, we sell the Big Mac in Manhattan, paying the sales tax there. Let's write a formula for our arbitrage profits:

$$\pi = P_{us}(1 - t_{us}) - S_{ask}P_c(1 + \tau_{us} + t_{c-us}). \tag{3.3}$$

When our transactions costs are reckoned in, arbitrage profits are likely to be nil. We incur these additional arbitrage costs:

1   We pay the ask rate, S_{ask}, a premium, for the yuan—these are currency exchange costs.
2   We pay the cost of shipping and insuring the Big Mac, t_{c-us}.
3   We pay the US customs rate on the Big Mac, τ_{us}.
4   Finally we pay the NY excise tax, t_{us}.

Net of these costs, we will not make a dime since arbitrage assures that the law of one price holds, assuring that arbitrage profits are zero, $\pi = 0$, or:

$$P_{us}(1 - t_{us}) = S_{ask}P_c(1 + \tau_{us} + t_{c-us}). \tag{3.4}$$

The bid–ask spread is part of the transactions costs that the arbitrageur must cover in order to make the arbitrage profitable. The other transactions costs—import duties and transport costs—are more obvious, but they must also be covered to make arbitrage profitable.

The strict law of one price

For the law of one price to exactly hold, taxes, transports costs, import duties, and the bid–ask spread all must be zero, in which case arbitrage (in either direction) imposes the strict law of one price, or:

$$P_{us} = SP_c. \tag{3.5}$$

With non-traded goods (in which no arbitrage takes place due to high transport costs or prohibitive duties), this condition cannot be satisfied. In general, the spot exchange rate, whether bid or ask, will not exactly satisfy the law of one price due to the presence of duties and transport costs on traded goods as well as the prohibitive costs of arbitraging non-traded goods. A weaker form of PPP—relative PPP, however, may save the day.

Relative purchasing power parity

Relative PPP does not require that the level of the exchange rate equal the ratio of purchasing powers, but that the change in the spot rate reflect the inflation rate differential. In other words, there is no change in the real exchange rate.

Relative PPP states:

$$\frac{E(S_{t+1}) - S_t}{S_t} = \frac{E(P^{us}_{t+1}) - P^{us}_t}{P^{us}_t} - \frac{E(P^j_{t+1}) - P^j_t}{P^j_t}, \qquad (3.6)$$

where the left-hand side of equation 3.6 is the expected appreciation of the foreign currency in terms of home currency and the right-hand side is the expected inflation rate differential: that is, the expected rate of inflation at home less the expected rate of inflation abroad.

The relative PPP theory of the exchange rate is depicted in Figure 3.7. When inflation at home is expected to be 1 percent greater than abroad, the expected price of foreign currency rises 1 percent. In fact, whenever the shocks are mainly monetary in nature, the PPP theory provides a good forecast of future exchange rates. It is not an arbitrage equation; rather, it says that movements in currencies reflect movements in their relative purchasing power.

THE IMF'S REAL EFFECTIVE EXCHANGE RATE

The International Monetary Fund's (IMF) real effective exchange rate index, RER (line rec, *International Financial Statistics*), is an exponentially weighted index that

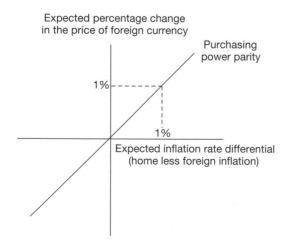

Figure 3.7 Purchasing power parity

measures the price of a home country's goods in terms of foreign goods. This type of index has excellent properties and is known as a "harmonic index," having exponential weights that sum to one:

$$RER = 100 \prod_{i=1}^{n} \left(\frac{P}{S_i P_i}\right)^{w_i} = 100 \left(\frac{P}{S_1 P_1}\right)^{w_1} \left(\frac{P}{S_2 P_2}\right)^{w_2} \left(\frac{P}{S_3 P_3}\right)^{w_3} \cdots \left(\frac{P}{S_n P_n}\right)^{w_n}. \quad (3.7)$$

As RER rises, the home currency is said to experience a real appreciation while, if RER falls, a real depreciation is said to occur. The Π symbol stands for the product of the i terms, in the same way that the Σ stands for the sum of various terms in a summation expression. P indicates the consumer price index of the home country, S_i indicates the home currency price of currency i, and the P_i indicates the consumer price index in country i. The exponential weights for each currency i are the W_i terms and must sum to unity (i.e. the equation is homogeneous of degree one so that a doubling of domestic prices relative to all exchange rate adjusted foreign prices leads to a doubling of the index). The W_i can represent simply trade weights with different countries, or, in the case of the IMF's RER, the weights are known as "effective trade weights."

Essentially, if the United States trades heavily with China and Mexico, the weights for the yuan and the peso would be relatively high in the US's RER. The *International Financial Statistics* are published in CD-ROM format monthly by the IMF, but lags in the data are a problem. *Bloomberg News* contains more current financial data on the real exchange rate.

FOREIGN CURRENCY FUTURES VERSUS FORWARD CONTRACTS

Futures are standard contracts per currency traded on the floor of an organized exchange. Maturities are usually less than one year and have fixed maturity dates. Prices are determined by the Chicago method of "open outcry." In Francesca Taylor's words:

This is very colorful to watch, and conveys "price transparency" by allowing every trader equal access to the same trade at the same price. Technically the meaning of open outcry is that your bid or your offer is good "whilst the breath is warm." What this actually means is that each trader on the exchange will shout out what trade he is trying to execute. He is not able to just shout it once and assume everyone heard him, he must keep shouting. If he stops shouting, it is assumed that he no longer wishes to execute his trade at that price level. Everyone around him is also shouting, resulting in a lot of noise

45

without too much clarity. The consequence of this is that not only do traders have to shout continuously what trades they are trying to fill, they must also "hand-signal" their trades, in case a trader a long way away cannot hear clearly. The hands and the mouth must say the same thing. Traders cannot just trade with hand signals and they must take examinations to comply with the requirements of the respective exchanges.

(1996: 26)

In the futures market, initial margin is required and is "marked to market" daily. Delivery rarely takes place—the purchase of an offsetting position unwinds the contract. A single commission is paid for the round trip purchase and sale. There is no counterparty risk as the exchange guarantees the contracts. Trading hours are regular exchange hours, but recently electronic trading takes place on a 24-hour basis. While liquid, the futures market is small in size.

Forwards, on the other hand, are any size desired, with maturities occasionally longer than a year. Trading occurs between firms and banks in the interbank market, with prices determined by bid–ask quotes—the spread providing profits for the banks. Standing bank "relations" are necessary, but not margin collateral. In the forwards market, banks are connected 24 hours a day via the SWIFT system and negotiate forward prices directly. In volume, the forwards market dwarfs the futures markets.

As a practical matter, international businesses hedge their risks through the forwards market, money market hedges, and foreign exchange swaps. Forwards give them the flexibility in terms of size of contract and maturity terms, and do not require the firm to tie up working balances in margin deposits.

Money market hedges allow for a matching of streams of payments and receipts in a foreign currency, thus reducing exchange rate exposure. Foreign exchange swaps do the same thing, but allow each firm to take advantage of its comparative advantage in borrowing in its local currency, swapping the proceeds of the loans through a swap dealer. Both borrowers are able to hedge their ongoing exposure through swaps at a lower cost. Nevertheless, the bid–ask spreads in foreign exchange and interest rates allow the swap dealer to make profits.

In forwards markets, money markets, and swap markets, there is counterparty risk, broadly defined as non-fulfillment or downgrading, either partial or complete, of the terms of financial contract.

Points quotations

A point is the last digit of a quotation. Thus, a point in foreign exchange quotations is typically equal to 0.0001 or 1/10,000 because currencies are usually quoted to four decimal points. A point is sometimes called a *pip* by foreign exchange traders. Consequently, when a forward quotation is given in terms of forward points (also known as swap points), it is necessary to adjust the spot quotation accordingly to obtain an outright forward quotation. For example, consider the following outright spot quotations on the pound sterling and the one-, two-, three-, six- and twelve-month forward points quotations in Table 3.5, as well as the corresponding outright forward rates.

As a general rule:

- When the bid in points is larger than the offer in points, the reference currency is at a discount, so the points are subtracted from the spot quotations to obtain the outright forward quotation.
- When the bid in points is smaller than the offer in points, the reference currency is at a premium, so the points are added to the spot quotations to obtain the outright forward quotation.

Notice again that the reciprocal of the American bid equals the European ask quotation. Likewise, the reciprocal of the American ask equals the European bid. This is obviously the case since, when bidding pounds for dollars, a bank or trader is simultaneously offering dollars for pounds. The corresponding European quotation is reported in Table 3.6.

FORWARDS AND FUTURES IN COMMODITIES

Like futures, forward contracts are agreements to exchange an underlying asset, such as gold, at an agreed price at some future date. Consequently, futures and

Table 3.5 Points and outright forward quotations

Forward points			Outright forward quotation ($/£)		
Period	Bid	Ask	Period	Bid	Ask
1 month	−0.00195	−0.00185	1 month	1.75853	1.76057
2 months	−0.00354	−0.00313	2 months	1.75694	1.75929
3 months	−0.00440	−0.00410	3 months	1.75608	1.75832
6 months	−0.00599	−0.00541	6 months	1.75448	1.75702
12 months	−0.00619	−0.00541	12 months	1.75428	1.75702
2 years	−0.00639	−0.00541	2 years	1.75408	1.75702

Source: OzFOREX Foreign Exchange Services, London, 10:19 a.m., July 14, 2005.

Note: Spot rate GBP/USD = 1.7609/1.7628.

Table 3.6 *Outright forward quotations in European terms*

Outright forward quotations (£/$)

Period	Bid	Ask
1 month	0.56800	0.56866
2 months	0.56841	0.56917
3 months	0.56872	0.56945
6 months	0.56915	0.56997
12 months	0.56915	0.57003
2 years	0.56915	0.57010

Source: OzFOREX Foreign Exchange Services, London, 10:19 a.m., July 14, 2005.

forward contracts may be used either to manage risk or for speculative purposes. However, there are important differences between forwards and futures that bear recalling:

1 A forward contract is negotiated directly between counterparties and is therefore tailor-made, whereas futures contracts are standardized agreements that are traded on an exchange.
2 Although forward contracts offer greater flexibility, there is a degree of counterparty risk, whereas futures contracts are guaranteed by the exchange on which they are traded.
3 Because futures contracts can be sold to third parties at any point prior to maturity, they are more liquid than forward contracts.
4 Futures prices are determined by the carrying costs at any time. These costs include the interest cost of borrowing gold plus insurance and storage charges.
5 The cost of a futures contract is determined by the "initial margin"—the cash deposit that is paid to the broker.

Speculative positions in forward contracts

A speculative position in a forward contract is the forward purchase or sale of an asset or commodity for delivery at some specified date in the future at a price, F, determined today. If a speculator who sold gold short purchases gold spot upon the delivery date at a price, S, to cover the short position, the profits/losses per unit of gold are $F - S$. Gold is usually traded forward in large units—metric tons.

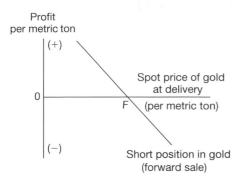

Figure 3.8 *A long forward position in gold*

On the other hand, if the spot price of gold is greater than F the trader loses $S - F$ in covering the forward contract. In Figure 3.8, the payoff for a forward sale of gold at the price F is illustrated.

A long position in gold is a purchase of gold for forward delivery. Consequently, if the spot price upon maturity of the forward purchase is higher than the forward price, a speculator gains $S - F$. If the spot price is less, the trader loses $F - S$. A hedged position is the combination of a long and a short position for the same amount and maturity of a security or asset. What is gained on the long position is lost on the short position, and vice versa. Graphically, the hedged position is the sum of the long and short positions, yielding the horizontal axis in Figure 3.9—a zero payoff.

Surprisingly, a gold mining company that sells its gold forward may not be perfectly hedged. If the spot price of gold rises before maturity, the company may be forced to sell its forward contract at a loss if it is illiquid.

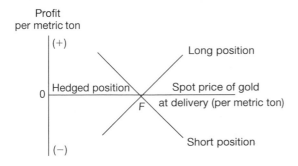

Figure 3.9 *A hedged forward position in gold*

The cost of carry and the forward arbitrage price

The forward price of an asset may be computed by the cost of carry and a no-profit arbitrage condition. Consider the following steps:

- Borrow S today at interest rate r.
- Purchase today one unit of the security at price S.
- Sell forward today one unit of the security at price F for delivery at time T.
- At maturity T, cash in the dividend k, on the security.
- Deliver the security at maturity T at agreed upon price F.
- Pay off loan at T.

The profit from this arbitrage can be computed as the forward sale price, plus the dividend received, less the principal and interest on the borrowed funds. That is:

$$\pi = F + \left[(1 + k)^T - 1\right] S - (1 + r)^T S. \tag{3.8}$$

Zero arbitrage profits imply:

$$F = \left[(1 + r)^T - (1 + k)^T + 1\right] S, \tag{3.9}$$

or, subtracting S from both sides of the equation yields the cost of carry:

$$F - S = \left[(1 + r)^T - (1 + k)^T\right] S. \tag{3.10}$$

When $T = 1$, the cost of carry is simply:

$$F - S = \left[r - k\right] S. \tag{3.11}$$

The carry trade requires that the forward price be at a premium when the borrowing rate is greater than the dividend rate or $r > k$. When the security has zero coupon, $k = 0$, or is a commodity with storage costs, $k < 0$, arbitrage pricing requires a premium over spot on the forward sale.

Let's take a few examples. First, suppose you sell 500 ounces of gold short for delivery in the futures market at $422 in three months. In a short sale, an investor borrows shares or gold from a brokerage firm and sells them, hoping to profit by buying them back at lower prices. If they rise, the investor faces a loss. Uncovered short sales are those shares or gold that have been borrowed and sold, but not yet covered by repurchase. If the spot price falls to $400, three months later when you cover your short position, you gain $22 per ounce or $11,000, as illustrated in Figure 3.10. However, if the price of gold rises in the spot market to $444, you will lose $22 an ounce, or $11,000, as shown in Figure 3.11.

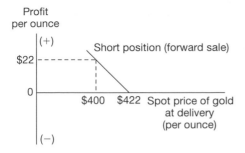

Figure 3.10 *Figure 3.10* A short forward position in gold

Since the forward rate is centered at the expected future value of gold, it is as likely you will gain at least $11,000 as you will lose at least $11,000. A hedged position combines a short with a long position, guaranteeing neither gains nor losses. However, you will pay the ask for the long forward and receive the bid for the short forward. That is, you will pay the spread. In addition, there is a commission. Ignoring the currency conversion costs, the hedged position is illustrated in Figure 3.12. By the same token, a long position—i.e. a forward purchase—gains when the spot price rises and loses upon covering when the spot price falls, as illustrated in Figures 3.13 and 3.14.

Gold is a hedge against inflation, as evidenced by these observations:

Gold prices climbed to an eight-month high in New York as US consumer prices rose more than forecast in July, increasing the precious metal's appeal as a hedge against inflation. . . . Some investors buy gold in times of inflation which erodes the value of fixed-income assets such as bonds.

(Itzenson, 2005)

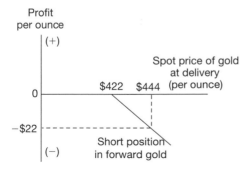

Figure 3.11 A loss on a forward short position in gold

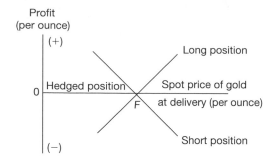

Figure 3.12 *A hedged forward position in gold*

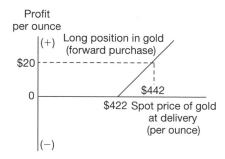

Figure 3.13 *A gain on a forward long position in gold*

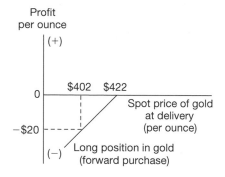

Figure 3.14 *A loss on a forward long position in gold*

ARBITRAGE DETERMINATION OF THE SPOT AND FUTURE RATES

"Arbitrage" means buying low, selling high, and profiting from differences in price when the same security, currency, or commodity is traded on two or more markets. An arbitrageur simultaneously buys one contract of, say, gold in New York and sells one contract of gold in Chicago, locking in a small profit because at that moment the price on the two markets is different. Arbitrageurs perform the economic function of making markets trade more efficiently by eliminating different prices for the same item.

Covered interest arbitrage hedges the foreign currency risk, thus covering the arbitrage from unexpected exchange rate losses in the future spot market. The hedge takes the form of a forward sale for foreign currency today at an agreed upon rate for delivery in the future, thus locking in the exchange rate conversion to home currency.

Uncovered interest arbitrage does not hedge foreign currency risk. The arbitrageur purchases foreign T-bills on the expectation that, when they mature, the foreign exchange proceeds—interest plus principal in pounds, for example —will be sold on the spot market in say 30 days for more dollars than would otherwise be earned by holding US 30-day T-bills. The uncovered arbitrageur may expect to sell at the forward rate in effect today, but the spot rate for the pound may be higher or lower than the forward rate today. If it is higher, the arbitrageur-speculator gains by selling pounds at the higher rate, but, if it is lower, there are unanticipated losses on the exchange conversion. Since the arbitrager does not cover foreign exchange exposure by selling pounds in the forward market, this type of interest arbitrage is called uncovered.

Covered interest arbitrage

Let's jot down some preliminary notation. To focus on strict interest rate parity, we will initially ignore the foreign exchange and Treasury bid–ask spreads. As we shall see later, these spreads are not insignificant and add substantially to the cost of arbitraging for an individual investor. Banks and financial intermediaries trading on their own accounts are spared the spreads and can arbitrage large amounts to take advantage of small deviations from interest rate parity.

- Spot rate for the pound: $S = (\$/\pounds)$ = number of dollars paid today for one British pound sterling delivered today.
- One month forward rate for the pound: $F = (\$/\pounds)$ = number of dollars received in three months for the sale of one pound sterling. This rate is agreed upon today.
- The US Treasury bill three-month rate: R_{us} = the interest rate on the three-month US Treasury bill (the quarterly rate).

- The UK Treasury bill interest rate: R_{uk} = interest rate on a three-month UK Treasury bill.

US Treasury bills (T-bills) are issued with different maturities in denominations beginning at $1,000. T-bills do not bear interest or pay coupons. Instead, investors purchase bills at a discounted price from their face value. At maturity, the Treasury redeems the bills at full face or par value. The difference between the discounted price paid and the face value of the bill is paid when redeemed. T-bills are also quoted by price. An investor pays the ask when buying T-bills and receives the bid when selling them. For the moment, we set the bid–ask spread at zero. To simplify the notation in the list above, this is the three-month interest rate, i.e. the quarterly rate, not the interest rate per annum. To convert the annual interest rate to a 90-day interest rate, the convention is to multiply the annual rate by 90/360 or 1/4 to convert to a quarterly rate; that is, just divide by four.

To take advantage of small profit opportunities by arbitraging short-term liquid capital, take the following two steps:

Step I: Compare dollars to dollars

Route 1:

With one million dollars, buy 90-day US T-bills. At maturity, they will yield principal plus interest of $(1 + R_{us})$ million dollars. Each dollar invested yields $1 + R_{us}$ dollars in 90 days.

Route 2:

1 Buy $[1/(S)]$ million pounds sterling in the spot market at S.
2 Invest $[1/(S)]$ pounds sterling in 90-day UK T-bills, yielding $[1/(S)(1 + R_{uk})]$ million pounds in three months.
3 Sell $[1/(S)(1 + R_{uk})]$ pounds sterling in the forward market at F, yielding $F[1/(S)(1 + R_{uk})]$ or:

$$\left(\frac{F}{S}\right)(1 + R_{uk}) \tag{3.12}$$

dollars at settlement in three months.

Step II: Select higher dollar return

If:

$$(1 + R_{us}) > \left(\frac{F}{S}\right)(1 + R_{uk}), \tag{3.13}$$

place short-term capital in US T-bills due to the higher yield. That is, sell pound T-bills from your portfolio, buy dollars spot, buy 90-day US T-bills, sell the proceeds 90 days forward. You have completed a round trip in pounds and gained the covered arbitrage differential.

If:

$$(1 + R_{us}) < \left(\frac{F}{S}\right)(1 + R_{uk}),$$ (3.14)

place short-term capital in UK T-bills due to the higher yield. That is, sell 90-day US T-bills from your portfolio, buy pounds spot, buy UK 90-day T-bills, and sell the pound proceeds forward for delivery in 90 days. You have completed a round trip and gained the covered arbitrage differential.

However, if:

$$(1 + R_{us}) = \left(\frac{F}{S}\right)(1 + R_{uk}),$$ (3.15)

covered interest rate parity holds, there are no unexploited arbitrage profit opportunities, so do nothing!

Covered interest parity can be expressed in terms of the percentage interest rate differential versus the percentage premium or discount on the forward pound. Subtract $(1 + R_{uk})$ from both sides of the interest rate parity equation and simplify:

$$(R_{us} - R_{uk}) = \left(\frac{F - S}{S}\right)(1 + R_{uk}),$$ (3.16)

which says that the interest rate differential in favor of US T-bills is just (approximately) offset by the premium on the pound sterling. If interest rates on US T-bills are 2 percent higher than on UK T-bills, the forward pound will be at a 2 percent premium. Covered interest rate parity can be illustrated in Figure 3.15. Along the interest rate parity line, it does not matter whether you invest your short-term funds in US or UK T-bills. To the right of the interest parity line, the

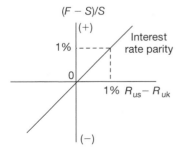

Figure 3.15 Covered interest rate parity

THE FOREIGN EXCHANGE MARKET

covered arbitrage differential (CAD) is in favor of US T-bills. To the left, the CAD is in favor of UK T-bills.

The covered arbitrage differential

The covered arbitrage differential (CAD) in favor of 90-day US T-bills is measured by:

$$CAD = (1 + R_{us}) - \left(\frac{F}{S}\right)(1 + R_{uk}), \tag{3.17}$$

which may be positive or negative. If positive, sell UK T-bills, buy dollars spot with the pound proceeds, buy US T-bills, and sell the dollars forward (buy pounds forward), thus gaining the CAD in the round trip arbitrage. If negative, sell US T-bills, buy pounds spot, buy UK T-bills and sell pounds forward (buy dollars forward), to gain the CAD in favor of UK T-bills.

Transactions costs

Of course, there are transactions costs, since the investor must pay the ask when buying and receives the bid when selling, effectively paying the bid–ask spreads on FOREX to the financial institution. Similarly, when buying US or UK T-bills, the investor pays the ask price, while, when selling, the investor receives the bid. For this reason, slight deviations from interest rate parity do not trigger covered arbitrage movements, except possibly by financial institutions. Ignoring transactions costs, capital will arbitrage until interest rate parity holds since the assets are risk-free. The CAD, including transactions costs, equals zero, yielding covered interest parity. Otherwise, unexploited riskless profits from arbitrage would exist.

Just what are these arbitrage costs? We can identify three spreads and commissions in the FOREX and T-bills markets:

1 the FOREX spread;
2 the US T-bill spread;
3 the UK T-bill spread;
4 commissions on FOREX and T-bills.

Taking into account the rates at which an individual transacts, the interest rate parity condition is a bit more complex. Equation 3.18 illustrates the interest rate parity condition for an investor's round trip to UK T-bills and back:

$$\left(\frac{1 + R_{us}^{bid}}{1 + R_{us}^{ask}}\right) = \left(\frac{F_{\$/£}^{bid}}{S_{\$/£}^{ask}}\right)\left(\frac{1 + R_{uk}^{bid}}{1 + R_{uk}^{ask}}\right), \tag{3.18}$$

which uses the convention that the bid rate is less than the ask rate, both for FOREX and T-bills. T-bills are quoted in terms of their price, of course, so an ask price discount of a T-bill yields the same as an interest rate bid.

An example of covered interest arbitrage

When the interest differential does not exactly offset the forward discount, it is possible to make small gains by arbitraging money. Consider an example of either investing $10,000 in three-month US T-bills, or converting into euros, purchasing European T-bills, and selling the euro proceeds in the three-month futures market. The basic data are given below:

Basic arbitrage data

US T-bill rate (3 months)	0.9625
Euro T-bill rate (3 months)	0.9000
Spot price of the euro	1.2500
Forward price of the euro (3 months)	1.2700.

In this case, the interest rate differential against euro T-bills is less than the percentage future premium on the euro. Consequently, small gains ($155.44) can be made by arbitraging toward euro T-bills, and selling the euro proceeds three months forward. Once again, we are covered in the futures market. Thus this riskless arbitrage (buying low–selling high) will eliminate arbitrage gains.

The steps in covered interest arbitrage are illustrated in Figure 3.16. For arbitrage activity to be truly profitable to the investor, the correct rate quotation must

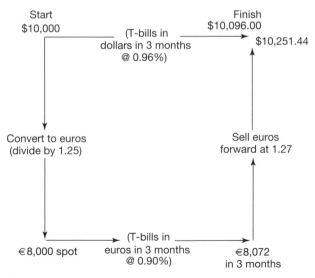

Figure 3.16 An example of covered interest parity

be used for each transaction. When US T-bills are sold, the bid rate is received; when pounds are bought spot, the dollar bid–pound ask rate is used, the ask rate for UK T-bills is paid and the forward bid price of the pound is received (or equivalently, the forward ask price of the dollar is paid.) Every transaction has a transactions cost. The round trip must cover all the transactions costs to be worthwhile.

An example of uncovered interest arbitrage

It is also possible to buy and hold euro T-Bills for three months, then at maturity sell the euro proceeds in the spot exchange market. This type of arbitrage is called uncovered interest arbitrage because it is subject to unexpected gains or losses. Uncovered interest arbitrage equilibrium occurs when the expected returns are equal. When there are riskless assets, it is generally true that $E(S_{90})$ = F_{90}. Consequently, when covered interest arbitrage equilibrium holds, the uncovered interest arbitrage equilibrium condition does too. Figure 3.17 illustrates an example of realized uncovered interest arbitrage where the euro proceeds are multiplied by the actual spot exchange rate realized after three months. If the realized spot rate of the euro is higher than the expected rate in one year, there are unanticipated gains, while, if it is less, there are unanticipated losses, hence the term "uncovered interest arbitrage." In Figure 3.17, the spot price of the euro has unexpectedly fallen to $1.20, so the arbitrage return is only $9,686.40. A loss of $409.60 is realized relative to the investment is US T-bills. Of course, the arbitrageur could liquidate the position at any time before maturity, thereby locking in any gains or losses. In general, we may define the unanticipated

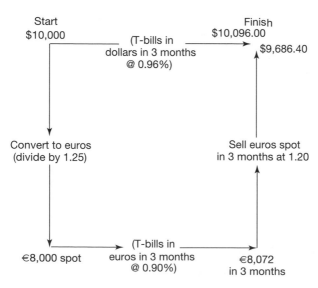

Figure 3.17 An example of uncovered interest parity

gain(+)/loss (−) by the difference between the spot price of the euro in 90 days (the bid), S_{90} and the future bid price of today, F_{90}.

The unanticipated gain, if positive, or loss, if negative, in uncovered interested arbitrage activity is measured as $S_{90} - F_{90}$ per unit of foreign exchange. We must still bear in mind that the rates refer to the dollar bid price of the euro in the spot and futures markets respectively (i.e. American quotation), and that the bid–ask spread is also paid on T-bills.

Cross rates and triangular arbitrage

Another type of arbitrage that is done by multinational financial institutions is known as "triangular arbitrage." Triangular arbitrage eliminates inconsistencies between direct and cross rates between two currencies, thereby enforcing the law of one price. It can take place in the spot or the futures markets to keep rates consistent.

The direct rate for the purchase of pounds by dollars is simply the American style quotation $/£. For an investor, this is the ask in dollars for one pound.

The cross rate, American quotation, between dollars and pounds via the yen is indicated by ($/¥)(¥/£) since this is the number of pounds obtained by buying yen for dollars, then buying pounds with the yen. Naturally, an investor pays the ask rate in dollars for yen, then the ask price in yen for pounds.

Triangular arbitrage equilibrium

There are no profit opportunities via triangular arbitrage when ($/¥)(¥/£) = ($/£). Whenever this condition is not satisfied, profit opportunities exist. Consider the following inconsistent quotations:

Direct rate:
Dollars per pound sterling ($/£)   1.7669

Cross rate:
Dollars per Japanese yen ($/¥)   0.009434
Japanese yen per pound sterling (¥/£)   186.3543
Therefore, the cross rate is (0.009434)(186.3543) = 1.7581.

An arbitrage opportunity exists! Buy yen with dollars, then pounds with yen. This will cost you $1.7581 per pound. Sell the pounds at $1.7669, earning one half of a US penny per pound. If you trade $1,000, your net profits are $5.02. Not bad for a few seconds' work. Note that the equilibrium cross rate is therefore ¥187.3543 per pound sterling.

In Figure 3.18, start with $1,000 in the upper right-hand starting position. Buy yen with dollars, then pounds with yen. At the end of the triangular arbitrage, you will have made about one cent per pound.

59

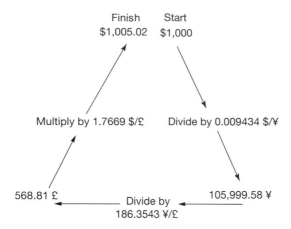

Figure 3.18 Triangular arbitrage

Profitable arbitrage will eliminate this price inconsistency, establishing the law of one price. Arbitrageurs take advantage of these opportunities until profit disappears and arbitrage equilibrium is satisfied. Arbitrage increases the dollar price of the yen and the yen price of the pound, until no further arbitrage profits exist.

Consider another arbitrage example: You have two prices for a pound:

$$(\$/\yen)(\yen/\pounds) = \$1.7669$$
$$(\$/\pounds) = \$1.7642.$$

In this case, buy a pound directly with dollars, and then sell it indirectly through yen for dollars, earning profits of [$1.7669 − $1.7642] = 0.0027 dollars per pound. Recall that you will pay the FOREX spread three times in converting currency in this example.

The law of one price

Interest rate arbitrage is another way of looking at the law of one price. A dollar is a dollar is a dollar. You should only pay one dollar for it! In general, the same item must have the same price, adjusting for transactions and shipping costs. An ounce of gold is worth the London fixing price all over the world. Even panners in Brazil know the day's market price of gold.

When prices for the same item are out of line, that is, are different in two markets, an arbitrage opportunity exists. Buy low in the low market and sell high in the high market, making sure your transactions and or transportation costs are covered in doing so. Buying in the low market makes the price rise there and selling in the high market makes the price fall there. The equilibrium requires the law of one price, accounting for transactions costs, to hold for the same item. Arbitrage makes markets more efficient, moving goods and assets from markets with lower returns to markets with higher returns. In the process, wealth and income are increased.

This is particularly true for riskless financial arbitrage, where the transactions costs are low and the commodity is currency. While the individual investor loses the spreads by paying the ask price when buying and receiving the bid when selling, multinational financial institutions trading on their own account have minute transactions costs and will therefore push the equilibrium back toward the interest rate parity line whenever there are slight deviations. This keeps markets efficient, moving capital from low-return environments to high-return environments. Bear in mind, naturally, that we are speaking of riskless assets that are otherwise identical.

Arbitrage with risk of default

When arbitrage takes place in presence of default risk, for example on sovereign bonds, a risk premium, ρ, appears on the risky asset to compensate for the risk of default. There is no net flow of capital when the risk premium just compensates for expected losses from default. Uncovered interest rate parity, therefore, no longer holds due to the presence of risky assets denominated in a foreign currency. If we write the expected rates of return in the Brazilian real, where $E(S_{90})$ is the expected spot price of the US dollar in one year in terms of the real, and S is today's spot price, respectively, and R_B and R_{us} are the interest rates in dollars on three-month T-bills in the United States and Brazil respectively, the expected rates of return in *reals* will differ by the risk premium plus the expected depreciation of the *real*. That is, Brazilian T-bills will bear a higher rate of return to compensate for the risk of default. It might not therefore make sense to sell US T-bills to gain a few percentage points in Brazilian T-bills.

Consider:

$$(1 + R_B - \rho) = \left(\frac{E(S)}{S}\right)(1 + R_{us}),$$ (3.19)

which yields a risk-adjusted uncovered parity condition.

A close approximation yields the risk premium:

$$\rho \cong \left(\frac{E(S) - S}{S}\right) + (R_B - R_{us}).$$ (3.20)

Notice that the risk premium, ρ, is the sum of the real expected premium on the dollar plus the interest differential in favor of Brazil.

61

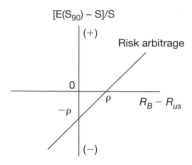

Figure 3.19 *Uncovered interest parity*

The equilibrium risk premium where there is no net portfolio capital flow in either direction is indicated in Figure 3.19. To the right of the risk arbitrage line, the interest rate in Brazil more than compensates for the expected depreciation and risk of default. Thus, capital flows in. To the left, capital flows out.

The interest differential is no longer a good predictor of the percentage rate of depreciation because a risk premium is imbedded into the risky asset. For emerging markets, therefore, expected inflation rate differentials (e.g. relative purchasing power parity) are a more reliable indicator of expected depreciation.

EXCHANGE RATE FORECASTING

If a forward rate, F, exists, it is centered at the expected exchange rate. Consequently, just buy *The Wall Street Journal* or The *Financial Times* and look up the forward rate. In the euro and the pound, there are futures up to two years. Consequently, today's forward quotations provided every bit of known information about the future, so they are unbiased predictors of the future spot exchange rate. However, forward and futures markets do not always exist for future delivery of foreign currency and their maturity is only up to two years. A forward bid and ask quotation could be gotten from a foreign exchange dealer, but the spread would be greater the further the quote is in the future. The foreign exchange dealer limits risk by widening the spread.

Forecasting the future exchange rate is conveniently done by the interest rate parity equation. First, let's create a hypothetical one-year T-bill that is composed of a six-month bill rolled over for an additional six months. That is, $(1 + R_{us180})$ $(1 + R_{us180}) = (1 + R_{us})$ yields an estimate of the comparable risk-free one-year rate, R_{us}. Alternatively, we could strip the interest rate futures to predict the 180- to 360-day six-month T-bill forward rate, or we could use the rate on a two-year T-bill with one year to maturity remaining. The main point of the exercise is to construct a one year synthetic riskless Treasury rate, R_{us}.

According to interest rate parity one year forward:

$$\left(\frac{F}{S}\right) = \frac{(1 + R_{us})}{(1 + R_{uk})}, \tag{3.21}$$

or equivalently:

$$F = S \frac{(1 + R_{us})}{(1 + R_{uk})}. \tag{3.22}$$

We can therefore use the interest rate parity equation to forecast the forward spot rate in one year—it is a no profit arbitrage condition that must hold. Similarly, by rolling over the Treasury asset an additional year or, in general, n years, we can forecast the future spot rate in n years by repeated application of interest rate parity:

$$F = S \left[\frac{(1 + R_{us})}{(1 + R_{uk})}\right]^n. \tag{3.23}$$

All information needed to make a five-year forecast of the future spot rate of the pound is available today: the spot rate, and one-year riskless interest rates in the United States and the UK. For example, if one-year riskless rate were 3.5 percent in the United States and 4 percent in the UK, interest rate parity implies that the dollar would be expected to appreciate approximately one half of a percent in a year relative to the pound. By rolling over the riskless pound investment each year, the successive dollar-pound future spot rates can be predicted using interest parity. That is, given the spot bid of $1.7609 per pound, we may predict the future spot bid rates by applying the n period forward interest parity formula, yielding a five-year forward forecast of the price of the pound:

$F_1 = 1.75243$
$F_2 = 1.74401$
$F_3 = 1.73562$
$F_4 = 1.72728$
$F_5 = 1.71898.$

The use of interest rate parity conditions—that is, the no expected profit arbitrage condition—as a forecasting tool is powerful and based in the best available finance theory. Despite the absence of a futures market five years ahead, a market-based forecast is still possible. It can be used to convert expected future cash flows in foreign currency, for instance.

AN APPLICATION TO FREE-CASH FLOW

Free-cash flow is defined as earnings after tax, plus depreciation (a non-cash expense) plus changes in net working capital. Table 3.7 indicates the forecasted free-cash flows for a possible expansion in the UK by a US firm in millions of pounds. (See Kester and Luehrman, 1993.)

Their approach is to convert foreign-currency cash flows to home currency, then discount to the present at the weighted average cost of capital in dollars, assumed to be 15 percent. Table 3.7 estimates the cost of acquisition of a subsidiary in the UK at 50 million pounds. In the first year of operations, it will generate a free-cash flow of £15.5 million, which peaks at £25.5 million in its third year, then goes to £12.5 in its fifth year of operations. During its fifth year, the firm is sold. Its terminal value is estimated to be £64.3 (a £10 million perpetuity discounted at 15.56 percent, our pound discount rate.) Alternatively, the terminal value could be the scrap value of the operation. The main issue is that the interest rate parity can be used to forecast the exchange rate of the pound in the second row of Table 3.7. This converts future free-cash flows from pounds to dollars in row three. Then discount at the firm's cost of borrowing in dollars, given as 15 percent. This yields a positive net present value of $71.5 million, representing a 35 percent internal rate of return (IRR; the rate of discount of free-cash flows in dollars that sets the net present value of the investment equal to zero.) Clearly, this expansion is worthwhile.

RANDOM INVESTING

Are darts better than financial advisors? Consider the following three tosses of a true (fair) coin that has a 50 percent (0.5) probability of landing heads and a

Table 3.7 Discounting and converting expected cash flows in pounds

Year	0	1	2	3	4	5	Terminal year
Free-cash flow (£)	−50	15.5	20	25.5	15	12.5	64.3
Exchange rates (forecast $/£)		1.76	1.75	1.74	1.74	1.73	1.72	1.72
Free-cash flow ($)	(88.0)	27.2	34.9	44.3	25.9	21.5	110.5
Present value of cash flows ($)	(88.0)	23.6	26.4	29.1	14.8	10.7	54.9
NPV ($)	71.49	–	–	–	–	–	–
IRR ($)	35%	–	–	–	–	–	–

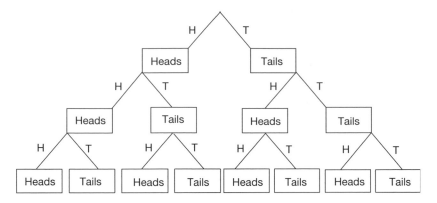

Figure 3.20 *Random investing*

50 percent probability of landing tails. There are eight possible outcomes after three tosses as illustrated by the binomial tree illustrated in Figure 3.20.

Consider eight investment funds associated with each branch of the binomial tree in Table 3.8. *Ex ante*, before the coin tosses, each has a 12.5 percent chance of winning, assuming three tosses of a fair coin. *Ex post*, after the coin tosses, there will only be one winner. Only one of the investment funds will be the successful investor, the others will be wrong. Nevertheless, the outcome was randomly determined. This random-walk view of investment suggests that indexed funds managed passively with low fees will do better on the average than actively managed funds with high fees. (See Reinker and Tower, 2004.) This is the efficient market hypothesis. For instance, if the winner takes $100, a fair investment would be $12.50 should the three tosses occur immediately. Notice that this example was a "fair" investment—neither bid–ask spread, nor fees associated with it—each

Table 3.8 *Random investing*

No.	Branches	Probability (%)	Investment fund
1	HHH	12.5	Fudelity
2	HHT	12.5	Local
3	HTH	12.5	Simpleton
4	HTT	12.5	Dubious
5	THH	12.5	Ponce de Leon
6	THT	12.5	GuarVan
7	TTH	12.5	T. Rut Price
8	TTT	12.5	Christopher Columbus

investor paid the expected value of investing. However, the house usually charges an entry fee and an ask price, so the investment is biased against the investor. This is especially true when a portfolio is actively managed and charges management fees. Yes, darts are usually better than financial advisors.

FOREIGN CURRENCY SWAPS

The principle of comparative advantage in borrowing leads to gains from a swap, just as comparative advantage in commodities leads to gains from trade. Each firm specializes in borrowing in the currency in which it enjoys its comparative advantage, then swaps that currency for another, thereby lowering its interest cost in the desired currency to be borrowed.

Firm A, an American firm whose credit rating is AAA, can borrow in euros at 12 percent or in dollars at 8 percent. Firm B, a Belgian firm, which has a BB+ rating and is thus more susceptible to adverse economic conditions, can borrow in euros at 14 percent and in dollars at 12 percent. Firm A exports to Europe and has accounts receivables in euros of about €11 million on an ongoing basis for the next five years. It is seeking matching interest and principal payments over the next five years. Similarly, Firm B sells around $14 million of Belgian waffles in the United States and wishes to hedge its ongoing dollar receipts by acquiring matching interest and principal payments in dollars. Forward markets at those maturities would be expensive. A currency swap is the appropriate instrument for both firms.

Comparative advantage in currency markets

For hedging purposes, Firm A thus prefers to borrow euros and Firm B prefers to borrow dollars. A swap dealer can exploit Firm A's comparative advantage in borrowing in dollars (8/12 < 12/14) and Firm B's comparative advantage in borrowing in euros (14/12 < 12/8). Firm A borrows in dollars while firm B borrows in euros for a maturity of five years; they swap the loan proceeds and payments through the swap dealer, both lowering their direct borrowing costs. In the process, the swap dealer earns the bid–ask spread in the foreign exchange rates and shares in the gains from each firm exploiting its comparative advantage in currency borrowing.

The direct borrowing rates are illustrated in Table 3.9. The American firm has a comparative advantage in borrowing in USD, while the Belgian firm has a comparative advantage in borrowing in euros. It does not matter that the American firm could conceivably borrow at less than the Belgian firm in euros—that only means it has an absolute advantage in borrowing in both currencies.

The swap dealer's bid–ask rates are given in Table 3.10. The swap dealer also charges 2 percent on the initial loans in up-front fees, and gains the bid–ask spread

■ *Table 3.9* Direct borrowing rates (%)

Currency	Firm A	Firm B
Euros	12	14
Dollars	8	12

■ *Table 3.10* The swap dealer's bid–ask rates

Currency	Rate	Currency	Rate
Bid ($/€)	1.2186	Bid (€/$)	0.8204
Ask ($/€)	1.2189	Ask (€/$)	0.8206

on the swap of both currencies. While the dealer loses interest on the euro loan, the gain in interest on the dollar loan just offsets the interest rate losses. Thus, the dealer is left with a little over $5 million in gains.

Consequently, the dealer agrees to pay Firm A's loan of $122.48 million at 8 percent and lends $120 million, after up-front fees of 2 percent and the bid–ask spread, to Firm B at an effective rate of 11.58 percent. This represents an interest savings of 0.42 percent over the direct borrowing rate of Firm B. Similarly, Firm B borrows €102.7 million at 14 percent, and the swap dealer agrees to assume the payments of interest and principal on the original loan, lending €102.7 million to Firm A at an effective rate of 11.57 percent, once again representing an interest rate savings of 0.43 percent over Firm A's direct borrowing costs in euros. Table 3.11 illustrates the effective euro and dollar loans to Firms A and B respectively.

The swap dealer makes 2 percent up-front profits, as well as the bid–ask spread in the loan swap, yielding a gain of $5.07 million at the time of the transaction. This is calculated in euros, then converted to dollars. In this instance, we assume that risk-free interest rates are the same, and simply convert at the spot bid rate. In the following years, the loans are structured so as to offset each other exactly, so no further profits are earned by the swap dealer.

Interest savings from the FOREX swap

The net gains to the swap dealer in dollars are:

5.0025
0.0000
0.0000
0.0000
0.0000
0.0000.

Table 3.11 Effective euro and dollar loans

Firm A	Effective euro loan to Firm A	Original euro bond issued by Firm B
Year 0	100.00	102.07
Year 1	(10.67)	(14.29)
Year 2	(10.67)	(14.29)
Year 3	(10.67)	(14.29)
Year 4	(10.67)	(14.29)
Year 5	(116.36)	(116.36)
All-in cost	11.57%	14.00%

Firm B	Effective dollar loan to Firm B	Original dollar bond issued by Firm A
Year 0	120.00	122.48
Year 1	(14.21)	(9.80)
Year 2	(14.21)	(9.80)
Year 3	(14.21)	(9.80)
Year 4	(14.21)	(9.80)
Year 5	(132.28)	(132.28)
All-in cost	11.58%	8.00%

Both firms save interest over direct borrowing. The FOREX swap exploits the gains from comparative advantage, so that both save nearly half a point in interest in the desired currency in which they wish to borrow, as illustrated in Table 3.12.

Figure 3.21 illustrates diagrammatically the cash flows of the swap. Firm B has now a little over $14 million in interest payments on an ongoing basis, matching its revenue in USD. It has therefore an operations hedge. Similarly, Firm A has acquired matching interest payments in euros of €10.67, an operations hedge against its expected receipts in euros. Neither have operational exposure to

Table 3.12 Interest rate savings by Firms A and B (%)

Firm	Direct borrowing rates	Effective swap rate	Interest rate savings
Firm A (€)	12	11.57	0.43
Firm B ($)	12	11.58	0.42

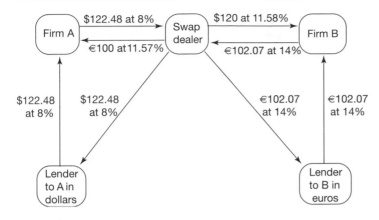

Figure 3.21 *A foreign exchange swap*

exchange rate changes, thanks to the FOREX swap. Notice that the gains from the swap are sufficient for both firms to experience reductions in their borrowing costs and for the swap dealer to benefit from the bid–ask spread and fees as a financial intermediary.

FOREIGN CURRENCY OPTIONS

A foreign currency call option is the right, but not the obligation, to buy a specified amount of foreign currency, known as the contract size, at an exercise price on or before the expiration date. A FOREX put option is the right to sell a specific quantity of foreign currents at strike price on or before maturity. Therefore, foreign currency options are derivatives whose value derives from the value of the underlying foreign currency. Like options on stocks, a European-style option cannot be exercised before the expiration date, while an American-style option can be exercised anytime between the moment it is written and its expiration.

- A call is an option to buy a foreign currency.
- A put is an option to sell a foreign currency.

The buyer of a foreign currency option pays a premium to purchase the option, but does not risk any further monies beyond the premium paid. Holding option positions can be risky and expensive. If the option expires "out-of-the-money," i.e. not profitable if exercised, the buyer loses all of the investment in the option premium. If the option expires "in-the-money," i.e. profitable if exercised, the buyer realizes a positive profit if the payoff of the option exceeds its cost, the premium.

69

The seller or writer of an FOREX option must honor the option contract if it is presented for exercise. Consequently, the seller of a put option risks the amount equal to the exercise price times the option contract size, should the currency become worthless. The seller of a call option faces potentially unlimited losses as the spot price of the underlying foreign currency could conceivably rise to infinity.

Exchange options in foreign currency are traded on the Philadelphia Stock Exchange (www.phlx.com/), and the International Money Market of the Chicago Mercantile Exchange (www.cme.com/). Exchange-traded options are standardized. The price of the option on an exchange is known as the premium. The contract is for a specified amount and the quoted exercise price is per unit of the underlying foreign currency, for example per pound sterling. Exchange-traded foreign exchange options do not carry default risk as the clearing house guarantees their performance.

Over-the-counter (OTC) options are sold by financial institutions to institutional buyers and are tailored to their needs in terms of amount (notional principal) and expiration date. These are mainly hedging transactions between multinational enterprises and banks. With OTC options, there is counterparty risk—the risk of deterioration in the terms of repayment, including default.

Payoff from a **FOREX** call option

We use a call option on pounds sterling to demonstrate the terminal profit to a long (buy) and a short (sell) call option position. Suppose that the call option premium were one cent per pound when the option positions were established. The exercise price of the call option is $1.77 per pound.

Figure 3.22 demonstrates the profit/loss to an investor who bought the call option and held it to the option's expiration date. As we can see from the figure,

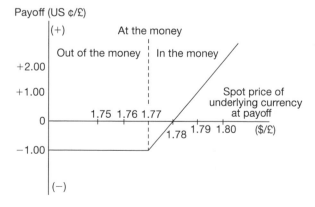

Figure 3.22 The payoff for the purchaser of a pound call option

the payoff is a negative one cent per pound when the option expires at $1.77 per pound or lower. The more the call option is "in the money," the higher is its payoff. The break-even point is at $1.78 per pound, which is the sum of the exercise price and call option premium. The payoff is potentially unlimited because the exchange rate could go to infinity.

At expiration at a spot price of $1.79 per pound, the call holder exercises the call option, buying pounds at $1.77 and selling them spot at $1.79, making two cents per pound. Net profits are one cent since the holder paid a premium of one cent per pound. The break-even point is $1.78 per pound. At a spot price of $1.75 per pound, the option would finish "out of the money." The call expires unexercised, leaving the holder with a net cost of one cent per pound of notional value. Because options are zero-sum games to their buyers and sellers, the seller of the call option has a profit diagram mirroring that of the buyer, but opposite in value, as in Figure 3.23.

The seller earns the premium of one cent per pound if the terminal spot exchange rate is no higher than $1.77 per pound. Beyond the exercise price of $1.77 per pound, the seller pays the difference between the spot price and the exercise price, keeping the option premium paid earlier. At $1.78 the seller pays out the premium collected, so $1.78 per pound represents the seller's break-even point also. At a price of $1.79, the seller of the call loses two cents per pound on the exercise, but keeps the one cent premium per pound. Since the price of the pound can in theory rise to infinity, the seller's potential losses are unlimited.

Profit from a FOREX put option

We use a put option on pounds sterling to demonstrate the terminal profit to a long and a short put option position. Suppose that the put premium was one cent

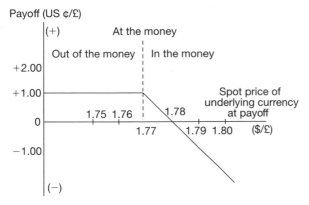

Figure 3.23 The payoff for the seller of a pound call option

per pound when the put option position was bought. The exercise price of the put option is $1.77 per pound. The put holder paid one cent per pound for the put. On expiration, the holder benefits if the spot exchange rate drops below $1.76 per pound, the break-even point. The lower the terminal spot rate, the higher are profits. The maximum profit is $1.77 per pound when the pound exchange rate drops to zero. The holder's maximum loss is the put option premium, one cent per pound if the put expires out of the money—above $1.77 spot at maturity, as shown in Figure 3.24.

The put seller collected one cent per pound of premium, which is the maximum profit the seller can expect to realize. If the put option finishes out of the money (when the spot exchange rate is more than $1.77 per pound), the seller keeps the premium without any further obligation. However, as the spot exchange

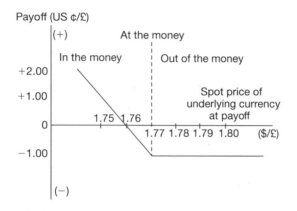

Figure 3.24 The payoff for the purchaser of a pound put option

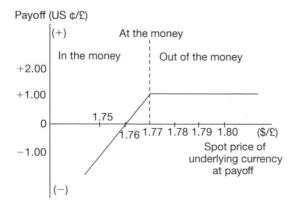

Figure 3.25 The payoff for the seller of a pound put option

72

rate decreases, so does the seller's liability up to $1.77 per pound. Because of the symmetry in payoffs, the seller's profit break-even point is also $1.77 per pound. Figure 3.25 illustrates the payoff for the seller of a put option.

The seller earns the premium of one cent per pound if the terminal spot exchange rate is no lower than $1.77 per pound. Below the exercise price of $1.77 per pound, the seller pays the difference between the spot price and the exercise price. At $1.76 the seller pays out the premium collected, so $1.76 per pound represents the seller's break-even point also. The seller of the put has a maximum liability of the exercise price of the currency, should its spot value fall to zero.

Valuation of options

An option is worth its expected present value. There is a specific formula due to Fischer Black and Myron Scholes for the valuation of a European-style option, and there are binomial tree pricing models for the valuation of American-style options.

In general, the expected value of the underlying asset is given by its forward price. Its volatility or standard deviation indicates how likely it is that the subsequent spot rate deviates from its expected value. The greater the volatility of the underlying asset, the greater the likelihood of large movements in its value. With large movements, options are more likely to be in the money. Therefore, they are worth more, the greater the volatility of the underlying asset.

The further away from expiration, the greater the volatility of the underlying asset. Consequently, for the same reason, options further away from expiration are worth more. Indeed, as the option expiration date approaches, the volatility approaches zero so that, at the time of expiration, the option is worth only its intrinsic value—the value if immediately exercised. The time value of the option is extinguished at expiration.

The value of an option equals the sum of its intrinsic value and its time value. The intrinsic value is its value if exercised immediately. It is zero if the option is out of the money, then rises cent for cent as the option moves into the money. The time value is the difference between the premium and the intrinsic value. It reflects the possibility that the option could move into the money or even further into the money. The time value is symmetric around the forward price, since it is characterized by a normal probability density distribution centered at the forward price.

Figure 3.26 illustrates the premium of a 180-day European-style call option with a strike price of $100, an annual volatility of 25 percent, and domestic and foreign interest rates at 6 percent per annum. If the current spot price is "at the money," or $100, the premium of the call is $6.835 according to the Black-Scholes formula.

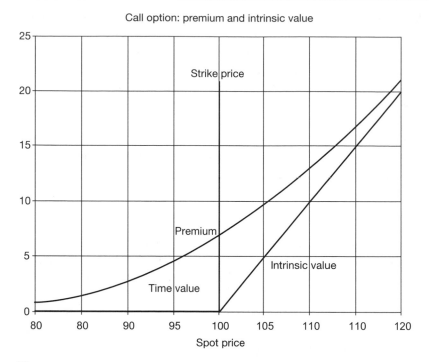

Figure 3.26 *The premium and intrinsic value of a call option*

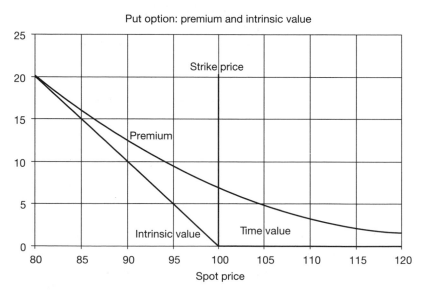

Figure 3.27 *The premium and intrinsic value of a put option*

The at-the-money put option has the exact same value, $6.835, since the expected forward value is a normal distribution centered at $100 with the same standard deviation (Figure 3.27). As the spot price rises to $105, for example, the intrinsic value of the call option is $5 if exercised immediately. It would be held, however, since its time value is $4.696, for a total premium value of $9.696. The put option is out of the money at a spot price of $105, and thus has an intrinsic value of zero. It could still move back into the money, so its time value (and premium) would now be $4.84.

In general, the value of a call option is summarized in Greek terms.

FOREX option Greeks

Option Greeks measure the sensitivity of option price changes with respect to small changes in underlying parameters. For an example, by raising the spot price of the foreign currency a very small amount, the call option premium rises. The rate at which the call option premium rises with respect to small increases in the underlying spot price of the currency is known as the option's delta. Table 3.13 summarizes the effect of changes in various parameters and the change in an option premium.

Options may be used to hedge foreign exchange exposure, as we will see in the next chapter on hedging techniques.

Table 3.13 Option Greeks

Greek	Meaning	Interpretation
Delta	The change in the option premium due to a small change in the spot rate	The higher the *delta* the more (less) likely a call (put) option will move into the money
Theta	The change in the option premium due to a small change in the time to expiry	Premia deteriorate in value as the time to expiration approaches
Vega	The change in the option premium due to a small change in volatility of the asset	An increase in volatility increases the value of call and put premia
Rho	The change in the option premium due to a small change in the domestic interest rate	An increase in the domestic interest rate causes rising call and falling put premia
Phi	The change in the option premium due to a small change in the foreign interest rate	An increase in the foreign interest rate causes falling call and rising put premia

Note: Vega is not a Greek language term, but is used for convenience.

CONCLUSION

The foreign exchange market is huge: in 2004, average daily turnover in the foreign exchange market was $1.9 trillion in foreign exchange markets—spot transactions, outright forwards, and swaps. These transactions facilitate trade and finance, and allow hedging of both transactional and operational exposure. We have tried to emphasize the idea that there is a bid–ask rate for nearly every FOREX transaction, as well as a commission. Unanticipated changes in exchange rates can cause large financial losses to unhedged international businesses. Yet hedges are not free. It is too costly to hedge all risk, but prudent risk management is in order when the firm has substantial foreign exchange revenues from transactions and operations. Often natural or matching hedges will do the trick, at less cost.

The BIS, the central bank's bank, has called for a world currency. So has Nobel Laureate Robert Mundell of Columbia University. This would remove exchange rate risk and reduce transactions costs considerably. However, nations would have to forgo seigniorage, an important source of tax revenue for many, and make their monetary and fiscal policies converge, thus giving up discretionary economic policy. In the meantime, as an asset, good monies will drive out bad monies and various currency unions are to be expected.

REFERENCES AND FURTHER READING

Abuaf, Niso and Philippe Jorion (1990) "Purchasing power parity in the long run," *Journal of Finance* 45(1): 157–74.

Ahtiala, Pekka and Yair E. Orgler (1995) "The optimal pricing of exports invoiced in different currencies," *Journal of Banking and Finance* 19(1): 61–77.

Aliber, Robert Z. (1973) "The interest rate parity theory: a reinterpretation," *Journal of Political Economy* 81(6): 1451–9.

Antl, Boris (ed.) (1983) *Swap financing techniques*, London: Euromoney Publications.

Apte, Prakash, Piet Sercu, and Raman Uppal (2004) "The exchange rate and purchasing power partity: extending the theory and the test," *Journal of International Money and Finance* 23(4): 553–71.

Beidelman, Carl R. (1991) *Cross-currency swaps*, Homewood, IL: Business One Irwin.

Bilson, John F. O. (1983) "The evaluation and use of foreign exchange rate forecasting services," in R. J. Herring (ed.) *Management of foreign exchange risk*, London: Cambridge University Press: 149–79.

Black, Fisher and Myron Scholes (1973) "The pricing of options and corporate liabilities," *Journal of Political Economy* 81(3): 637–59.

Cassell, Gustav (1918) "Abnormal deviations in international exchanges," *Economic Journal* 28(112): 413–15 .

Cincibuch, Martin (2004) "Distributions implied by American currency futures options: a ghost's smile," *Journal of Futures Markets* 24(2): 147–78.

Connolly, Michael (1982) "The choice of an optimum currency peg for a small, open country," *Journal of International Money and Finance* 1(2): 153–64.

Connolly, Michael (1983) "Optimum currency pegs for Latin America," *Journal of Money, Credit and Banking* 15(1): 56–72.

Connolly, Michael and Dean Taylor (1984) "The exact timing of the collapse of an exchange rate system," *Journal of Money, Credit and Banking* 16(2): 194–207.

Connolly, Michael, Alvaro Rodriguez, and William Tyler (1994) "The use of the exchange rate for stabilization: a real interest arbitrage model applied to Argentina," *Journal of International Money and Finance* 13(3): 223–31.

Cox, J. C., Stephen A. Ross, and M. Rubinstein (1979) "Option pricing: a simplified approach," *Journal of Financial Economics* 7(79): 229–63.

DeRosa, David F. (1992) *Options on foreign exchange*, Chicago, IL: Probus Publishing.

Fama, Eugene F. (1976) "Forward rates as predictors of future spot rates," *Journal of Financial Economics* 3(4): 361–77.

Fernald, Julia D. (1993–4) "The pricing and hedging of index amortizing rate swaps," *Quarterly Review of the New York Federal Reserve Bank* 18 (Winter): 71–4.

Frenkel, Jacob A. and Richard M. Levich (1975) "Covered interest arbitrage: unexploited profits?," *Journal of Political Economy* 83(2) (April): 325–38.

Friedman, Milton and Anna Jacobson Schwartz (1993) *Monetary history of the United States: 1867–1960*, Princeton, NJ: Princeton University Press.

Geman, Helyette (2005) "Commodities and commodity derivatives," Chichester: John Wiley & Sons.

Giddy, Ian H. (1979) "Measuring the world foreign exchange market," *Columbia Journal of World Business* 14(4): 36–48.

Giddy, Ian H. and Guner Dufey (1995) "Uses and abuses of currency options," *Journal of Applied Corporate Finance* 8(3) (Fall): 49–57.

Globecom Group Ltd (1995) *Derivatives engineering: a guide to structuring, pricing and marketing derivatives*, Homewood, IL: Irwin.

Goodhart, Charles A. and Thomas Hesse (1986) "Central bank forex intervention assessed in continuous time," *Journal of International Money and Finance* 12(4): 386–9.

Hanke, Steve. H. (2002) "On dollarization and currency boards: error and deception," *Journal of Policy Reform* 5(4): 203–22.

Hull, John, C. (1997) *Options, futures, and other derivatives*, 3rd edn, Upper Saddle River, NJ: Prentice Hall.

International Monetary Fund (no date) *International Financial Statistics*, Washington, DC: IMF.

Itzenson, Jennifer (2005) "Higher US consumer prices spur inflation concern," *Bloomberg News*, August 16.

Kester, W. and T. Luehrman (1993) "Note on cross border valuation," in W. Kester and T. Luehrman, *Case problems in international finance*, Boston, MA: McGraw-Hill.

Lessard, Donald R. (1979) "Evaluating foreign projects: an adjusted present value approach," in D. R. Lessard (ed.), *International financial management*, Boston, MA: Warren, Gorham, and Lamont.

Lessard, Donald R. (1985) "Finance and global competition: exploiting financial scope and coping with volatile exchange rates," in M. Porter (ed.) *Competition in global industries*, Boston, MA: Harvard.

Levich, Richard M. (1998) "Interest rate parity and the Fisher parities," in Richard M. Levich, *International financial markets: prices and policies*, Boston, MA: Irwin/McGraw-Hill.

77

Mahlotra, D., Rand Martin, and Vivek Bhargava (2004) "An empirical analysis of yen–dollar currency swap market efficiency," *International Journal of Business* 9(2): 143–58.

Marshall, John F. and Kenneth R. Kapner (1993) *The swaps market*, Miami, FL: Kolb Publishing.

Melvin, Michael (2004) *International money and finance*, Reading, MA: Addison-Wesley.

Melvin, Michael and David Bernstein (1984) "Trade concentration, openness, and deviations from purchasing power parity," *Journal of International Money and Finance* 3(3): 369–76.

Mill, John Stuart (1894) *Principles of political economy* (ed. William J. Ashley, 1909, 7th edn), New York: Longman, Green & Co.

Mundell, Robert A. (1961) "A theory of optimum currency areas," *American Economic Review* 57(4): 509–17.

Mundell, Robert A. (1973) "Plan for a European currency," in Harry G. Johnson and Alexander K. Swoboda (eds), *The economics of common currencies*, Cambridge, MA: Harvard University Press.

Officer, Lawrence H. (1976) "The purchasing power parity theory of exchange rates: a review article," *IMF Staff Papers* 23(1).

Ong, Li Lian (2003) *The Big Mac index: applications of purchasing power parity*, New York: Palgrave Macmillan.

Pan, Ming-Shiun, Angela Y. Liu, and Hamid Bastin (1996) "An examination of the short-term and long-term behavior of foreign exchange rates," *Financial Review* 31(3): 603–22.

Popper, Helen (1993) "Long-term covered interest parity: evidence from currency swaps," *Journal of International Money and Finance* 12(4): 439–48.

Reinker, Kenneth and Edward Tower (2004) "Index fundamentalism revisited," *The Journal of Portfolio Management* 30(4): 37–50.

Riehl, Heinz and Rita Rodriguez (1989) *Foreign exchange and money markets*, Englewood Cliffs, NJ: Prentice Hall.

Rolnick, Arthur J., Bruce D. Smith, and Warren E. Weber (2001) *Establishing a monetary union in the United States*, Minneapolis, MN: Federal Reserve Bank of Minneapolis.

Rosenberg, Michael (2003) *Exchange rate determination: models and strategies for exchange rate forecasting*, New York: McGraw-Hill.

Shapiro, A. C. (1978) "Capital budgeting for the multinational corporation," *Financial Management* 7(1): 7–16.

Solnik, Bruno (1990) "Swap pricing and default risk: a note," *Journal of International Financial Management and Accounting* 2(3): 79–91.

Stapleton, Richard C. and Marti Subrahmanyam (1977) "Market imperfections, capital asset equilibrium, and corporation finance, *Journal of Finance* 33(2): 307–19.

Sweeney, Richard J. and Edward J. Q. Lee (1990) "Trading strategies in the forward exchange markets," *Advances in Financial Planning and Forecasting* 4(1): 55–80.

Taylor, Dean (1982) "Official intervention in the foreign exchange market, or bet against the bank," *Journal of Political Economy* 90(2): 356–68.

Taylor, Francesca (1996) *Mastering derivatives markets*, London: Prentice Hall.

Wong, Kit (2003) "Currency hedging with options and futures," *European Economic Review* 47(5): 833–9.

PROBLEMS

3.1 The time value of money

Consider the following cash flows from today (year zero) to year 3 in pounds sterling:

Year	Cash flow in pounds sterling
0	−100
1	50
2	50
3	50

Your interest rate (or discount rate) in pounds is 10 percent.

a   Compute the net present value (NPV) at a 10 percent discount rate and the internal rate of return (IRR) of this investment in pounds.

b   If you were to sell this investment today (its NPV in pounds), how much would it be worth in USD at 1.76 dollars per pound?

3.2 The equilibrium exchange rate

Consider the following quantity of dollars demanded and supplied daily in millions as a function of the dollar's peso price, S:

Quantity demanded $Q_D = 90 - 2S$
Quantity supplied $Q_S = -10 + 3S$

a   Solve for the equilibrium exchange rate under a freely floating exchange rate regime, S (pesos per dollar). What is the quantity sold at the equilibrium price?

b   If the central bank maintained a fixed exchange rate of 15 pesos per dollar, how many millions of dollars of foreign reserves would it have to sell to maintain the fixed exchange rate regime? (Hint: Solve for $Q_D - Q_S$ at $S = 15$ pesos per dollar.)

c   If the central bank only had $15 million left in foreign reserves, what would its policy alternatives be?

d   If it instead wished to add $10 million to its holdings of foreign reserves, to what exchange rate would the central bank have to devalue the peso?

3.3 Intervention in the foreign exchange market

Argentina pegged its currency, the peso, to the US dollar at a rate of 1 to 1 from April 1991 to November 2001. Under the rules of the currency board, the central bank

79

must intervene to buy and sell dollars at this rate. For this reason, the Banco de la Republica Argentina backed its domestic currency issue with foreign exchange by the Convertibility Law, principally dollars. In Figure 3.28, the supply and demand for dollars is indicated:

a If the Argentine government were to abandon the currency board, what would be the equilibrium exchange rate and the volume of dollars traded daily?
b What amount of dollar reserves must the central bank of Argentina sell to the foreign exchange market daily in order to maintain its rigidly fixed exchange rate to the US dollar?
c What is the impact of the sale of dollars on the Argentine money supply? Does this cause any adjustment process?

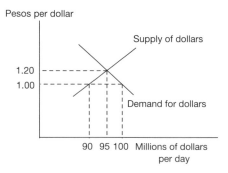

Figure 3.28 Foreign exchange intervention

3.4 The bid–ask spread (I)

In Table 3.14, consider the bid and ask spot quotations in dollars per pound ($/£), i.e. in American terms:

a Compute the bid and quotations in European terms, i.e. in pounds per dollar (£/$).
b Compute the bid–ask spread in terms of £ and $.

Table 3.14 Bid–ask spread quotation: American style

Quotations	European (£/$)		American ($/£)	
	Bid	Ask	Bid	Ask
Spot			1.7669	1.7675
Spread				
Mid-point				

c   Compute the mid-point quotations in both European and American terms. (Hint: midpoint = (bid + ask)/2.)

d   Compute the bid–ask spread as a percent of the mid-point quotation.

3.5 The bid–ask spread (II)

Consider the spot quotations in pounds per dollar (£/$) and dollars per pound ($/£) in Table 3.15:

a   Compute the bid quotations in American and European terms.

b   Compute the bid–ask spread in terms of £ and $.

c   Compute the mid-point quotations in both European and American terms.

d   Compute the bid–ask spread as a percent of the mid-point quotation.

Table 3.15 *Bid–ask spread quotation: American and European style*

Quotations	European (£/$)		American ($/£)	
	Bid	Ask	Bid	Ask
Spot		0.5660		1.7675
Spread				
Mid-point				
Spread/mid-point (%)				

3.6 Points quotations

In Table 3.16, consider the spot quotations in dollars per pound ($/£) and the forward quotations in basis points (1/10,000).

On the basis of the points quotations in Table 3.16, derive the outright quotations.

Table 3.16 *Points quotations for forward exchange: American style*

Quotations ($/£)	Bid	Ask
Spot	1.7669	1.7675
Points	*Bid*	*Ask*
1 month	214	220
2 months	283	398
3 months	388	416

3.7 Interest rate parity

Consider Figure 3.29, which indicates (approximately) the difference between interest rates in the United States and the UK, $R_{us} - R_{uk}$ on a one-year T-bill (i.e. a two-year bill with one year left to maturity) on the horizontal axis, and the forward premium on the pound for delivery in one year, $(F - S)/S$, on the vertical axis. If you wish, assume you already hold a portfolio of both T-bills. Note:

F is the US dollar price of the British pound for delivery in one year (the bid).
S is the US dollar price of the British pound for spot delivery (the ask).
R_{us} is the interest rate on a hypothetical US one-year T-bill (the ask).
R_{uk} is the interest rate on a hypothetical UK one-year T-bill (the bid).

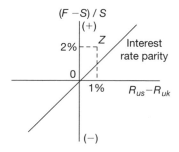

Figure 3.29 *Interest rate parity and arbitrage*

a At point Z, in what direction will short-term arbitrage capital flow and what will be the arbitrage profits?
b What steps will arbitrageurs take from point Z in order to make their profits and what will be the consequences on the forward discount on the pound and the interest rate differential?

3.8 Purchasing power parity

You are given the data in Table 3.17 on prices in local currency in the United States, Mexico, and England.

▨ **Table 3.17** *Purchasing power parity*

Country	Shoes	Hats	Haircuts
United States	$20	$10	$5
England	£10	£10	£3
Mexico	N$200	N$100	N$20

Suppose that a representative consumer bundle of these goods is:

Shoes	Hats	Haircuts
2	1	2

a   What are the rates of currency exchange suggested by the absolute version of the purchasing power parity doctrine?

b   Would you be surprised to learn that the equilibrium exchange rates were 0.566 pounds per dollar and 11 pesos per dollar?

c   Why might the PPP prediction for the peso be further off than for the pound?

d   Now suppose that all prices doubled in the United States and tripled in England and Mexico in the next ten years. What would you predict the equilibrium exchange rates to be in ten years?

e   How might real shocks to, say, the world price of wheat or oil modify your answer?

Chapter 4

Hedging foreign exchange risk

HEDGING DEFINED

A firm or an individual hedges by taking a position, that will rise (or fall) in value to offset a drop (or rise) in value of an existing position. A "perfect" hedge is one eliminating the possibility of future gain or loss due to unexpected changes in the value of the existing position.

Why hedge? Shareholders can, in principle, perform any foreign exchange hedging that the corporation can. Consequently, the corporation need not devote resources to the elimination of diversifiable or hedgeable risk. Indeed, hedging might be counterproductive by harming the interests of shareholders. Similarly, a firm that takes over other firms in different industries might displease share holders who can diversify their portfolio directly by purchasing shares themselves in those industries.

When there are neither transactions costs, nor bankruptcy costs, shareholders with perfect information on the firm's foreign exchange exposure can undertake any hedging they feel necessary. In short, a cogent argument can be made that the firm should not hedge foreign exchange risk—that is, exposure to unexpected changes in the exchange rate.

However, the majority of international firms hedge foreign exchange risk selectively, if not completely. Furthermore, shareholders do not have the same information that the firm has regarding its FOREX risk, or it would involve considerable search costs to ascertain the foreign exchange risk exposure of the firm. It is unlikely that pension fund managers, for example, have any idea about the currency flows involved in the global operations of General Motors or Ford, although fewer pension funds will be holding GM or Ford bonds now that they have been classified below investment grade or as junk bonds.

A counterargument in favor of foreign exchange hedging is made by Ian Giddy:

> Exchange-rate volatility may make earnings volatile and thus increase the probability of financial distress. If hedging reduces the nominal volatility of the

firm's earnings, it will in turn reduce the expected value of the costs of financial distress (including bankruptcy) . . . Some of these costs are borne by
creditors, in which case a reduction in expected distress costs will reduce
lenders' required rate of return. In addition, for a given level of debt, lower
earnings volatility will entail a lower probability of a negative net worth.

(1994: 481)

In Figure 4.1, there is a discrete drop in the return to creditors when the firm
goes bankrupt. Their return further declines as the value of its assets is further
downgraded. For instance, under Chapter 7 of the US Bankruptcy Code or liquidation proceedings, the return on the dollar to creditors deteriorates, the lower
the value of assets to be liquidated by court.

As illustrated, the expected value of the hedged firm, V_h, is less than the value
of the unhedged firm, V_u, because the cost of hedging, $V_u - V_h$ is assumed to be
positive.

This may not be true, however, since the greater the exchange rate risk, the
greater the costs of financial distress and risk of bankruptcy. Increased volatility
in earnings and risk of financial distress lead creditors to charge a higher risk
premium on loans to the firm. Greater leverage becomes more expensive and
thus there are fewer gains from tax shields. As Giddy argues:

The double taxation of corporate income and the worldwide practice of tax
deductibility of interest payments provide an incentive for debt finance. This
incentive is weakened, however, by the direct and indirect costs of financial

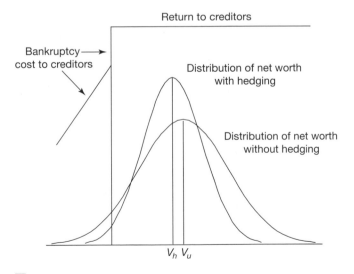

Figure 4.1 Hedging and the net worth of the firm

85

distress and bankruptcy; the greater the volatility of earnings, the greater the costs. More leverage means more volatile earnings, so the tax shield gains from leverage are, at some point, offset by the deadweight costs of financial distress. The greater the probability of distress, the lower the leverage level that is optimal for the firm and the lower the tax shield. Because currency matching reduces the probability of financial distress, it allows the firm to have greater leverage and therefore a greater tax shield. Thus, the greater the degree of bankruptcy-cost-hedging, the greater the value of the firm and the lower the cost of capital.

(1994: 482)

In this simple framework, the value of the firm to shareholders can be divided into the following parts:

The value of a firm to shareholders

equals	the value of existing assets;
less	the value of existing debt and obligations;
less	the present value of the expected costs of financial distress;
less	the present value of the cost of hedging;
plus	the present value of tax shields;
plus	the present value of lowered borrowing costs;
plus	the present value of growth and operating options.

Consequently, in comparison to the unhedged firm, a firm that hedges selectively may increase its net worth rather than reducing it. This would be the case when the reduced costs of financial distress and the lowered borrowing costs offset the costs of the hedges. In that case, the distribution of the net worth of the hedged firm in Figure 4.1 would have a higher expected value and a lower volatility. Indeed, the total cost of hedging would be negative. While possible, this is unlikely since managing risk usually entails a cost.

Another way of putting the argument is that hedging reduces the β, or market risk, of a company by reducing the volatility of its earnings, thus reducing the risk premium at which expected earnings are discounted. With hedges, a company's β is lower so its market risk premium is lower.

To summarize the arguments: on the one hand, expected earnings are discounted at a lower interest rate; on the other, earnings may also be lower due to the costs of the hedges. The firm's net worth could therefore conceivably be higher or lower. The theory of comparative advantage should shed some light on this unsettled issue. A firm that does not hedge its foreign exchange exposure is not only producing goods and services, but is also a currency speculator by taking unhedged positions in foreign currencies. It may have a comparative advantage in producing its goods, but surely does not as a currency speculator. To focus on its core business, production, it should selectively hedge through FOREX forwards, swaps, and contracts that do not leave it exposed to large unexpected losses in foreign exchange that could put it in financial distress.

Consider a specific example of long exposure to euros. Take the example of a Boeing 777 contract for delivery in one year in exchange for initial deposits and a final settlement payment of €10 million in one year. Boeing's reporting and functional currency is the US dollar, so it is exposed to the risk that the euro might fall below the one-year forward bid rate if it does not hedge. Similarly, by not hedging it could just as easily make foreign currency gains. However, Boeing's comparative advantage is not as a foreign exchange speculator, but rather as an aircraft builder; and the euro is a volatile currency. From February 24, 2004 to February 21, 2005, comprising 256 trading days, the euro's annual volatility (standard deviation) was over US 5.5 cents (0.055413), while its average price was $1.25264. Let's assume equal interest rates in the United States and Europe, so the one-year forward bid rate for the euro is also $1.25264. With a volatility of over 5.5 cents, there is a 16 percent probability that Boeing would lose $554,130 or more by remaining exposed to foreign exchange risk. That is, there is a 16 percent probability that the euro would fall to or below $1.1972, one standard deviation, as illustrated by the area under the lower left tail of Figure 4.2. By the same token, there is a 16 percent probability that Boeing could gain $554,130 or more.

Boeing would probably not want to run the risk of large losses, and consequently could hedge, by, for example, a forward sale of the €10 million either on the futures exchanges or on the forward OTC market with a bank. Other contractual hedges are elaborated upon below. In addition to foreign exchange risk, let's also discuss credit risk.

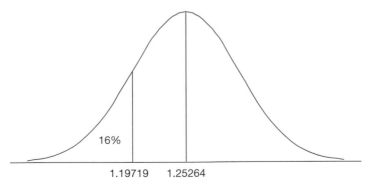

16%

1.19719   1.25264

Figure 4.2 Foreign exchange risk exposure

CREDIT RATINGS

Credit ratings are an assessment of the creditworthiness of a corporation's debt, whether equities or corporate bonds, agency debt, or that of sovereign, state, and local governments. The definitions of creditworthiness are based on how likely the firm, agency, or government is to default and the protection that creditors receive in the event of a default. Creditworthiness is rated by Standard & Poor's (S&P), Fitch, and Moody's.

The highest rating a firm or government security, can have is AAA or Aaa, and such debt is judged to be the best quality and to have the lowest degree of risk. This rating is not awarded very often; AA or Aa ratings indicate very good quality debt and are much more common. Low-quality, speculative, and "junk" (below BBB–) bonds have higher probabilities of default than investment grade (BBB– or above) bonds. S&P reduced General Motors two notches to BB and Ford to BB+, both junk bond status. This, following their low earnings, high pension liabilities, and outstanding debts, caused their bonds to plunge in value (*The New York Times*, May 6, 2005). In the 1980s, a growing part of corporate borrowing took the form of junk bonds. The lowest corporate rating is D for debt that is in default. For sovereign debt that is in default, the rating is SD. Both Moody's and S&P use adjustments to these ratings. S&P uses plus and minus signs: an A+ is higher than an A rating and an A– is lower. Moody's uses a 1, 2, or 3 designation, with 1 being the highest. A favorable creditworthiness rating reduces the interest that a borrower has to pay for new loans because the risk premium is lower, while an unfavorable rating increases the interest that investors require. Table 4.1 illustrates the 22 notches of the S&P ratings.

Default risk premium

Consider a corporate coupon bond with a face value of $100 and a coupon of $5 payable at maturity in one year. The risk-free rate is 5 percent for T-bills one year before expiration. If there is no default risk, its present value is $100:

$$\$100 = \frac{\$105}{1.05}.\tag{4.1}$$

Now consider the same coupon bond, but having a probability of complete default of p, in which case nothing is paid, and a probability of $(1 - p)$ of no default in which case $105 is paid at maturity. The expected payment is a weighted average of zero with weight p and $105 with weight $(1 - p)$. That is:

$$E(V) = p(0) + (1 - p)105 = (1 - p)105.\tag{4.2}$$

Table 4.1 *Debt ratings, S&P*

Grade	Rating	Description
Upper investment	AAA	Capacity to pay interest and principal is extremely strong
	AA+	
	AA	Very strong capacity to pay interest and repay principal
	AA−	
	A+	Strong capacity to pay, but susceptible to adverse economic conditions
	A	
	A−	
Lower investment	BBB+	Adequate capacity to pay, but likely to have weakened ability to pay
	BBB	
	BBB−	
Non-investment	BB+	Speculative or "junk" with respect to payment
	BB	
	BB−	
Lower non-investment	B+	Large uncertainties regarding ability to pay; some issues in default
	B	
	CCC+	
	CCC	
	CCC−	
	CC	
	C	Income bonds on which no interest is being paid
Default	D	Default; payment of interest and/or principal is in arrears

For instance, suppose that the probability of default is 0.3 or 30 percent. Then the expected value of the payment at maturity is given by:

$$E(V) = 0.7(105) = \$73.5 \,. \tag{4.3}$$

Therefore the present value of the expected payment at maturity is:

$$PV = \frac{\$73.5}{1.05} = \$70 \,. \tag{4.4}$$

This should equal the market value of the bond, given that there is a 30 percent chance of full default. Accordingly, the yield to maturity, R, is given by the IRR, which sets the present value of face plus coupon equal to the market price of the bond, or:

$$\$70 = \frac{\$105}{1 + R} \quad \text{or} \quad R = \frac{105}{70} - 1 = 0.5 = 50\%. \tag{4.5}$$

Therefore the default risk premium, p, for this bond is approximately 45 percent since 50 percent − 5 percent approximately yields the risk premium. The exact risk premium is 42.9 percent—very close to the approximate value, 45 percent, given by the rule of thumb. The exact risk premium is found by solving $(1 + r)$ $(1 + p) = (1 + R)$ where r is the risk-free rate.

An equivalent technique for measuring the default risk premium on a corporate bond is simply to use the market price discount of the bond to compute the risk premium. That is:

1 Compute the present value of the riskless bond and compare it to the market price of the risky bond.
2 Compute the risk premium p from the ratio of the market price of the asset to its present value discounted at the risk-free rate, and subtract one.

Default risk graphically

Default risk is measured by the percentage discount of the market value of an asset relative to the present value of its payments at a risk-free interest rate (say US Treasury rate). In Figure 4.3, the present value of the bond is indicated along the horizontal axis, discounted by the risk-free rate. If there is no default risk, the market value of the bonds plotted on the vertical axis would be the same, as plotted along the 45-degree line from the origin. When there is default risk, the market value falls below the risk-free value indicated along the 45-degree line. As

Market value of debt

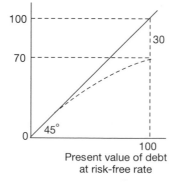

Figure 4.3 The risk premium (discount)

90

indebtedness increases, holding other things such as income constant, it becomes more difficult to service the foreign debt, so a discount emerges. It is entirely conceivable that additional debt might reduce the expected present value of repayment—more debt would have in fact less market value. In that case, the market value curve slopes downward. In the previous example of a risky coupon bond with a present value of $100 at the risk-free rate, the present value of expected repayment is only $70 in one year, since there is a 30% chance of full default. Both cases are illustrated in Figure 4.3.

In general, bonds that are rated poorly have a high yield to maturity, incorporating a risk premium.

HEDGING FOREX TRANSACTIONS EXPOSURE

A firm may have foreign currency exposure, either long or short, due to a future receipt or payment of a specified amount in a foreign currency. For example, when a British firm has accounts receivable in euros at some point in the future, say 90 days, it is exposed to transactions exposure—losses or gains due to unexpected changes in the exchange rate—in the pound price of the euro. The UK firm is said to be "long foreign exchange." If our firm has accounts receivable in euros, we might sell them spot for pounds in 90 days at the bid rate in pounds. Let's indicate the expected exchange rate (pound price of the euro) in 90 days by F_{90}, the futures or forward bid rate. If a forward rate does not exist, just forecast the rate using interest rate parity. In 90 days, there will be a realized spot rate, S_{90}, also the bid rate for the euro. Consequently, the unanticipated change in the exchange rate or forecast error is indicated by $F_{90} - S_{90}$. This represents the gain or the loss per unit of the euro in which the firm has foreign exchange exposure. If the firm is long 1,000,000 euros—accounts receivable, for example—it will gain if the spot price of the euro is above the forward price upon receipt of the euros. If the spot price is less than the forward, the firm will lose $(F_{90} - S_{90})1,000,000$ in terms of pounds.

The long position

If unhedged, the long position in euros due to accounts receivable has the payoff diagram shown in Figure 4.4.

For example, let's say the 90-day pound bid price of the euro is £0.69. This would be the expected rate of settlement of the €1,000,000 accounts receivable. If we go unhedged, we risk possible losses or gains from unanticipated changes in the exchange rate. For instance, the euro may fall in the spot market to £0.64, so we would lose £0.05 per euro, or five pence, when we sell in the spot market. On €1,000,000, this amounts to −£50,000. This is illustrated in Figure 4.5.

On the other hand, by going unhedged, we also may gain from a rise in the spot price of the euro, to say £0.74. In this case, we would gain £50,000 from the sale of our euro receipts, five pence per euro. This is illustrated in Figure 4.6.

91

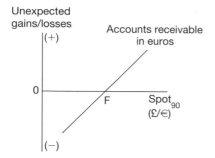

Figure 4.4 *A long position in foreign exchange — accounts receivable*

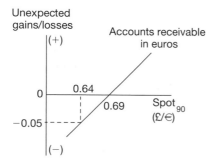

Figure 4.5 *A loss on a long position in foreign exchange — accounts receivable*

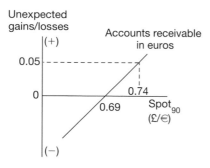

Figure 4.6 *A gain on a long position in foreign exchange — accounts receivable*

With €1,000,000 accounts receivable in 90 days, a one-time transaction, the hedging choices would be to acquire one of the following contractual hedges:

- a forward market sale of €1,000,000;
- a money market hedge by borrowing the present equivalent of €1,000,000; or
- the purchase of a put option on €1,000,000.

A forward market sale

To hedge the long position in euros using a forward market hedge, sell €1,000,000 in the forward market for delivery in 90 days. The forward sale is a short position in euros that exactly offsets the existing long position from accounts receivable. What is gained on the short position is lost on the long position. Or what is gained on the long position is lost on the short position. The combined position is perfectly hedged—no chance of either gain or loss from unanticipated movements in the euro. The forward market sale is illustrated in Figure 4.7.

What is lost on the long position—accounts receivable—is just offset by gains on the short position—the forward sale, if the spot price of the euro falls to £0.64 in 90 days, for example. The horizontal axis is the hedged position, the sum of the long and the short positions, showing neither gains nor losses, independent of the subsequent spot rate in 90 days.

A money market hedge

To hedge the long position in pounds using a money market hedge, borrow euros today for 90 days, and sell them in the spot market. In 90 days, repay your loan with the €1,000,000 accounts receivable. How many euros would you need to borrow today? That would depend on the cost of borrowing. Say you can borrow euros for 90 days at 2 percent quarterly interest. Borrow exactly $1,000,000/1.02 = 980,392.16$ euros today, and repay the loan with €1,000,000 in 90 days. This is a perfect hedge using the money market. Be sure to sell the euros you borrow in the spot market—otherwise you are acquiring another long position in euros. Your intent is to acquire a short position, the euro loan, to offset your existing long position, accounts receivable in euros in 90 days.

The money market hedge is depicted graphically in Figure 4.8, exactly as the forward sale is illustrated.

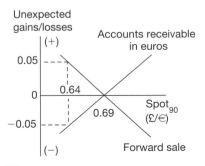

Figure 4.7 A hedged position in accounts receivable from a forward sale

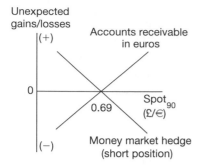

Figure 4.8 *A hedged position in accounts receivable from a money market loan*

A call option

Buying a put option at a strike price of £0.69 would be a hedge against unforeseen losses, while retaining the possibility of unexpected gains. The cost of the hedge is the option premium, not illustrated in Figure 4.9.

When the positive put option and the losing position below £0.69 per euro are added, and a hypothetical one cent cost per euro of the hedge is subtracted, the net position of the put option hedge is illustrated in Figure 4.10. The break-even point is at a spot price of the euro of £0.70, the one cent gain in the long position in accounts receivable just offsetting the cost of the option.

The short position

Consider now a short position in euros. If your firm has a €1,000,000 account payable in 90 days, the choices are as follows:

- buy euros for delivery in 90 days—a forward market hedge;
- buy three-month euro T-bills—a money market hedge; or
- purchase a call option for €1,000,000.

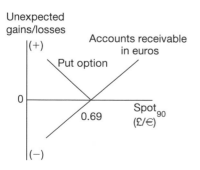

Figure 4.9 *A put option hedge of a long position in accounts receivable*

94

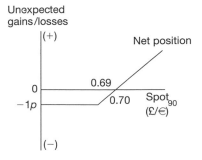

Unexpected
gains/losses

Figure 4.10 *The payoff from a put option of accounts receivable*

Remain unhedged

The payoff diagram if unhedged is a straightforward short position in euros, as illustrated in Figure 4.11. The expected spot rate in 90 days is the forward ask rate for the euro in terms of pounds, which, for simplicity, we assume is £0.69 per euro. This is because we are short euros and will have to pay the ask price in pounds when we purchase euros spot in three months. The difference between the bid and the ask rates is typically around £0.0005 per euro in the 90-day forward market.

As illustrated in Figure 4.11, we lose £0.05 when we cover our short position in euros at a spot price of £0.74 per euro, once again amounting to a loss of £50,000.

On the other hand, if we do not hedge, we may cover our short position at a lower spot price, for example £0.64 per euro, should the euro fall £0.05 on the spot market as illustrated in Figure 4.12. In this case, we gain £50,000 by not hedging our short position.

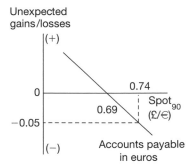

Unexpected
gains/losses

Figure 4.11 *A loss from a short position in foreign exchange —*
accounts payable

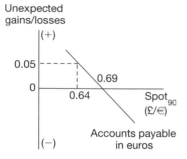

Figure 4.12 *A gain from a short position in foreign exchange—*
accounts payable

A forward market hedge

We can simply cover our short position by a forward purchase of €1,000,000 at
£0.69 per euro. That is, by acquiring an offsetting long position in euros, we have
a perfect hedge. Any loss made in one position is recovered in the other position,
as illustrated in Figure 4.13.

As illustrated in Figure 4.13, the gains from the short position—accounts
payable in euros—are just offset by the forward purchase of euros, the long
position.

A money market hedge

The short position in euros could be covered by a money market loan made by
the firm. It would simply lend enough principal in euros so that principal plus
interest repaid in 90 days would represent €1,000,000. The money market hedge
is illustrated in Figure 4.14.

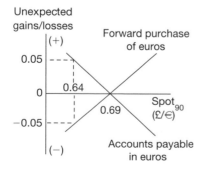

Figure 4.13 *A hedged position in accounts payable from a forward purchase*

96

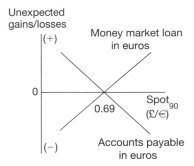

Figure 4.14 *A hedged position in accounts payable from a money market hedge*

A call option

Finally, we sketch the purchase of a call option with a strike price of £0.69 costing one penny per euro. To simplify, we only sketch the net position in Figure 4.15 with a break-even point of £0.68 per euro.

Collars as hedges

A collar is an options hedge that simultaneously limits a loss in one direction by giving up a gain in the other direction. A zero premium collar is a hedge in which the premium received from selling one option exactly offsets the premium paid for purchasing an opposing option. For example, consider again €1,000,000 accounts receivable in 90 days. This transaction represents long exposure in the euro. The firm could simultaneously buy an at-the-money put and sell an at-the-money call for €1,000,000 expiring in 90 days. The premium paid for the put would just equal the premium received for the call—i.e. the hedge is known as a zero premium collar. In Figure 4.16, the payoff from the put eliminates downside losses and the payoff from the call offsets upside gains. Since both are

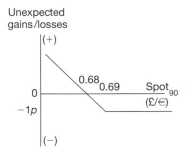

Figure 4.15 *A call option hedge of accounts payable*

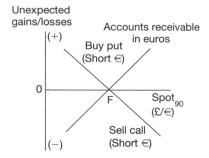

Figure 4.16 *A collar hedge of accounts receivable*

at the money, the premium received for selling the call equals the premium paid for the put.

To summarize the steps in financing a hedge by a collar: the initial position is long euros—accounts receivable of €1,000,000 in 90 days. Buy an at-the-money put to sell €1,000,000 in 90 days at the at-the-money rate. Simultaneously sell an at-the-money call for €1,000,000 in 90 days. The collar is equivalent to a sale of euros at the forward price, with the exception that the sale of the call finances the purchase of the put. IBM uses this financing strategy for its hedges.

Hedging a short position in pounds by using a collar

A collar can be used to hedge a short position in foreign exchange. Consider €1,000,000 accounts payable in 90 days, a short euro position. To hedge a short foreign exchange exposure, the firm simultaneously sells a put and buys a call, both with 90-day maturity. If the sale of the put and the purchase of the call are both at the money, the premium is the same. Thus, the sale of the put finances the purchase of the call—another zero premium collar. This collar is illustrated in Figure 4.17.

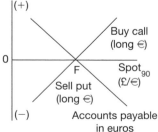

Figure 4.17 *A collar hedge of accounts payable*

RELATED TECHNIQUES FOR HEDGING FOREIGN EXCHANGE RISK

Risk-shifting by currency invoicing

By invoicing in pounds, the British firm can shift the foreign currency exposure to the European importer. The pound may be specified as the currency of payment in the L/C. However, the shifting of the FOREX exposure to the European importer may risk the loss of the contract since it raises its cost to the European firm. The latter may shift its source of supply to another European firm.

Risk-sharing by currency contingency clauses

In the terms and conditions of the L/C, a risk-sharing currency clause may pass part of the currency risk onto the European firm. For instance, if the euro declines by more than 10 percent between today and settlement, the European firm may agree in advance to pay 5 percent more euros at settlement. Thus, at settlement, the European firm pays 5 percent more in euros and the European firms receives 5 percent less in pounds if the euro declines more than 10 percent.

A single large transaction involving foreign currency can be best and efficiently hedged by a contractual hedge. However, when the accounts receivable or payable are on an ongoing, operational basis a natural, matching flow of offsetting amounts of the foreign currency is more appropriate.

OPERATING EXPOSURE

Operating exposure measures the changes in the NPV of a firm due to unexpected changes in exchange rates. It is a forward-looking concept that re-estimates the discounted cash flow in home currency from overseas operations in a local currency following an unexpected change in the exchange rate. Parker Pen's European operations involve both the production and sale of pens in the European Community. It has a partial natural hedge in that its direct costs of production are in euros. When the dollar price of the euro rises, both expected revenues and costs in dollars rise. If the cash flow in euros is positive, the euro appreciation adds to earnings in dollars. When the dollar price of the euro falls, expected net earnings in euros suffer a fall in value in terms of dollars. This is known as "operating exposure."

However, the firm can make economic decisions in its operations to offset the effect of the change in the exchange rate on its earnings translated into dollars. Table 4.2 illustrates the effect of unanticipated euro devaluation from 0.7765 euros per dollar to one euro per dollar or $1.2878 per euro on January 1, 2007

Table 4.2 Parker Pens, Europe: unexpected euro depreciation

Expected cash flow (2007)	Values
Cash flow from operations in euros	€3,000,000
Existing exchange rate ($ per €)	$1.2878
Cash flow from operations in dollars at existing exchange rate	$3,863,400
New exchange rate ($ per €)	$1.0000
Cash flow from operations at new exchange rate in dollars	$3,000,000
Expected gain or loss from unanticipated change in exchange rate	$(863,400)

on expected cash flows in euros and dollars from forecasted operations of Parker Pen's French subsidiary, Parker Pen, Europe, SA. Table 4.2 reports the estimated cash flow from European operations in 2006. In terms of euros, net cash flow from operations is about €3 million which translates into $3.863 million at the initial exchange rate of 1.2878 dollars per euro. The unanticipated devaluation of the euro to $1 per euro reduces net cash flow in USD to $3 million, entailing a loss of $863,400 from operations if there is no change in operations.

This is the benchmark case of no change in any of the economic variables: volume of production, prices, or costs. With no change in the business plan, an unexpected loss in operations of $863 millions takes place. If 2008 were also similarly adjusted in the business plan to the new exchange rate, there would be an even greater fall in the NPV of profits in terms of dollars. However, management has an opportunity to adjust the business plan to offset these losses. For one thing, prices in the euro zone will rise in some proportion of the rate of depreciation. For another, the product may be exported from the euro zone so that constant foreign prices imply higher euro prices—by the exact percent of the devaluation Alternatively, by holding euro prices constant, the firm can expand its share of the market and plan not to lose relative to its initial expectations. In short, Parker Pen Europe can increase its sales revenues in euros by approximately 28.9 percent in euros to offset the decline in the value of the euro. The change in the business plan can involve:

- a rise in the profit margin in euros by raising prices;
- a rise in revenues in euros by expanding the volume of output; or
- a combination of higher prices and increased output

Table 4.3 *Parker Pens, Europe: changes in operations to offset exchange rate exposure*

Expected cash flow (2007)	Values
Cash flow from operations in euros	€3,863,400
New exchange rate ($ per €)	$1.0000
Cash flow from operations at new exchange rate in dollars	$3,863,400
Expected gain or loss from unanticipated change in exchange rate	$–

Thus, free-cash flow in euros is increased to offset the unanticipated euro depreciation, as illustrated in Table 4.3.

Each of the three cases is plausible since the devaluation of the euro will be inflationary, so all goods and services prices will rise. Or, if Parker Pen holds the line on prices, it is effectively lowering its relative price and can expand its sales at the expense of competitors. Finally, the most realistic outcome is a simultaneous increase in price and expansion in volume, ideally to fully offset the effects of the unexpected devaluation of the euro. Table 4.4 illustrates an unexpected appreciation of the euro from 1.2878 to 1.5 dollars per euro. Parker Pen now benefits from the exchange rate change: should it do nothing, it will have an additional $637 million in cash flow in USD.

Clearly, Parker Pen could expand European operations in the hope of generating higher free-cash flow in euros that would translate into higher dollar profits at the new exchange rate.

Table 4.4 *Parker Pens, Europe: unexpected euro appreciation*

Expected cash flow (2007)	Values
Cash flow from operations in euros	€3,000,000
Existing exchange rate ($ per €)	$1.2878
Cash flow from operations in dollars at existing exchange rate	$3,863,400
New exchange rate ($ per €)	$1.5000
Cash flow from operations at new exchange rate in dollars	$4,500,000
Expected gain or loss from unanticipated change in exchange rate	$636,600

MANAGING OPERATING EXPOSURE BY DIVERSIFICATION

Management can also diversify the firm's operations and financing in order to reduce operating exposure. Common techniques are as follows.

Diversifying operations

International diversification of production, sourcing, and sales

Parker Pens, NY has shifted the production or assembly of its pens to France, purchasing parts and hiring labor there. Its pens are paid for in euros on a regular basis, and Parker uses the euros from its sales to pay for parts, assembly, distribution, and after-sales service on a matching basis. This is a natural hedge. Similarly, Japanese automobile firms have managed their foreign exchange risk (and "voluntary" export quota) by opening plants in the United States. Their dollar revenues can be used in part to pay wages, salaries, and other operational expenses in dollars. Their net income is less adversely affected by the yen appreciation relative to the dollar. The decline in yen revenue due to dollar devaluation is offset in large part by the decline in costs when reckoned in yen. Net income, however, is adversely affected, particularly since the Japanese auto makers have difficulty increasing their price due to competition from US auto makers.

Another example of operations hedging concerns the low-cost US carrier, Southwest Airlines. In the first quarter of 2005, "Southwest said it saved $155 by capping 86% of its fuel expenses at the equivalent of just $26 a barrel of crude oil, close to half the actual cost of oil during the quarter" (*The Wall Street Journal*, April 15, 2005: A2). Its fuel hedges run through 2009, but cover a smaller portion of its fuel needs. In 2006, an estimated 60 percent of fuel use is capped at the equivalent of $30 a barrel, falling to 20 percent at $35 in 2009. In hindsight, these hedges have led to Southwest being one of the few profitable airlines in 2004 and 2005.

Risk-shifting by currency invoicing

By invoicing in US dollars, Parker Pens, NY could in principle shift the foreign currency exposure to the wholesale purchasers from the French affiliate. The US dollar would be specified as the currency of payment. However, the shifting of the foreign exchange exposure to the wholesale purchasers may cost Parker Pens, NY the contract since it imposes currency risk on the wholesaler. They may shift to a European source of supply that invoices in euros. However, when the currency of the country is unstable or inconvertible, invoicing in US dollars or a hard currency becomes the best vehicle to protect from rapid declines in the value of revenues due to high inflation and currency depreciation. When the rouble was depreciating 20 percent a month, contracts were routinely specified in dollars or in countertrade terms, that is barter.

Risk-sharing by currency contingency clauses

In the terms and conditions of an L/C, a risk-sharing currency clause may pass part of the currency risk onto the foreign importer. For instance, if the pound declines by more than 10 percent between today and settlement for exports of a Boeing aircraft, British Airways may agree in advance to pay 5 percent more pounds for the plane at settlement. Thus, at settlement, the British airline pays 5 percent more in pounds and Boeing receives 5 percent less in dollars if the pound declines more than 10 percent.

Leads and lags in currency payments

A firm can pay its "hard" foreign currency commitments early with "soft" currency before the latter's anticipated devaluation. A US firm can purchase dollars with pesos before they depreciate, then pay its dollar liability early. The idea is to spend the soft currency before it loses value. Similarly, it can delay paying its soft currency liabilities by lagging the payment so as to purchase the soft currency after it loses value. That is, it delays its payment, waiting to purchase the peso at a lower rate. Leading and lagging payments on liabilities benefit the firm by actively managing the timing of the transfer of funds, but worsens the position of the corresponding firm. If the latter is a subsidiary, the profits are transferred from the subsidiary to headquarters. If the transfer is between the firm and a totally separate firm, the latter could easily be bankrupted from currency losses and delays in payments. This procedure may also be used to transfer profits to a subsidiary, for example (see "Transfer pricing," p. 118).

Reinvoicing centers

A reinvoicing center is a subsidiary that has no inventory but centralizes invoices and manages operating exposure in one center. Manufacturing affiliates ship goods directly to distribution affiliates, but invoice the reinvoicing center, which then receives title to the goods and invoices the affiliate in a separate currency. Transactions exposure thus resides in the reinvoicing center. Naturally, some of its accounts receivable and accounts payable will be in the same currency, providing a natural hedge. The invoicing center thus centralizes the net exposure to each currency.

A reinvoicing center could also transfer profits from a high-tax affiliate to a low-tax affiliate, i.e. practice aggressive transfer pricing. This is not the purpose of the reinvoicing center and it violates "arm's length" pricing rules established by the US Internal Revenue. A reinvoicing center's purpose is to centralize and manage foreign exchange risk in one place. The diagram in Figure 4.18 depicts the flow of invoices and payments.

103

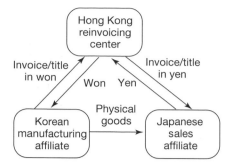

Figure 4.18 *An international invoicing center*

Diversifying financing

Natural hedges

A firm that has an ongoing inflow of foreign currency as accounts receivable can borrow the same currency so as to have matching accounts payable as a natural hedge. This is illustrated in Figure 4.19, where a US firm sells goods for pesos in Mexico, but offsets its operating exposure by obtaining a loan in pesos.

Foreign currency swaps

A foreign currency swap is an agreement between two parties to exchange a given amount of one currency for another and to repay these currencies with interest in the future. One counterparty borrows under specific terms and conditions in one currency while the other counterparty borrows under different terms and conditions in a second currency. The two counterparties then exchange the net receipts from their respective issues and agree to service each other's debt.

In Figure 4.20, a German firm borrows euros, a US firm borrows dollars, and they exchange the interest and principal payments, agreeing to service each other's debt through the swap dealer. This swap arrangement benefits each due to their comparative advantage in borrowing in their respective national markets. The swap enables both firms to have lower borrowing costs in foreign currency.

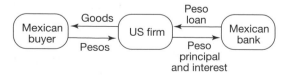

Figure 4.19 *A natural hedge*

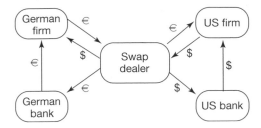

Figure 4.20 A foreign exchange swap

The US firm may have euro receipts from its exports and the German firm may have dollar receipts from its exports, so the swap dealer arranges for matching payments in foreign currency at a lower interest rate. Thus, a currency swap is a way of managing foreign exchange risk. The swap dealer captures some of the lowered borrowing costs by earning the bid–ask spread on foreign currency and other fees from serving as an intermediary.

Alternatively, had the two firms known of each other's matching needs and maturities, they could have done the swap directly with each other, but then would have counterparty risk. A swap dealer can provide insurance against non-performance of the counterparty as well as general intermediation. In case of default by one of the counterparties, the swap dealer has the right of offset, that is, to stop servicing the defaulting party's original debt.

Back-to-back (parallel) loans

Indirect financing can be done by a German firm lending euros to the US affiliate in Germany and simultaneously a US firm lending dollars to the German affiliate in the United States. A parallel loan is also known as a credit swap loan since the firms are borrowing each other's currency for a specified period of time. This is illustrated in Figure 4.21.

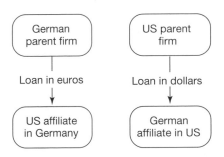

Figure 4.21 Back-to-back (parallel) loans

105

The firms do not go through the foreign exchange market, so do not pay the foreign exchange spread or fees. They also benefit from lowered interest rates. In short, they save intermediation costs and benefit from comparative advantage in lending. At the same time, they may use a parallel loan to hedge their foreign exchange risk. Naturally, there is counterparty risk, but the right of offset exists. A swap dealer is better able to match the size, timing, and condition of foreign exchange swaps by avoiding the "double coincidence of wants" implicitly involved in direct counterparty swaps.

Accounting exposure

Accounting exposure arises from changes in the parent's net worth due to changes in exchange rates. Accounting exposure is also known as "translation exposure," since it is associated with the translation of foreign currency assets and liabilities. Foreign currency financial statements must be translated into the parent company's reporting currency to consolidate worldwide financial and income statements. If exchange rates have changed since the previous reporting period, the restatement of financial and income statements that are denominated in foreign currencies will result in foreign exchange gains or losses. Re-measurement of different line items using different exchange rates results in changes in current income or equity reserves.

A firm is long in a currency if its net exposed assets in the currency are positive (i.e. its exposed assets in a currency are greater than its exposed liabilities in that currency). It is short if its exposed liabilities exceed exposed assets in the currency.

FASB 52

The rules that govern translation in the United States are devised by the Financial Accounting Standards Board. FASB 52—*Foreign Currency Translation* established US translation standards, requiring a functional currency and a reporting currency. A functional currency must be selected for each subsidiary; that is, the currency of its primary working environment. Any foreign currency income is translated into the functional currency at current exchange rates if measured at current cost and at historical rates if measured at historical cost. Then, all amounts are translated at the current exchange rate from the functional currency into the reporting currency. The reporting currency is the currency in which the parent firm prepares its own financial statements; that is, US dollars for a US firm. In the case of a hyperinflationary country—defined as one that has cumulative inflation of approximately 100 percent or more over a three-year period—the functional currency of a US affiliate must be the dollar. Translation gains and losses bypass the income statement and are accumulated in a separate equity account on the parent's balance sheet called a "cumulative translation adjustment."

106

Translation methods vary from country to country, but most use a cumulative translation adjustment equity line to account for translation gains or losses.

A simple technique is to multiply the difference between exposed assets and exposed liabilities by the change in the exchange rate in each currency. The resulting number is the gain/loss due to translation exposure in that currency. That is:

$$(A_i - L_i)(S_i^2 - S_i^1), \tag{4.6}$$

where $(A_i - L_i)$ represents the net position in currency i. If $A_i > L_i$, the firm is long in currency i; if $A_i < L_i$, the firm is short in currency i; while, if $A_i = L_i$, the firm is hedged in currency i from an accounting point of view. $(S_i^2 - S_i^1)$ represents the change in the spot price of currency i terms of USD or the home currency between re-measurement periods.

The total gain or loss between reporting periods due to translation at new exchange rates is the sum of the gains or losses in each individual currency, or:

$$\sum_{i=1}^{n}(A_i - L_i)(S_i^2 - S_i^1). \tag{4.7}$$

This amount is added to or subtracted from the cumulative translation adjustment item.

Hedge accounting

Hedge accounting refers to the inclusion of gains and losses in earnings from financial hedge instruments at the same times losses and gains from changes in the value of the asset are recorded. FASB 52, paragraph 21, indicates that the financial hedge must be designated as, and be effective as, a hedge of a definite, foreign currency commitment. That is, the value of the hedge must move opposite to the value of a definite foreign currency commitment.

Trade finance

Trade finance can play a useful role in hedging. An L/C specifies, for example, the currency of payment as well as the conditions of payment. When it is confirmed, the bank substitutes its credit for that of the importer should the importer default on payment. Naturally, there are fees associated with an L/C, but it assures the payment for international trade, a very important role in the world trade and financial system.

In general, trade can be financed by:

- cash-in-advance: the seller receives cash from buyer prior to shipment. This shifts the credit risk to the buyer.
- an open account: goods are shipped to the buyer, then payment is made to account. This shifts the credit risk to the seller.
- collections: goods are shipped to the buyer, and the seller's draft and documents covering the shipment are presented through his/her bank to the buyer's bank for payment. In this case, both share in the credit risk.
- an L/C: after the seller receives an L/C with acceptable terms, the seller ships the goods. The bank that issued the L/C assures the seller of payment when the terms of the L/C are met by confirming the L/C. A confirmed L/C is a negotiable instrument.

STEPS IN OBTAINING A LETTER OF CREDIT

1 The importer obtains an L/C promising to pay on the importer's behalf.
2 The bank promises the exporter to pay on behalf of the importer by advising and/or confirming the L/C.
3 The exporter "ships to the bank," trusting the bank's promise.
4 The bank pays the exporter.
5 The bank "turns over" the merchandise to the importer.

Diagrammatically, an L/C can be depicted as in Figure 4.22.

DOCUMENTS IN TRADE FINANCE

- L/Cs are documentary or standby, irrevocable or revocable, confirmed or unconfirmed, revolving or non-revolving. An L/C may be transferable to a second party, i.e. discounted on a secondary market. It is typically irrevocable and confirmed to be marketable on the secondary market.
- The exporter ships the merchandise to the importer's country. Title to the merchandise is given to the bank on an order bill of lading.

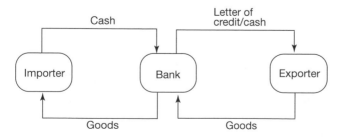

Figure 4.22 A letter of credit

- The exporter asks the bank to pay for the goods and the bank (or its correspondent or affiliate) does so. The document to request payment is a sight draft (also known as a bill of exchange). The bank passes title to the importer. At that time, or later, depending upon the terms of the agreement, the importer reimburses the bank.
- Both sight drafts and time drafts are negotiable instruments, if properly drawn. When a time draft is drawn upon and accepted by a bank, it becomes a banker's acceptance. When a time draft is drawn on and accepted by a business firm, it becomes a trade acceptance.
- Countertrade takes place when "the sale of goods and services by a producer is linked to an import purchase of other goods and services" (Downes and Goodman, 2005). Countertrade is thus a form of barter or bilateral clearing resulting from shortages of hard currency, central planning, political risk, and barriers to international trade and investment. It is also a vehicle for avoiding taxation.

CONCLUSION

A firm's free-cash flow from overseas operations is subject to exchange rate risk. By changing economic variables or seeking offsetting matching currency flows, the firm can hedge against exchange rate losses. To hedge, there are contractual hedges, operational hedges, and trade documents that cover against unexpected changes in exchange rates. The contractual hedges are mainly useful for one-time large future receipts or expenses in foreign exchange, while operational hedges provide matching natural offsetting flows in foreign currency on an ongoing basis. Accounting hedges insulate the balance sheet and income statement from transla- tion losses, and trade finance can set up risk-sharing contingency clauses or invoic- ing in the reporting currency of the exporter. While the case for hedging may be debated, large multinational businesses hedge their foreign exchange exposure on a routine basis. Their core business and comparative advantage is in the produc- tion of goods and services, not in speculating on movements in the exchange rate by implicitly taking long or short positions in different currencies.

REFERENCES AND FURTHER READING

Akemann, Michael and Fabio Kanczuk (2005) "Sovereign default and the sustainability risk premium effect," *Journal of Development Economics* 76(1): 53–69.
Aliber, Robert Z. and C. P. Stickney (1975) "Accounting measures of foreign exchange exposure: the long and short of it," *Accounting Review* 50(1): 44–57.
Ball, Ray (1995) "Making accounting international: why, how, and how far will it go?," *Journal of Applied Corporate Finance* 8(3): 19–29.

Banks, Gary (1983) "The economics and politics of countertrade," *World Economy* 6(2): 159–82.

Bilson, John F. O. (1994) "Managing economic exposure to foreign exchange risk: a case study of American Airlines," in Y. Amihud and R. Levich (eds), *Exchange rates and corporate performance*, Burr Ridge, IL: Irwin Publishing: 221–46.

Bishop, Paul and Don Dixon (1996) *Foreign exchange handbook: managing risk and opportunity in global currency markets*, New York: John Wiley & Sons.

Clark, Ephraim (2004) *Arbitrage, hedging, and speculation: the foreign exchange market*, Westport, CT: Praeger.

Donnenfeld, Shabtai and Alfred Haug (2003) "Currency invoicing in international trade: an empirical investigation," *Review of International Economics* 11(2): 332–45.

Downes, John and Jordan Elliot Goodman (2005) *Dictionary of Finance and Onvestment Terms*, 7th edn, Hauppage, NY: Barron's Financial Guides.

Eiteman, David K., Arthur I. Stonehill, and Michael H. Moffett (2000) "Translation exposure," in David K. Eiteman, Arthur I. Stonehill, and Michael H. Moffett, *Multinational Business Finance*, 10th edn, Reading, MA: Addison-Wesley Publishing Company.

Euromoney Publications (1988) *The guide to export finance*, London: Euromoney Publications.

Financial Accounting Standards Board (1981) *Foreign currency translation, statement of financial standards No. 52*, Stamford, CT: FASB.

Francis, Dick (1987) *The countertrade handbook*, Westport, CT: Quorum Books.

Giddy, Ian H. (1994) *Global financial markets*, Lexington, MA: D. C. Heath & Co.

Heckerman, Donald (1972) "The exchange rate risks of foreign operations," *Journal of Business* 45(1): 42–8.

Henderson, Callum (2002) *Currency strategy: the practitioner's guide to currency investing, hedging, and forecasting*, Hoboken, NJ: John Wiley & Sons.

Jesswein, Kurt R., Chuck C. Y. Kwok, and William R. Folks, Jr (1995) "Corporate use of innovative foreign exchange risk management products," *Columbia Journal of World Business* 30(3): 70–82.

Jokung, Octave (2004) "Risky assets and hedging in emerging markets," *Economic and Financial Modeling* 11(2): 66–98.

Kerkvliet, Joe and Michael H. Moffett (1991) "The hedging of an uncertain future foreign currency cash flow," *Journal of Financial and Quantitative Analysis* 26(4): 565–78.

Lecraw, Donald J. (1989) "The management of countertrade: factors influencing success," *Journal of International Business Studies* 20(1): 41–59.

Levi, Maurice D. (1994) "Exchange rates and the valuation of firms," in Y. Amihud and R. Levich (eds), *Exchange rates and corporate performance*, New York: Irwin: 37–48.

Pilbeam, Keith (2004) "The stabilization properties of fixed and floating exchange rate regimes," *International Journal of Finance and Economics* 9(2): 113–23.

Ross, Derek (1992) "Investors: for or against translation hedging?," *Accountancy* 109(1182): 100.

Ross, Stephen A., Randolph W. Westerfield, and Bradford D. Jordan (2003) *Corporate finance*, 5th edn, Irwin/McGraw-Hill.

Schwartz, Robert and Clifford W. Smith (1990) *Handbook of currency and interest rate risk management*, New York: New York Institute of Finance.

Smith, Clifford W. Jr and Rene M. Stulz (1985) "The determinants of firms' hedging policies," *Journal of Financial and Quantitative Analysis* 20(4): 391–405.

Smith, Clifford W. Jr, Charles W. Smithson, and D. Sykes Wilford (1993) "Five reasons why companies should manage risk," in Robert J. Schwartz and Clifford W. Smith, *Advanced strategies in financial risk management*, New York: New York Institute of Finance.

Soenen, Luc A. (1991) "When foreign exchange hedging doesn't help," *Journal of Cash Management* 11(6): 58–62.

Solnick, Bruno (1990) "Swap pricing and default risk: a note," *Journal of International Financial Management and Accounting* 2(1): 79–91.

Stultz, Rene M. (1984) "Optimal hedging policies," *Journal of Financial and Quantitative Analysis* 19(2): 127–40.

Stultz, Rene M. (1996) "Rethinking risk management," *Journal of Applied Corporate Finance* 9(3): 8–24.

Zysman, John and Stephen S. Cohen (1986) "Countertrade, offsets, barter and buy-backs," *California Management Review* 28(2): 41–56.

PROBLEMS

4.1 Hedging (I)

There are several schools of thought regarding hedging and its impact on the value of the firm. One school argues that, if the owners of the firm wish to hedge, they can do so in their own portfolios. If the firm hedges, the costs outweigh any benefits. Another school argues that the comparative advantage of the firm is production of goods and services, and that, if it does not hedge, it is essentially speculating. However, not all risk can be hedged by contracts and the cost of reducing some risks is prohibitively expensive. Write two short essays defending the following opposing positions:

a "I never hedge, since it reduces my bottom line!"
b "I always hedge, since I cannot take the risk of exchange rate losses bankrupting my firm."

4.2 Default risk

Consider the following basic data on a one-year Ecuadorian Brady Bond (dollar denominated sovereign obligation). It has a face value of $100 payable at maturity, but no coupon. Today it is trading at $80. Your risk-free rate is 5 percent.

a What is the Brady Bond's "yield to maturity" (that is, its IRR)?
b What is its "risk premium"?

4.3 Stock options as executive compensation

You were hired by Sparkle.com, a telecommunications company, last year (exactly a year ago today). The company agreed to pay you £12,000 annual salary plus an option to buy in one year (i.e. today) 1,000 shares in Sparkle.com at £80. Today's share price on the market is £50.

a   What was your total annual compensation?
b   What percent of your compensation was in the form of stock options?
c   Answer question (a) on the assumption that today's share price is instead £100.
d   Answer question (b) on the assumption that today's share price is instead £100.

4.4 Foreign exchange options

a   Claudia Speculator, IB Investments Ltd, bought 100 euro call options at $0.01 per option (i.e. one cent per option) with a strike price of $1.25. She exercised them and sold the proceeds at a spot price of $1.27. How much profit did Claudia make?
b   Thomas Banker, NPI Bankers, sold 100 euro put options with a strike price of $1.25, receiving a premium of $0.005 (i.e. one-half of one cent per option). The put expired when the spot price was $1.20.
   (i)   Was the put in or out of the money from the point of view of the buyer?
   (ii) How much money did Thomas make or lose as the seller (what is his profit/loss on the put he sold)?
   (iii) Did he have to honor the put?

4.5 Hedging (II)

Martha Exporter, Miami Baking Ltd, exports her delicious Martha's Brownies to the United Kingdom and has accounts receivables in pounds sterling of £100,000 in 90 days.

Basic data:
US interest rate at which Martha can borrow dollars is 10 percent p.a.
UK interest rate at which Martha can borrow pounds is 8 percent p.a.
Spot price of pound is $1.763, bid.
Spot price of pound is $1.769, ask.
Forward bid price of pound is $1.78 for 90-day delivery.
Premium on £ put option at $1.78 (at-the-money) strike price is $0.0028 per £.

a   What are the various contractual hedges that Martha might purchase to hedge her pound exchange exposure?

Now suppose that Martha decides to invoice British Baking Imports in US dollars to shift the exchange rate exposure to the importer. She thus invoices $178,000 dollars deliverable in 90 days. British Baking is assumed to face the same market conditions as Martha's Brownies, namely:

US interest rate at which British Baking can lend dollars is 10 percent p.a.
UK interest rate at which British Baking can borrow pounds is 8 percent p.a.
Spot ask price of the dollar is £0.56527 per dollar.
Forward ask price of the dollar is £0.5618 per dollar for 90-day delivery.
A £0.5618 at-the-money call option to buy dollars costs £0.0028 per dollar.

b   What are the various contractual hedges that British Baking might purchase to hedge their dollar exchange exposure?

4.6 Balance sheet hedging

Gateaux Antoinette, SA, a subsidiary of Antoinette Cakes Inc., New York, had cash of €100,000 and accounts receivable of €100,000 each on its books (or €200,000 in total) when the euro suddenly appreciated from $1 per euro to $1.20.

a   Indicate what effect the revaluation would have on the translation of these assets into US dollars on the consolidated balance sheet of the US parent firm.
b   How could Gateaux Antoinette have acquired a "balance sheet" hedge for its cash and accounts receivable in euros prior to the revaluation (even though it benefited from the exposure in this instance)?

4.7 Operating exposure (I)

You are a French company exporting widgets to the United States from your plant in France where the widgets are produced. You sell them for dollars in the United States. Last year you sold 100,000 widgets in the United States for $10 a widget, converting your dollar revenues to euros at €0.9 per US dollar. Next year you expect the dollar to be worth less, €0.8, but to export 110,000 widgets to the United States. You are considering selling them at $10 a widget, but may reconsider the US price.

a   Are you subject to operating exposure in dollars for the next year? If so, how much?
b   What are some techniques you can use to hedge against this operating exposure in the United States?

4.8 Operating exposure (II)

Tiny Tots Toys of Miami, Florida projects second quarter 2006 sales in Argentina to be 10,000 pesos, and expects the exchange rate to be $0.5 per peso (dollar earnings are therefore expected to be $5,000).

a If the exchange rate unexpectedly changes to $0.25 per peso and Tiny Tots has not hedged, what are losses due to ''operating exposure''?
b How could Tiny Tots eliminate its operating exposure?
c Suppose that Tiny Tots relocates production to Argentina and expects second quarter costs of production and distribution to be 5,000 pesos, leaving a net profit of 5,000 pesos if sales remain constant. Would you recommend that Tiny Tots hedge the entire 10,000 pesos?
d In either event, what will Tiny Tots' hedging activity do to the expected profitability in US dollars and in Argentine pesos of Tiny Tots? Explain.

4.9 Accounting exposure

Your European subsidiary has cash and accounts receivable of 100 and 300 euros respectively, and accounts payable and short-term debt of 100 and 200 euros respectively. US headquarters re-measures these line items in dollars on November 1, when the dollar price of the euro rose from $1.20 per euro to $1.30 per euro.

a Did headquarters experience translation losses or gains in terms of US dollars?
b How are any such translation gains or losses entered into the balance sheet?
c How could the European subsidiary have acquired balance sheet hedge against losses or gains from translation exposure?

Chapter 5

International financial management

CAPITAL STRUCTURE

There are two ways of financing your firm: by contracting debt (business loans) or issuing equity (shares). Creditors have senior debt that must be paid or satisfied, except in the case of bankruptcy. They only share in bankruptcy risk. Shareholders participate in ownership of the firm, so they share in business risk and risk of bankruptcy, in which case they usually get nothing. Due to the greater risk, shareholders typically require a higher rate of return to their equity. Interest payments to creditors are treated as an expense, so they are a "tax shield" for the firm.

The cost of capital is thus a weighted average of the after-tax cost of borrowing (D) and the cost of issuing equity (E):

$$WACC = R_D(1 - t_c)\left(\frac{D}{D + E}\right) + R_E\left(\frac{E}{D + E}\right), \tag{5.1}$$

where $WACC$ indicates the weighted average cost of capital, R_D the cost of debt, R_E the cost of equity, $D/(D + E)$ the degree of financial leverage (the ratio of debt to the value of the firm), E the value of equity shares in the firm, and t_c the marginal corporate tax rate. For example, assume your corporation has 30 percent debt and 70 percent equity. It can borrow at 10 percent by selling its corporate bonds, while its shareholders require a 14 percent return on investment due to a 9.5 percent market risk premium on your company. Consequently, the weighted average cost of capital is:

$$11.75\% = 10\%(1 - 0.35)(0.3) + 14\%(0.7). \tag{5.2}$$

Due to the tax shield of borrowing and to the low degree of risk to the initial loans, the WACC initially declines with greater financial leverage, $(D/(D + E))$. With a high degree of financial leverage, $(D/(D + E))$ approaching one, the

115

risk of financial distress and bankruptcy increases. This causes both the borrowing rate and the equity rate to rise sharply. Consequently, there is an optimum capital structure that minimizes the weighted average cost of capital, indicated in Figure 5.1.

The optimal degree of leverage appears to be around 40 percent in Figure 5.1. The degree of curvature is exaggerated for illustration purposes. In practice, the WACC is likely to have fairly flat ranges. Start-ups are often too leveraged and fail to reach their break-even point due to fixed interest and principal payments. Equity-based finance is less risky to the firm because shareholders participate in operational and economic risk. Dividends need not be paid out should profits be small or negative. However, venture capitalists often seek management fees, in addition to 40 percent of ownership control. Marketing is often the greatest challenge to the start-up firm. The four "Ps"of marketing—product design, pricing, promotion, and placement (distribution)—are critical in generating positive cash flow as soon as possible.

Tight financial controls are indispensable. A monthly, if not weekly, profit/loss (P/L) statement should be accurately done, including the opportunity cost of the owners, if they are involved in the management. Positive cash flow is the aim of the firm and its owners. Records must be kept and discussed at regular meetings of the board of directors and managers. This is what gives value to the firm and ultimately dividends to its owners.

The managers can have fun and enjoy their jobs. But, as agents, they must be loyal to the principals, taking decisions that increase the value of the firm. Revenue growth is fine, but costs must grow at a lower rate. The tax shield advantage of additional debt must be weighted against the rising cost of financial distress. Theoretically, a firm has an optimal level of debt that balances increased value of the tax shield against the increased cost of borrowing with financial distress.

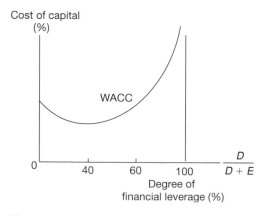

Figure 5.1 The weighted average cost of capital and financial leverage

International capital structure

Some basic rules apply to the optimal capital structure from an international point of view. First, the basic rule for conversion of the WACC in dollars to, say, pounds for purposes of discounting pound cash flows (the interest rate parity rule) is:

$$\left(\frac{1 + WACC_{£}}{1 + WACC_{\$}}\right) = \left(\frac{1 + R_{uk}}{1 + R_{us}}\right), \tag{5.3}$$

or equivalently:

$$WACC_{£} = (1 + WACC_{\$})\left(\frac{1 + R_{uk}}{1 + R_{us}}\right) - 1. \tag{5.4}$$

If your WACC is 11.75 percent in USD, R_{us} = 4.5 percent, and R_{uk} = 3 percent, the WACC in GBP is 10.14 percent, reflecting the lower expected inflation in the UK. That is:

$$10.14\% = (1.1175)\left(\frac{1.030}{1.045}\right) - 1. \tag{5.5}$$

The key idea is to seek the lowest WACC in whatever currency it is the least, and then use the conversion rule to measure the WACC in the other currency. It is important to use the interest rate on risk-free T-bills for conversion purposes. That allows the costs of capital to be adjusted for different inflationary expectations, as in the Fisher equation.

It is appropriate to consolidate all debt and equity at current exchange rates in order to correctly measure the debt-to-equity ratio for global operations.

CROSSLISTING ON FOREIGN STOCK EXCHANGES

By crosslisting its shares on foreign stock exchanges—despite additional disclosure, listing, and reporting costs—a firm can improve the liquidity of its existing shares by making it easier for foreign shareholders to acquire shares at home in their own currencies. Crosslisting may also increase the share price by overcoming mispricing in a segmented, illiquid, home capital market.

There are other advantages to crosslisting: (1) It may also provide a liquid secondary market to support a new equity issue in the foreign market; and (2) it may establish a secondary market for shares used to acquire local firms or to compensate local management and employees in foreign affiliates.

117

American depositary receipts

Crosslisting is usually accomplished by depositary receipts. In the United States, foreign shares are usually traded through American depositary receipts (ADRs). These are negotiable certificates issued by a US bank in the United States to represent the underlying shares of stock, which are held in trust.

"Sponsored" ADRs are created at the request of a foreign firm wanting access to equity finance in the United States. The firm applies to the Securities and Exchange Commission (SEC) and a US bank for registration and issuance. The firm bears the costs of creating sponsored ADRs. However, a US bank may issue "unsponsored" ADRs if the foreign firm does not wish to sponsor them.

INTERNATIONAL LIQUIDITY AND MARKET INTEGRATION

By seeking access to international capital markets, a firm can benefit from two distinct, important effects: first, increased liquidity of its own securities; and, second, overcoming market segmentation. Both effects tend to lower the cost of capital to the firm compared to borrowing from solely domestic sources.

The firm has a list of investment projects ranked according to the marginal rate of return on investment, sometimes called the marginal efficiency of investment (MEI). High-return projects are taken on before low-return projects. As the firm spends more of its capital budget, the MEI declines. Its level of capital expenditure is therefore constrained by the marginal cost of borrowing.

Increased liquidity increases the supply of capital at existing interest rates, so that an increase in borrowing causes a smaller rise in the cost of borrowing. In addition, market integration overcomes market segmentation, thus additionally lowering the cost of borrowing.

TRANSFER PRICING

Transfer pricing refers to the pricing of the transfer of goods, services, and technology between related units of the firm. Transfer pricing takes place both domestically and internationally. In the case of the international firm, several considerations come into play. In principle, there is an optimal transfer price to provide the right incentives to the affiliate to supply the appropriate quantity of the intermediate input.

Optimal transfer prices

Assume there are a marketing division and a production division. Each unit of output requires one unit of marketing production, that is, marketing and production are joint products. The marketing division purchases the intermediate input

118

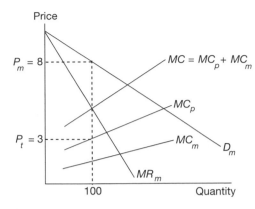

Figure 5.2 *Transfer pricing*

from the production division, then markets the final product. The intermediate input is neither sold to other firms, nor bought from other firms, by assumption.

In Figure 5.2, the marginal cost of the marketing and the production divisions is summed vertically to yield the marginal cost of the final product. Setting marginal cost of the final product equal to its marginal revenue yields the profit-maximizing level of production, 100, and a price of \$8. To provide the correct incentives to the production division, a transfer price of \$3 is optimal. In its production decisions, the production division sets marginal cost equal to \$3 to maximize profits. It produces exactly the required amount of intermediate inputs and sells them to the marketing division. Any other transfer price would distort the incentives of the overseas affiliate.

Transfer pricing with external sales or purchases

When there is a possibility to buy or sell the intermediate input externally to other firms at a fixed price, the firm should regard this price as the opportunity cost of the intermediate input. In this case, the marketing department will maximize profits by having a transfer price equal to the market price of the intermediate input.

Any excess supply of the intermediate input at the market price would be sold externally, while any excess demand for the intermediate input would be outsourced; that is, purchased externally.

Imperfectly competitive market for the intermediate good

When the market for the intermediate good is not competitive, the marketing division should set a higher transfer price to its internal division, and restrict its purchases slightly from the external market. Indeed, profit-maximization requires:

119

$$\frac{P_t}{P_x} = 1 + \frac{1}{\varepsilon}, \tag{5.6}$$

where P_t represents the transfer price, P_x represents the price at which the firms purchases the input on the external market, and ε the elasticity of supply of the intermediate input to the marketing division. Equation 5.6 reflects the fact that, by curtailing purchases on the external market somewhat, the marketing division pays a lower price for outsourced intermediate goods. For example, if $\varepsilon = 2$, the transfer price would be 50 percent higher than the external price. If the external market were perfectly competitive, ε approaches infinity, and the optimal transfer price equals the market price of the intermediate good.

If the production division produces more of the intermediate input than sold to the marketing division and has monopoly power in the market for the intermediate input, its optimal transfer price is below the price at which it sells the intermediate input to the external market:

$$\frac{P_t}{P_x} = 1 - \frac{1}{\eta}, \tag{5.7}$$

where η is the absolute value of the elasticity of market demand for the intermediate good. For example, if $\eta = 2$, the optimum transfer price is 50 percent below the price at which the intermediate input is sold on the external market. Again, if the external market were perfectly competitive, η approaches infinity, and the optimal transfer price equals the market price of the intermediate good.

Transfer pricing may be a technique by which funds may be relocated. A lowering of transfer prices may finance the foreign affliate. A parent firm wishing to transfer funds out of a particular country can charge higher prices on goods sold to its affiliate there, thus evading exchange controls. By setting transfer prices to shift taxable income from a country with a high income tax rate to a jurisdiction with a low income tax rate, the firm may lower its taxable income. It may do so legally since profits earned in the lower tax jurisdiction may not be taxed until repatriated under some circumstances.

However, according to the IRS guidelines, the "correct transfer price" is one that reflects an arm's length price for a sale of the same goods or service to an unrelated customer. An advanced pricing agreement (APA) may be negotiated with the tax authorities of both home country and host country. An APA may save trouble and litigation resulting from an IRS challenge to transfer prices. The incidence of import duties may also offset the favorable income taxes in transfer pricing—an additional consideration.

The aggressive use of transfer pricing can transfer profits from high-tax jurisdictions to tax havens, thereby reducing global tax liabilities. Profits can be

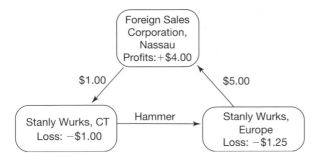

Figure 5.3 *Abusive transfer pricing*

accumulated in an offshore tax haven, no income taxes being paid in the home country of headquarters. Say you are a hardware equipment manufacturer, Stanly Wurks, in Connecticut, where you are not only subject to federal taxes, but also to state and local taxes. You export hardware equipment to Europe through an FSC in Nassau, the Bahamas. Take a hammer, for example. It costs a constant $2.00 to produce per unit. You sell it to the foreign sales corporation (FSC) in Nassau for $1.00, thereby incurring losses of $1.00 per hammer exported. Thus far, you have saved headquarters $0.35 in corporate income taxes. Next, the FSC sells it in euros to your affiliate in Europe for $5.00 (or €4.00), which in turn distributes it for €3.00, losing one euro, or $1.25, per hammer. Thus, the affiliate incurs a loss of $1.25. Consequently, its taxes are down approximately $0.44. The FSC bought the hammer at $1.00 and sold it at $5.00, making $4.00 in profits on each hammer. These profits are deposited in an offshore bank and are not subject to income taxes. If this sounds like eating your cake and having it too, it is! Taxes are down $0.79, and the affiliate is accumulating $4.00 of untaxed profits in Nassau. These can be used to make payments or deposits of one sort or another.

Clearly, this would be an example of abuse of the national and international laws of taxation. Yet, it takes place. Figure 5.3 depicts this example of transfer pricing. If caught, the firm would be fined.

INTERNATIONAL TAXATION

The General Agreement on Tariffs and Trade (GATT) of the World Trade Organization (WTO) governs the tax treatment of branches and subsidiaries located abroad. If a branch or subsidiary is located in a signatory country, it is entitled to "national treatment"—that is, tax and regulatory treatment no less favorable than that accorded to national enterprises. Article III, *National Treatment on Internal Taxation and Regulation*, explicitly forbids discrimination against foreign subsidiaries. Consequently, a firm with a foreign subsidiary may appeal any discriminatory treatment to the WTO/GATT in Geneva, Switzerland. Its corporate income tax cannot be higher than that of local companies, and it cannot be charged higher duties to import intermediate goods, or be required to purchase inputs locally to protect domestic production.

US taxation of foreign-source income

In general, US taxation of foreign income is consolidated into the income statement of the parent firm. Income derived from a minority-controlled foreign affiliate is taxed when remitted to the US parent. This treatment sometimes leads to tax avoidance by the creation of tax-shelter affiliates such as FSCs and international financial offshore centers (IFOCs) located in offshore banking havens. Income from foreign subsidiaries is eligible for tax credits on taxes deemed paid abroad up to its headquarter's marginal tax rate. A tax credit thus typically reduces the tax liability of the parent firm by the full amount paid in foreign taxes. If the foreign corporate rate is above 35 percent, a deferred tax credit is given on the amount above 35 percent or is mingled with sources of foreign income taxed at less than 35 percent, reducing the rate to an effective 35 percent.

Foreign sales corporations (FSC)

An FSC allows firms having export operations to enjoy exemption of most export income from US taxes, even when the good is produced in the United States. Exempt foreign trade income derives from "export property" sold, leased, or rented outside the United States by the FSC. The portion of income exempted is either 34 percent when arm's length pricing is used, or 17/23 (approximately 74 percent) if the transfer price is set by administrative pricing rules applicable to FSCs. The WTO has ruled that the FSC amounts to an export subsidy and as such violates Article VI of the GATT/WTO, *Anti-dumping and Countervailing Duties*.

Examples of taxation of international operations

A foreign majority-controlled branch is treated as part of the parent firm and thus must repatriate profits and pay home taxes contemporaneously. A subsidiary incorporated locally need not repatriate profits nor pay home country taxes unless it remits the profits. Foreign income tax credits apply in both cases. The value-added tax and sales taxes are deducted from income, and thus treated as expenses.

The following examples attempt to capture these various aspects of international taxation. Country A, where the affiliate is located, is a high-tax country, so that the home country, assumed to be the US, issues an excess tax credit

Table 5.1 *International tax treatment of firms: high tax jurisdiction (Country A)*

Income/taxes	Exemption*	Credit*	Deduction
Foreign income	100	100	100
Foreign taxes paid	40	40	40
Home taxes paid	0	0	21
Net income	60	60	39

Note: *Excess tax credit of 5.

Table 5.2 *International tax treatment of firms: comparable tax jurisdiction (Country B)*

Income/taxes	Exemption	Credit	Deduction
Foreign income	100	100	100
Foreign taxes paid	35	35	35
Home taxes paid	0	0	22.75
Net income	65	65	42.25

Table 5.3 *International tax treatment of firms: low tax jurisdiction (Country C)*

Income/taxes	Exemption	Credit	Deduction
Foreign income	100	100	100
Foreign taxes paid	15	15	15
Home taxes paid	0	20	29.75
Net income	85	65	55.25

to the parent firm in Table 5.1. Country B in Table 5.2 is a comparable tax country.

No US taxes would be paid, the firm receiving a full tax credit for the 35 percent corporate income tax. The tax burden would thus be the same as in the United States, unless Country B imposed its taxes by the value-added and sales tax alone. Table 5.3 depicts a low-tax country.

A US subsidiary that reinvested profits in the host country would be exempt from US taxes; a branch would receive a tax credit of 15 percent, and pay an

Table 5.4 *International tax treatment of firms: tax havens (Country D)*

Income/taxes	Tax haven, no deferral	Tax haven with deferral*	Tax haven, no repatriation
Foreign income	100	100	100
Foreign taxes paid	0	0	0
Home taxes paid	35	0	0
Net income	65	100	100

Note: *Taxes paid upon repatriation.

additional 20 percent to the US Treasury on its repatriated profits, while it would pay an additional 29.5 percent if the 15 percent tax were a value-added tax or a sales tax. The tax treatment of affiliates located in tax havens is shown in Table 5.4.

In some instances, special regimes are applied to a tax haven, thereby further lightening the tax burden. Table 5.5 illustrates the special cases of FSCs located in tax havens, which benefit either from 34 percent exemption, or 17/23 exemption of foreign source income depending on whether arm's length pricing or administrative rules pricing is applied. The total exemption of foreign source income or possessions derived investment income is also shown in Table 5.5.

A US parent firm can take advantage of these special regimes, but may be tempted to abuse them. In these cases, the IRS takes a "guilty until proven innocent" approach. The firm may end up tricking itself, especially if it uses aggressive transfer pricing to shift profits into the tax haven, then does not repatriate the profits, thus evading corporate income taxes in the United States.

A US amnesty was applied in the 2005 tax year to permit a repatriation of accumulated overseas funds at a 5 percent rate, ostensibly to encourage investment in the United States. Large sums were repatriated on these favorable terms by companies such as Hewlett Packard.

Table 5.5 *Special international taxation regimes*

Income/taxes	FSC (arm's length pricing)	FSC (administrative rules)	US possession income from foreign sources or possessions source investment income
Foreign income	100	100	100
Foreign taxes paid	0	0	0
Home taxes paid	23.1	9.13	0
Net income	76.9	90.87	100

WORKING CAPITAL MANAGEMENT

Net working capital consists of cash, accounts receivables, and inventories less accounts payable and other current liabilities. A firm must have operating balances to manage its receivables, inventories, and payables. Its net working capital finances the cash conversion cycle from raw inputs to final product and sale. As indicated in Figure 5.4, short-term borrowing and repayment plays an important role in the cash management process.

In addition, the international firm may hold cash reserves for its anticipated cash needs (*transactions motive*) and its unanticipated cash needs (*speculative motive*). A multinational firm with many affiliates may, for example, reduce its cash reserves by pooling them in a centralized facility (see Eiteman *et al.*). Cash netting may also reduce the settlement costs of a multinational firm with several affiliates having separate foreign exchange transactions between themselves and the parent firm. For instance, if subsidiary A must pay €150 to subsidiary C for widgets, and C must pay A €100 for intermediate inputs for assembling widgets, rather than having two separate transactions, subsidiary A (or a centralized facility) can simply pay subsidiary C €50. The single transaction netting the payment saves the multinational firm transactions and spread fees in its cash operations. In short, the cash management process attempts to not tie up cash unnecessarily, without risking liquidity crises.

INTERNATIONAL MERGERS AND ACQUISITIONS

International mergers and acquisitions are not for the faint of heart. Political risk, hostile trade unions, and governmental regulations protecting employment and working conditions are fraught with pitfalls. Every foreign investor is guaranteed "national treatment" by the WTO/GATT, meaning the same treatment as domestic firms, but in most cases this is not particularly business-friendly. The

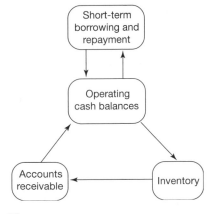

Figure 5.4 Working capital management

125

firm's cultures may differ significantly in terms of goals and means of communication, introducing an additional layer of difficulty in managerial decision-making. The tax burden is invariably higher in developed countries, especially high payroll taxes to finance social programs—health, unemployment, retirement, and disability. As a result, the growth of temporary employment agencies in Europe, for example, is phenomenal. Temporary workers do not "benefit" from the same high payroll tax treatment.

In emerging markets, securing large contracts—for example, the exploitation of mineral rights, or the acquisition of a state enterprise that is being privatized—is often a matter of putting a bundle of cash on the President or Minister's desk, or depositing some percent of the contract in an offshore bank account in his or her name (or that of his wife or sons or daughters), or some numbered account. These practices are illegal for US corporations under the Foreign Corrupt Practices Act, as well as under the OECD Anti-corruption Agreement. Consequently, an acquisition of a former state enterprise in a rigged bid involving bribery of government officials would not be admissible. Political risk is great as it may damage the firm's global reputation, for example in the case of the sale of computers by IBM, Argentina to the Banco de la Nación, Argentina: an Argentine federal judge investigated "allegations that IBM gave Government officials up to $21 million in 1994 and 1995 to win a contract with the state-owned Banco de la Nacion. IBM officials in the United States have repeatedly denied any involvement, saying local executives who have since left the company were acting on their own" (Krauss, 1998).

On the other hand, there are potential gains:

- Economies of scale (global output may be maintained by reducing inputs or output may be expanded at reduced average costs).
- Marketing economies (advertising costs are spread over the merged firm).
- Economies of scope (wider and complementary product range).
- Economies of global standardization of product and manufacturing processes.
- Exploitation of comparative advantage within the merged firm by greater vertical integration.
- Leapfrogging of import barriers by producing, distributing, and marketing locally.
- Anti-competitive acquisitions (reduce market competition and increase market share, but there is a risk of violating anti-trust laws).
- Acquisition of technologies.
- Economies of R&D (sharing fixed costs).
- Diversifying the risk of R&D (exploring competing technologies within the merged firm).

- Restructuring (takeover, eliminating inefficient management, and cost reducing).
- Natural hedging (acquiring accounts payable in a currency in which there are accounts receivable).
- Tax gains from the acquisition of tax shields from net operating losses, unused debt capacity, and surplus funds.

A merger is the absorption of one firm by another. Firm A might acquire firm B by offering two shares in A for each share of B. B would then cease to exist. Typically, two thirds of the voting shares of each firm must approve the merger. In general, a merger is only worthwhile is there is some *synergy* in combining the firms:

$$V_{AB} > V_A + V_B, \tag{5.8}$$

that is to say, the value of the merged firm should be greater than the individual firms taken alone. When firm A and firm B consolidate into a new firm C, in general it should be true that:

$$V_C > V_A + V_B. \tag{5.9}$$

In practical terms, a consolidation is equivalent to a merger.

Acquisition by cash

Consider the simple example below:

	Firm A	Firm B
Value	$100	$50
Shares outstanding	20	10
Share value	$5	$5

Let's say that, after the acquisition, the combined firms are worth $170. Synergy is thus $20. Firm A could acquire firm B by paying $60 in cash, a premium of $10 over its market value in order to secure the 2/3 vote necessary of B's shareholders. Each share would be tendered at $6 while it was previously worth $5. For Firm A to benefit from this, the combined value of the firms must increase to more than $160 (the sum of their values, $150, plus the premium offered, $10). After the acquisition, the combined firms are worth $170. The value of Firm A after the acquisition will therefore be $170 minus the $60 paid to B's stockholders. A is thus worth $110 after the acquisition, as shown:

	Firm A
Value	$110
Shares outstanding	20
Share value	$5.5

The acquisition has a positive net present value, increasing shareholders' value. The price of the share rises to $5.50. Shareholders of both firms benefit and should go along with the merger. The firms share equally in the synergy. Notice that, if the NPV of firm B was $50, but it had present value of debt of $10, firm A could equivalently offer cash of $50 and assumption of debt of $10.

Acquisition by stock

It would seem that the same purchase price of $60 could be paid by the issue of 12 shares of A in exchange for the 10 shares of B. At the current market value of $5 for A's shares, this would be equivalent to $60. However, this is not correct, because, due to the rise in the value of A after the merger, 12 shares would be worth more than $60. To see this, consider the exchange ratio 12:10.

Firm A would then look like this:

	Firm A
Value	$170
Shares outstanding	32
Share value	$5.31

Former stockholders in B would now own $5.31 × 12 = $63.75 worth of A's stock, receiving more than the purchase price of $60 in cash. How many shares should A therefore offer to B's shareholders? The correct amount would equal the ratio: $a170 = 60$, giving them shares worth $60. That is, $a = 60/170 = 0.352941176$ of the combined company. Setting this ownership share equal to the fraction of new shares in the merged company, we can solve for n_w the number of new shares issued in addition to the existing number of shares, $n = 20$.

$$a = \frac{n_w}{n + n_w}, \tag{5.10}$$

or, solving for n_w:

$$n_w = \frac{an}{(1 - a)} = 10.90909. \tag{5.11}$$

Firm A's situation is now:

	Firm A
Value	$170
Shares outstanding	30.91
Share value	$5.50

128

The 10.91 shares offered to shareholders of B are worth exactly $60 at the new market price of $5.50!

Acquisition by stock and cash

Suppose firm A acquires firm B by an offer of both cash and stock; for instance, $30 in cash and the rest in stock. How many shares of stock will firm A have to offer? Firm A will therefore be worth $140 after the cash payment of $30. In this case $a = 30/140 = 0.21428571429$, or inputting the basic data directly into equation 5.11, we get:

$$n_w = \frac{\left(\dfrac{30}{140}\right)20}{\left(1 - \dfrac{30}{140}\right)} = 5.45455. \tag{5.12}$$

By offering exactly 5.45455 shares and $30 in cash, Firm A would be offering the same premium as with pure cash or pure stock. Notice that the 5.45455 new shares are worth exactly $30 at the new share price of A, $5.5. Firm A's new situation would be as follows:

	Firm A
Value	$140
Shares outstanding	25.45
Share value	$5.5

The co-insurance principle

The increased value of the firm from an acquisition benefits both shareholders and bondholders. The reduced variability in the sum of the value of the firms (due to less than perfect correlation) reduces the cost of borrowing and thus mainly benefits bondholders at the expense of shareholders. The reduced likelihood of financial distress mainly benefits creditors. Some consider the co-insurance effect as a cost to shareholders (see Ross *et al.*, 2005: 844–5).

Alternatives to acquisition

- Joint ventures involve local partners who share in the managerial and financial decision-making in the local venture. This has advantages in their knowledge of the local market, but may not properly align the motivation of firm and local managers. In the case of China, until 2006 foreign companies typically had to be minority partners in joint ventures.

129

- Direct licensing agreements and management contracts allow headquarters to share in some of the profits from a locally owned operation. On the other hand, direct foreign investment should be considered as an alternative.
- A strategic alliance takes place when two firms exchange stock and form a separate joint venture to develop and manufacture a product or service.

Case study

Deutsche Telekom negotiated the acquisition of VoiceStream Wireless, a mobile telephone firm in Bellevue, Washington, for the price of 3.2 Deutsche Telekom shares plus $30 in cash for each share of the US firm. Based on the 2.3 million subscribers to VoiceStream, the German group offered $24,000 per subscriber in shares and cash. Deutsche Telekom plans to issue 828.8 million additional shares to finance the acquisition. The 30 percent premium offered to shareholders of VoiceStream over market value, the losses of VoiceStream of $1.5 billion in 2000 and projected $1.2 billion in 2001, along with the dilution of Deutsche Telekom shares, all led to a 12.3 percent fall in Deutsche Telekom in Frankfurt upon the announcement of the deal. On the NASDAQ, VoiceStream fell in US dollars by 4 percent (*Le Figaro*, July 26, 2000). In general, if firm A acquires firm B, it is because its net present value increases. For Deutsche Telekom, the option value of access to the US telecommunications market may be great—however, the market did not seem favorably impressed. The German government is a minority shareholder in Deutsche Telekom (25 percent), and has a voice whose interest may not always be compatible with maximizing shareholder wealth—the US model. The European model has constituents—the government, labor unions, shareholders, and the general public—whose interests are taken into account simultaneously. For example, Air France is still majority state owned and has received millions in operating subsidies in the past. Its initial public offering as EADS has received a lukewarm reception. An update from *The Financial Times* stated:

> Deutsche Telekom has joined the growing list of European technology companies whose foreign takeovers are being called into doubt by plunging share prices. Shares in the German phone group have fallen below the level that could force it to renegotiate the terms of its agreed cash-and-shares acquisition of VoiceStream Wireless of the US. The fall in Telekom shares to a new 12-month low of €36.15 ($31.40) yesterday also means the price is within €3.15 of the level where VoiceStream has the right to walk away from the deal. However, analysts do not believe this will happen. Earlier this week, France Telecom shares crossed a threshold which means the French company is likely to face the embarrassment of having to buy back its own shares from Vodafone for significantly more cash than they currently fetch in the market.
>
> (Bertrand *et al.*, 2000)

OFFSHORE BANKING

Offshore banking refers to deposits and loans that are made in a country other than the depositor's or borrower's country of origin. The Eurodollar market was one of the earliest examples of an offshore banking market. An offshore deposit or loan can be characterized simply as in Figure 5.5.

The key differences between offshore banking and domestic banking are the currency of denomination, the tax jurisdiction, and the regulatory framework. For accounts payable and hedging purposes, it is often convenient to hold cash balances in a foreign currency. In some cases, however, offshore banking is used for money laundering. A recent example is a shell Argentine bank in the Cayman Islands, which had no personnel in the Cayman Islands but was used to launder money. It was ordered to close recently by the Cayman banking regulators. The Bank of New York has experienced regulatory trouble resulting from the laundering of Russian monies, as have some Swiss banks.

In the United States, an Edge Act bank is a branch of a foreign bank that is allowed to take in offshore deposits, but not domestic deposits. Edge banks are subject to the regulation and the supervision of the US monetary authorities (the Federal Reserve Bank and the Comptroller of the Currency), who are keen to discover money laundering and close the offending banks.

An Edge bank may make US and foreign loans and investments for its offshore clients. Examples are Banco Santander Central Hispano (BSCH), which has Edge Act facilities for private banking in New York and Miami. Its depositors are mainly from Europe, primarily Spain, and Latin America. It complies with international and US banking regulations and best banking practice, which it has observed since the fifteenth century. Today, BSCH has the greatest volume of assets of any bank in Latin America. Its policy is to acquire 100 percent of existing or new banks, and to install BSCH management to avoid taking the risk of a partner doing illegal or irresponsible banking. Additionally, they take no deposits from politicians nor former politicians from Latin America.

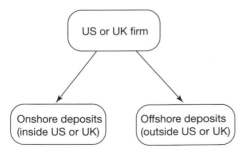

Figure 5.5 Offshore banking

International financial offshore centers (IFOC)

The primary purpose of an IFOC is to centralize, net, and track international cash flow and defer taxes on profits before repatriation or investment. It may also serve as an invoicing center. The Internal Revenue Act of 1962 and the Tax Reform Act of 1984, which created FSCs, permit IFOCs in an attempt to reduce the tax burden on exports from the United States.

However, by the use of aggressive transfer pricing and shell banks and corporations, IFOCs have been vehicles for tax avoidance rather than deferment, and, even worse, money laundering. The Edge Act created IFOCs in the United States for the rest of the world, so this is not a statement only about a few small Caribbean islands. The larger jurisdictions—the United States and Europe—are pressuring smaller IFOCs to remove coveted banking secrecy laws that have shielded money laundering. However, it is clear that a great deal of money is laundered through New York and Miami, despite mandatory notification to the Treasury of deposits over $10,000, an amount so small that it triggers too many notifications.

Other special regimes

A US possessions corporation is not subject to US income tax on income received in the US possession, provided it is not received in the United States. This is an incentive for US firms to set up separate corporations in the US possessions. These special incentives are being phased out gradually.

Blacklisted countries (Non-Cooperative Countries and Territories)

The Financial Action Task Force (FATF)—an international body created by the G-7 to combat terrorist financing and money laundering (the movement of profits from illicit activities through the banking system or legitimate business)—has established a blacklist of countries that do not take enough action to curb money laundering. It also requires greater identification of customers involved in wire transfers in order to combat terrorism. The FATF removed the Cook Islands, Indonesia, and the Philippines from the Non-Cooperative Countries and Territories (NCCTs) list in February 2005. The currently blacklisted countries are Myanmar, Nauru, and Nigeria. The list fell from 17 countries in June 2001 to the only three remaining countries in 2005. While the FATF cites considerable progress in this respect, there is no hard evidence that neither money laundering nor terrorist finance has abated. More worrisome, in their 2005 NCCT Report, they welcomed the substantial progress made by Myanmar, Nauru, and Nigeria

132

in enacting legislation that addresses money laundering deficiencies (FATF/ OECD, 2005: 5). Presumably, when all countries have been removed from the NCCTs list, the FATF will close its doors at the OECD in Paris, declaring the money laundering and terrorist finance problem solved by the implementation of legislation.

AN INTERNATIONAL BUSINESS PLAN

Forms of business organization

The principal ways of organizing a business are:

- a sole proprietorship involving an individual acting on his or her own behalf in a business context. It is the least specially regulated and least complex form, but has greatest asset exposure.
- a partnership formed by the independent action of the partners whose rights and duties are spelled out in business charters.
- a limited partnership involving one or more investing partners and at least one operating partner. An investing partner is liable only to the extent of that partner's investment.
- a corporation is a single entity, a "person," which may sue or be sued without its members being held liable. It is chartered by the jurisdiction in which it is located. A corporation is a business in which large numbers of people are organized in a single venture. They may enter or withdraw from the venture at any time, by buying or selling shares.

The principal–agent problem

The legal cornerstone of business transactions is agency law. An agent is a person empowered to act so as to legally bind another, the principal. An agent must be loyal to the principal. So long as the agent acts with authority, the principal is bound to perform the obligations to third parties. There are several possible solutions to the principal–agent problem. Each tries to align the interests of the agent with those of the owners:

- Ownership means selling part of the firm to the agent, or having the agent buy shares in the corporation, or granting the agent shares.
- Incentive pay means including incentives in the agent's compensation package that reflect the principal's interest. However, there are several problems with stock options as solutions to the principal–agent problem. First, the holdings of current shareholders are diluted since the firm issues

133

more shares to fulfill a stock option plan. The existing shares will decline in value relative to what they would otherwise be. Second, when the market turns downward, many of the manager's call options are under the water—that is, way out of the money—and are practically worthless. Thus, their incentive effect is nearly nil. Under some conditions, the exercise price may be reset so as to restore managerial incentives, but this seems unfair to shareholders who have purchased their stock on the open market. At times, the shares have also been backdated to a lower exercise price to build in intrinsic profits. Third, when a manager has inside information, he/she may exercise early or book earnings for goods not delivered so as to cash in the options before the bad news hits the market. Fourth, managers have an incentive to book earnings early, to exaggerate them, or remove negative items from income statements in order to cash in their bonus or stock options. In short, stock options may distort incentives.

- Monitoring. Who will "monitor" the monitor? Many international accounting firms have been fined for signing off on obviously fraudulent earnings and income statements. Partly this is due to conflicts of interest when the auditing firm also seeks investments from the firm.

Financial distress and bankruptcy

Financial distress can be defined in several ways:

- Business failure (a business has terminated with a loss to creditors).
- Legal bankruptcy (firms or creditors petition the court for bankruptcy).
- Chapter 7 of the US Bankruptcy Code, or liquidation cases, where the debtor's property is sold by a trustee to pay the debts owed to creditors. An individual debtor can keep a modest amount of household property or realty. The states of Texas and Florida are famous for their bankrupt managers and owners with multi-million-dollar homes sheltered from the bankruptcy court due to "Homestead Laws."
- Chapter 11 of the Code, or business reorganization, where the business is continued by its management or a trustee while creditors' claims are frozen pending approval of a restructuring plan. With court approval, the plan can reduce debts, recapitalize a corporation, provide for a takeover, or sell its assets.
- Chapter 13 of the Code, or adjustment proceedings, where individuals with a regular income may elect for adjustment proceedings instead of liquidation. In these cases, claims of creditors are frozen until a plan to pay off the creditors from income is approved by a trustee, while the debtor still retains all property.

- Technical insolvency, which occurs when a firm defaults on a legal obligation, for example by not paying a bill. Solvency means the ability of the firm to pay its liabilities on time. The short-term solvency of a firm is measured in two ways: the current solvency ratio (the ratio of its current assets to its current liabilities); and the quick solvency ratio (the ratio of its liquid assets such to its current liabilities). Rules of thumb suggest a minimum current ratio of 2:1, and a minimum quick ratio of 1:1.
- Accounting insolvency, which occurs when the total book value of liabilities exceeds the book value of total assets. Owner's equity—the difference between assets and liabilities—is negative.

The break-even point and the profit-maximizing point

In principle, the valuation of a firm requires only three things: a forecast of its profits or free-cash flow, an estimate of its terminal value when sold in, say, five years, and a weighted average cost of capital of the firm with which to discount free-cash flows and the terminal value. The exercise is part art, part science. When these three variables are estimated, the NPV of the firm is given by substitution into the standard NPV formula:

$$NPV = \pi_0 + \frac{\pi_1}{(1+i)} + \frac{\pi_2}{(1+i)^2} + \frac{\pi_3}{(1+i)^3} + \frac{\pi_4}{(1+i)^4} + \frac{\pi_5}{(1+i)^5} + \frac{T_5}{(1+i)^5} \qquad (5.13)$$

where π represents profits (or rather free-cash flow) in each year, T_5 the terminal value when the firm is sold in the fifth year, and i the WACC. In the start-up year, costs typically exceed revenues, or $\pi_0 < 0$. For the NPV to be positive there must be positive cash flow in at least one of the future years. In each period, it is assumed that production is at the profit-maximizing level, requiring that marginal revenue equal marginal costs (the slope of the revenue curve equals the slope of the cost curve, as depicted in Figure 5.6).

Note that a second-order condition requires that costs be rising faster than revenues, otherwise marginal cost equals marginal revenue would imply a profit minimum. This can easily occur with economies of scale where average cost is declining.

Financial and operating leverage

A start-up business faces two serious questions: how much financial leverage and how much operating leverage it should take on? Higher financial leverage—as measured by the debt to debt plus equity ratio—benefits the owners greatly when the firm does well. Earnings per share are more responsive to a rise in earnings

135

Revenue and cost

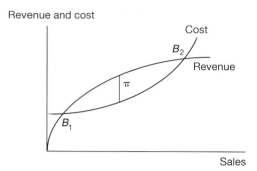

Figure 5.6 *Profit maximization and break-even points*

before interest, because the debt obligations—interest and principal payments to bondholders—are fixed. Shareholder dividends thus rise elastically with respect to earnings before interest. That is the positive side of financial leverage.

However, if the firm does poorly after getting started, the creditors are nevertheless legally entitled to interest and principal payments, but the shareholders can only hope for dividends. Earnings per share can easily be negative yet paying creditors required. However, it may be forced into bankruptcy after only a few months if it does not reach a break-even point quickly. New restaurants often do not stay in business for over a year, partly due to financial leverage, as was the case of the Aztec Café (see below), whose start-up was 100 percent debt financed.

The degree of operating leverage at start-up is another critical decision that may jeopardize a company's survival. Operating leverage is the extent to which a company's costs of operating are fixed—rent, insurance, and salaries, as opposed to variable—costs that vary with output, such as wages and the costs of material inputs.

Operating leverage is measured by the ratio of fixed to fixed plus variable costs. In a company whose costs are virtually all fixed, every dollar of increase in sales is a dollar of increase in operating income once the break-even point has been reached. In contrast, a company whose costs are largely variable would show relatively little increase in operating income when production and sales increased because costs and production rise together.

Operating leverage comes into play because a small change in sales has a magnified effect on operating income. The degree of operating leverage—the ratio of the percentage change in operating income to the percentage change in sales—measures the sensitivity of a firm's profits to changes in sales volume. A firm with a high degree of operating leverage has a break-even point at a relatively high sales level.

136

An international business plan: the Aztec Café

This is all very well and good, but how is it put into practice, particularly abroad?

Let's take the example of the Aztec Café, whose revenues and costs are in Mexican pesos, its functional currency. As a start-up in 2001, its initial investment costs were N$500,000 for the oven and hood with fire extinguisher, grease trap, tables, chairs, and dinnerware, plus renovation of the existing facility. The owner/manager, Juan Olive, elected for straight-line depreciation of his investment over five years. His forecast of free-cash flow in pesos is indicated in Table 5.6.

He had borrowed from a local bank the entire amount at 22 percent in pesos, which gives us the WACC (no equity was brought to the project). The Aztec's forecasted revenue and costs yielded a free-cash flow projection for five years. In addition, a terminal value was predicted as a no-growth perpetuity of its fifth year's free-cash flow. Unfortunately, the business plan was done at the end of the Aztec's first year of operations. Had it been done earlier, the project would not have taken place.

In the first year, Juan accumulated arrears in his rent, his loan, and in payment of the 15 percent value-added tax in Mexico. His cash flow was negative so he sought finance by running arrears. The business plan was prepared in May 2001 to value the restaurant in pesos. Naturally, the value of debt arrears had to be subtracted from the NPV of forecasted free-cash flow. The business plan summary is presented in Table 5.7.

In addition, the landlord could padlock the restaurant door at any moment with a court order, and the lender could seize the oven and equipment on which he held the lien. The state was about to file criminal charges for tax evasion. The Aztec Café was clearly in serious financial distress. Could it be sold? The NPV of free-cash flow was negative, but the restaurant was worth even less. Let's deduct debts from the NPV of free-cash flow:

Present value of free-cash flow	*N$(86,750)*
Rent arrears	N$(225,000)
Loan arrears	N$(50,000)
Value-added tax arrears	N$(60,000)
Estimated NPV of the Aztec Café	*N$(421,750)*
Spot exchange rate (USD per peso)	US$0.1098
Estimated NPV of the Aztec Café	*US$(46,308).*

Table 5.6 An international business plan: free-cash flow in Mexican pesos

2001	2002	2003	2004	2005
N$(332,683)	N$(108,046)	N$60,553	N$123,615	N$82,554

Table 5.7 An international business plan: valuation of the Aztec Café

Year	2001	2002	2003	2004	2005	2005 (terminal value)
Free-cash flow in Mexican pesos (N$)	(332,683)	(108,046)	60,553	123,615	82,554	375,247
Present value in Mexican pesos (N$)	(272,691)	(72,592)	33,347	55,799	30,545	138,841
Present value of free-cash flow in Mexican pesos (N$)	(86,750)	22.0% WACC in N$				
Spot exchange rate (US$ per peso)	0.1098					
Present value of free-cash flow (US$)	(9,525)					

New equity financing was sought to recapitalize the restaurant and repay the tax, loan and rent arrears. Meetings of potential investors took place, but the decision was taken that any more money put into the venture would be lost. In any case, ignoring the arrears, the NPV of cash flow was negative. The potential investors informed the restaurant's lawyer that they would not invest in the Aztec Café. The owner declared a liquidation bankruptcy in June 2001, turning in his keys to the landlord. The bank took the equipment and sold it at auction. It also required the owner, Juan, to sell his home and took the equity in the home. Finally, it rescheduled the remaining balance of his loan. The state forgave his tax arrears.

The moral of the story is: look before you leap! That is, do a reasoned business plan.

OPTIMAL INVESTMENT ANALYSIS

Market and unique risk

Market risk, also known as systematic risk, represents risk factors that are common to the whole economy. Firm specific risk, also known as diversifiable risk, represents risk factors that can be eliminated by diversification. The variance of security i, σ_i^2, can be written as the sum of the market risk and the firm specific risk:

$$\sigma_i^2 = \beta_i^2 \sigma_M^2 + \sigma_{\epsilon_i}^2, \tag{5.14}$$

where:

$$\beta_i^2 = \frac{\sigma_{iM}}{\sigma_M^2} \tag{5.15}$$

and σ_{iM} is the covariance between security i's return and the market return, and σ_i^2 is the variance of the market return. The beta (β) of an individual security measures the security's sensitivity to market movements and therefore is known as its market risk. For example, the beta of the S&P 500 index share should be about one since it reflects a broad selection of market stocks. A riskier security would have a beta greater than one, and a less risky security would have a beta less than one.

Portfolio diversification

Non-systematic risk is diversifiable by increasing the number of securities. By sufficiently diversifying, the investor can virtually eliminate firm-specific risk. By holding both domestic and international securities, portfolio diversification is more

139

efficient since the universe of assets is the choice set. Figure 5.7 illustrates the reduction of portfolio risk as the number of securities in the portfolio increases.

Asset allocation with one domestic and one foreign asset

Here we consider the allocation of the investment budget between two risky funds—a domestic fund and a foreign fund. If the proportion invested in the domestic fund is w_d, then the remainder is invested in the international (g for global) fund, $w_g = 1 - w_d$.

Some basic relationships hold:

$$r_p = w_d r_d + w_g r_g;$$ (5.16)

$$E(r_p) = w_d E(r_d) + w_g E(r_g);$$ (5.17)

$$\sigma_p^2 = (w_d \sigma_d)^2 + (w_g \sigma_g)^2 + 2(w_d \sigma_d)(w_g \sigma_g)\rho_{dg}.$$ (5.18)

That is:

- The rate of return on the portfolio is a weighted average of the rates of return on the domestic and global funds.
- The expected rate of return on the portfolio is a weighted average of the expected rates of return on the domestic and global funds.
- The variance of the portfolio is the sum of the square of weighted volatilities plus a term involving the correlation coefficient, ρ_{dg}, between the domestic and the global funds.

The correlation coefficient is the term that permits efficient diversification. Only in the case of a perfect positive correlation, $\rho_{dg} = 1$, are there no gains to be had from diversification. In the case of a perfect negative correlation, $\rho_{dg} = -1$, the potential benefits from diversification are the highest. In general, the efficient investment portfolio has the shape depicted in Figure 5.8.

Figure 5.7 *Risk and diversification*

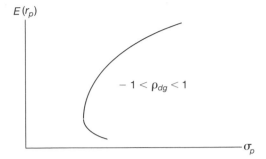

Figure 5.8 *Portfolio expected return and diversification*

The minimum risk portfolio

The minimum risk portfolio is found by differentiating (5.18) with respect to the portfolio weights, setting the result equal to zero, and solving. The weight of global shares in the minimum variance portfolio is given by:

$$w_g^* = \frac{\sigma_d^2 - \sigma_g \sigma_d \rho_{dg}}{\sigma_d^2 + \sigma_g^2 - 2\sigma_g \sigma_d \rho_{dg}}. \tag{5.19}$$

The minimum risk portfolio, while a point on the efficient investment frontier, will not be chosen because higher expected reward can be achieved by a small increase in risk.

The efficient investment frontier

The efficient investment frontier is derived by maximizing the expected return, subject to a given risk. Alternatively, it can be derived by minimizing the risk for a given expected rate of return on the portfolio. For a given level of risk, σ_p^2, the efficient weight of the global asset is given by:

$$w_g = \frac{E(r_g)\sigma_d^2 - E(r_d)\sigma_g \sigma_d \rho_{dg}}{E(r_g)(\sigma_d^2 - \sigma_g \sigma_d \rho_{dg}) + E(r_d)(\sigma_g^2 - \sigma_g \sigma_d \rho_{dg})}. \tag{5.20}$$

Note that this is the share of the global asset necessary to be on the efficient investment frontier—a purely technical condition. This share maximizes expected portfolio return for each level of risk. Our next step in the optimal efficient portfolio analysis is to maximize the Sharpe "reward to risk" ratio.

141

The asset allocation decision

Investors may be risk averse, demanding a higher rate of return—a risk premium—for holding risky assets. Risk may be reduced either by converting risky assets into safe assets such as money market assets or by constructing a risky portfolio efficiently, diversifying away unsystematic risk. Consider an investor holding a risky portfolio, P, along with a risk-free asset, T, such as US T-bills. The risky portfolio consists of some domestic and some foreign assets.

For example, a hypothetical portfolio might be as shown in Table 5.8. This investor is holding 62.5 percent of her risky portfolio in General Motors, US and 37.5 percent of P in Tiger International. Let w represent the holdings in US securities and $w*$ indicate the holdings of international securities in the risky portfolio, so that $w + w* = 1$. Thus, $w = 0.625$ and $w* = 0.375$. The weight of the risky portfolio, P, in the complete portfolio, C, including risk-free investments, is denoted by z. Thus the weight of the risk-free asset in the complete portfolio is $1 - z$. T-bills represent 20 percent of the complete portfolio, or $1 - z = 0.2$, and risky assets 80 percent of C, or $z = 0.8$. General Motors, US represents 50 percent of the complete portfolio and Tiger International 30 percent.

The investor is thus holding a risk-free asset and a bundle of risky assets, which can be thought of as one risky asset. In this way, the investor can keep the relative shares of the two risky assets constant in the risky portfolio P, and at the same time reduce risk by selling them off proportionately to acquire more of the risk-free asset, T-bills.

By changing the distribution of the risky asset relative to the risk-free asset, yet maintaining the mix of assets in the risky portfolio, the investor can reduce the risk of the complete portfolio yet remain on the efficient investment frontier. That is, z can be reduced in C while maintaining w and $w*$ fixed in P.

Table 5.8 A complete portfolio

Company	Assets	Complete portfolio weights	Risky portfolio weights
General Motors, US	$50	0.5	0.625
Tiger International	30	0.3	0.375
Portfolios			
(Portfolio *P*)	80	0.8	1.0
US T-bills (Portfolio *T*)	20	0.2	
Complete portfolio (Portfolio *C*)	100	1.0	

Portfolio expected return and risk

Notation

r_P	Rate of return on the risky portfolio.
r_f	Rate of return on the risk-free asset.
$E(r_P)$	Expected rate of return on the risky portfolio.
σ_P	The standard deviation ("volatility") of the risky portfolio.
$E(r_f) = r_f$	Expected rate of return on the risk-free asset.
$E(r_C)$	Expected rate of return on the complete portfolio.

Consequently, with a fraction, z, of risky assets in the portfolio and $1 - z$ of risk-free assets, the rate of return on the complete portfolio is:

$$r_C = zr_P + (1 - z)r_f. \tag{5.21}$$

Consequently, the expected rate of return on the complete portfolio is:

$$E(r_C) = zE(r_P) + (1 - z)r_f, \tag{5.22}$$

or, equivalently:

$$E(r_C) = r_f + z[E(r_P) - r_f], \tag{5.23}$$

which has a perfectly natural interpretation: The complete portfolio has a base return equal the risk-free rate, r_f, plus an expected market risk premium, $[E(r_P) - r_f]$, on its exposure to risky assets, z. Risk-averse investors demand a positive market risk premium. The standard deviation of the complete portfolio is indicated by:

$$\sigma_C = z\sigma_P, \tag{5.24}$$

since the volatility of the risk-free asset is zero.

Figure 5.9 plots the capital allocation line (*CAL*) depicting the rise in expected portfolio return against the standard deviation of the risky asset. It is the investment opportunity set resulting from different values of z.

When $z = 0$, the *CAL* begins at r_f and $\sigma_C = 0$. When $z = 1$, the portfolio has only the risky asset and its standard deviation is σ_P and its expected rate of return is $E(r_P)$.

The slope of the investment opportunity schedule is the Sharpe "reward to risk" ratio:

$$\frac{E(r_P) - r_f}{\sigma_P}. \tag{5.25}$$

143

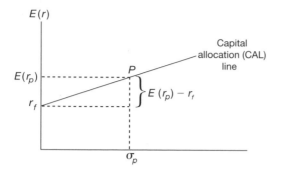

Figure 5.9 *Expected portfolio return and risk*

The slope is also called the reward-to-volatility ratio since it is the ratio of the market risk premium to the standard deviation of the risky portfolio.

Financial leverage (purchases "on margin")

By borrowing, an investor can invest on the *CAL* line to the right of point *P*, thereby levering her investment in the risky asset. Our investor has an investment budget of $100 and borrows, for example, on margin an additional $50 at the risk-free rate, thereby investing $150 in the risky asset. In this case $z = 1.5$, reflecting a levered position in the risky asset, and $1 - z = -0.5$, reflecting a short or borrowed position in the risk-free asset.

Borrowing to invest in the risky asset requires a margin account with a broker. Purchases "on margin" may not exceed 50 percent of the purchase value. If the net worth of the margin account is $100, the investor can borrow up to $100, for a total investment of $200. In this case, $z = 2$, assets in the account would equal $200 and liabilities $100. In practice, an investor can borrow from his or her credit card, deposit this with a broker, and lever the borrowed sum. In most instances, the leveraged borrower cannot borrow at the risk-free rate, so therefore faces a lowered *CAL* line beyond *P* because she pays a higher interest rate to borrow. That is, there is a kink at the point *P*.

Risk aversion and asset allocation

Consider the following utility (happiness or choice) function:

$$U = E(r_C) - \frac{A\sigma_C^2}{2}.$$

(5.26)

This investor enjoys a higher expected return, $E(r_C)$, but dislikes higher risk, σ_C. The level of risk aversion is $A > 0$. The higher A, the more risk averse the investor.

Utility maximization: mathematically

The investor's objective is to maximize utility (happiness!) by selecting the fraction, z, of the investment budget to be invested in the risky portfolio, P. The expected return and variance of the complete portfolio are $E(r_C) = r_f + z[E(r_P) - r_f]$ and σ_C^2, respectively. To choose the best allocation to the risky asset, we maximize utility, equation 5.26, with respect to z, that is, maximize the quadratic utility function with respect to z:

$$U(z) = E(r_C) - \frac{A\sigma_C^2}{2} = r_f + z[E(r_P) + r_f] - \frac{Az^2\sigma_P^2}{2} \tag{5.27}$$

yielding the optimal share of the risky portfolio in the complete portfolio:

$$z^* = \frac{E(r_P) - r_f}{A\sigma_P^2}, \tag{5.28}$$

where z^* indicates the optimal share of the risky asset. The optimal share of the risky asset:

- rises with increases in the market risk premium, $E(r_P) - r_f$;
- falls with increases in the degree of risk aversion, A;
- falls with increases in market volatility, σ_P^2.

Utility maximization: graphically

Figure 5.10 illustrates the optimal allocation of assets for a risk-averse investor who chooses to hold approximately half the portfolio in the risky asset and half in the safe asset. This optimal allocation yields the highest level of utility (at point C, the tangency of the capital allocation line and the highest indifference curve).

Figure 5.11 illustrates a levered portfolio where the investor has borrowed on margin of approximately 50 percent. In our example, if the net worth in the account is $100, margin purchases may be up to 50 percent of the purchase, so the investor can buy "on margin" an additional $100 of the risky asset. The investor would then have $200 on the asset side of the account and $100 on the liability side, yielding $z = 2$.

145

Naturally, a levered portfolio has a greater expected rate of return and a higher risk than an unlevered one.

The tangency of the capital asset line to the investment opportunity frontier at point P yields the highest expected reward–risk ratio. It is therefore the optimal risky portfolio. The optimal risky portfolio is found by the CAL with the steepest slope tangent to the efficient investment frontier at P. The optimal complete portfolio is found by allocating z percent of the portfolio to the risky asset composed of domestic and international assets. The remainder of the optimal complete portfolio, $1 - z$, is composed of US T-bills.

Let's consider an application of the theory of the optimal complete portfolio. The risk-averse investor has the following utility function:

$$U = E(r_C) - 0.5A\sigma_C^2 = E(r_c) - \sigma_C^2. \tag{5.29}$$

Once again, $E(r_C) = r_f + z[E(r_p) - r_f]$. This investor has a degree of risk aversion, $A = 2$, since $0.5A = 1$. We are also given the following data: $E(r_p) = 0.15$,

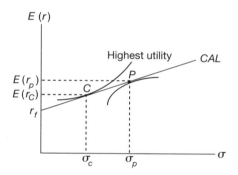

Figure 5.10 *Optimal asset allocation*

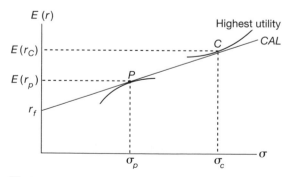

Figure 5.11 *A levered portfolio*

146

$r_f = 0.05$, $\sigma_p^2 = 0.10$. Consequently, the market risk premium is 10 percent, as is the variance of the market portfolio. We may directly substitute the data into the optimal share of the risky portfolio of the investor:

$$z^* = \frac{E(r_p) - r_f}{A\sigma_p^2} = \frac{0.15 - 0.05}{2 \times 0.10} = \frac{0.10}{0.20} = \frac{1}{2}. \qquad (5.30)$$

The optimal solution for this investor is to hold half her portfolio in the optimal risky asset and half in the risk-free asset. The expected return on the complete portfolio is:

$$0.05 + \frac{0.10}{2} = 0.10, \qquad (5.31)$$

or 10 percent. The variance of the complete portfolio is:

$$\left(\frac{1}{2}\right)^2 (0.10) = 0.025. \qquad (5.32)$$

Its volatility is the square root of 0.025, or 0.158. Finally, the utility of the investor is $0.100 - 0.025 = 0.075$.

Figure 5.12 illustrates graphically the optimal complete portfolio for this investor with degree of risk aversion equal to 2. Half of her complete portfolio is in risk-free bonds, the other half in the risky asset. Her expected rate of return is mid-point between the risky and the risk-free portfolio, and the volatility of her portfolio is also half the volatility of the risky portfolio.

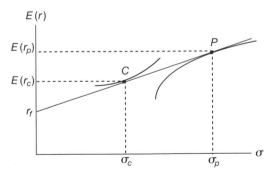

Figure 5.12 The optimal risky and complete portfolios

The separation property

Portfolio choice is separated into two separate parts: first, selection of the optimum risky portfolio at (P), which is a purely technical consideration, and, second, the personal investor choice of the best mix of the risky portfolio and the risk-free asset (C). Risk aversion plays no role in the first part; it enters into play in the second part of the portfolio choice. The optimum risky portfolio is the same for all investors, independent of their degree of risk aversion. It is the point of tangency of the highest CAL line to the efficient investment portfolio. The second part, construction of the complete portfolio composed of US T-bills and the risky portfolio, depends on personal preference, that is, risk tolerance. This separation theorem is due to James Tobin (1958), the 1983 Nobel Laureate in Economics. Since the optimal investment portfolio comprised of domestic and global securities is the same for all investors, a passive index fund of domestic and global securities will usually yield better results than an actively managed fund since the latter have higher management and trading fees.

Determination of the market risk premium

The market portfolio of all assets in the universe, each held in proportion to its market value, represents an efficient fund of risky assets. This is known as the mutual fund theorem. A passive index fund holding both domestic and international assets may therefore be viewed by the rational investor as a close approximation to the optimal risky portfolio. In addition, a passive index fund saves management and transaction fees.

Net aggregate lending (borrowing) is zero, viewing T-bills as the liabilities of the citizens who both issue and hold them. Some investors are net lenders, $z_i < 1$, while others are net borrowers, $z_j > 1$, but, on aggregate, the average z must equal 1. Therefore, for the average investor, $z = 1$.

Since the optimal portfolio of the individual investor with average risk aversion, $A*$, is:

$$z^* = \frac{E(r_p) - r_f}{A^* \sigma_p^2},$$
(5.33)

and the average investor has $z = 1$, the risk premium on the market portfolio is proportional to its risk and average risk aversion:

$$E(r_p) - r_f = A^* \sigma_p^2,$$
(5.34)

which states that the market risk premium depends on the average degree of risk aversion times the degree of risk of the market portfolio, as measured by its

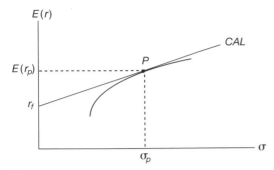

Figure 5.13 *The mutual fund theorem*

volatility. The average investor's portfolio is thus the marked portfolio having expected value, $E(r_p)$, and volatility, σ_p, as illustrated in Figure 5.13.

The CAPM (capital asset pricing model)

The individual contribution of an individual security to the standard deviation of the market portfolio is $\beta_i \sigma_p$. Furthermore, by definition $\beta_p = 1$ for the market portfolio. The investor's trade-off between risk and return should be the same for the market portfolio and an individual security's per unit contribution to the market portfolio's risk:

$$\frac{E(r_p) - r_f}{\beta_p \sigma_p} = \frac{E(r_i) - r_f}{\beta_i \sigma_p}. \tag{5.35}$$

Noting that $\beta_p = 1$ and rearranging equation 5.35, yields the CAPM's expected return *beta* relationship:

$$E(r_i) = r_f + \beta_i \left[E(r_p) - r_f \right], \tag{5.36}$$

which states that the expected return on asset *i* equals the risk-free rate plus the market risk premium times the market risk coefficient, β_i, of the individual security.

CONCLUSION

The Markowitz-Sharpe model of risk aversion is a powerful tool for application to the analysis of the optimal portfolio of a client, based upon her degree of risk aversion. It rests solidly on the idea of portfolio diversification, showing that portfolios offer higher returns for given risk than do individual securities, thereby

149

revolutionizing the theory of investment finance. In 1990, Merton Miller, William Sharpe, and Harry Markowitz were jointly awarded the Nobel Prize in Economics for their contributions.

International financial management covers the international cost of capital, working capital balance management, offshore banking, international tax management, transfer pricing, mergers and acquisitions, currency forecasting and conversion, and optimal investing. As this chapter has suggested, there are perfectly legal and reasoned ways of reducing tax liabilities, yet there may be the temptation to abuse some of these tools. Chapter 6 deals with some of the more abusive international financial deals that cross the line in terms of accounting, legal, and ethical standards.

REFERENCES AND FURTHER READING

Abdallah, Wagdy (2004) *Critical concerns in transfer pricing and practice*, Westport, CT: Praeger.

Adler, Michael (1974) "The cost of capital and valuation of a two-country firm," *Journal of Finance* 29(1): 167–84.

Al-Eryani, Mohammed F., Pervaiz Alam, and Syed H. Akhter (1990) "Transfer pricing determinants of US multinationals," *Journal of International Business Studies* 12(3): 409–25.

Aliber, Robert Z. (1980) "The integration of the offshore and the domestic banking system," *Journal of Monetary Economics* 6(4): 509–26.

Anderson, Ronald (2003) "Capital structure, firm liquidity, and growth," in Ronald Anderson, *Firms' investment and finance decision: theory and empirical methodology*, Cheltenham: Edward Elgar.

Azzara, Thomas (2003) *Tax havens of the world*, Chicago, IL: New Providence Press.

Bangs, David H. Jr (1998) *The business plan*, Chicago, IL: Upstart Publishing.

Barrett, M. Edgar (1977) "The case of the tangled transfer price," *Harvard Business Review* 55(3): 20–36.

Bertrand, Benoit, Dan Roberts,and Richard Waters (2000) "Falling telecoms shares hit takeover: Deutsche Telekom purchase of Voice Stream is latest deal to be imperilled," *Financial Times*, October 13: 25.

Bradshaw, Mark, Brian Bushee, and Gregory Miller (2004) "Accounting choice, home bias, and US investment in non-US firms," *Journal of Accounting Research* 42(5): 795–841.

Cumming, Douglas (2005) "Capital structure in venture finance," *Journal of Corporate Finance* 11(3): 550–85.

Dye, Ronald and Sri Sridhar (2005) "Moral hazard severity and contract design," *RAND Journal of Economics* 36(1): 78–92.

Eckbo, E.B. (1983) "Horizontal mergers, collusion and stockholder wealth," *Journal of Financial Economics* 11(2): 241–76.

Eiteman, David K., Arthur I. Stonehill, and Michael H. Moffett (2000) "Principles of multinational taxation," in David K. Eiteman, Arthur I. Stonehill, and Michael H. Moffett, *Multinational Business Finance*, 10th edn, Reading, MA: Addison-Wesley.

Emery, Douglas, R., John D. Finnerty, and John D. Stove (1998) *Principles of financial management,* Upper Saddle River, NJ: Prentice Hall.

FATF/OECD (2005) *NCCTs report* (June 5), Paris: FATF/OECD.

Ganguin, Blaise (2005) *Fundamentals of corporate credit analysis,* New York: McGraw-Hill.

Ghauri, Pervez and Peter Buckley (2003) "International mergers and acquisitions: past, present, and future," in Cary L. Cooper and Alan Gregory (eds), *Advances in mergers and acquisitions,* vol. 2, Amsterdam, Boston, and Oxford: Elsevier Science.

Grauer, Robert R. and Nils Hakansson (1987) "Gains from international diversification: 1968–85 returns on portfolios of stocks and bonds," *Journal of Finance* 42(3): 721–39.

Gup, Benton (2004) *Too big to fail: policies and practices in government bailouts,* Westport, CT: Praeger.

Harris, Milton and A. Raviv (1991) "The theory of capital structure," *Journal of Finance* 46(1): 297–355.

Harvey, Campbell R. (1991) "The world price of covariance risk," *Journal of Finance* 66(1): 111–58.

Haugen, R. A. and L. Senbet (1988) "Bankruptcy and agency costs: their significance to the theory of optimal capital structure," *Journal of Financial and Quantitative Analysis* 2(3): 73–86.

Ioannou, Lori (1995) "Taxing Issues," *International Business* 8(3): 44–5.

Isenbergh, Joseph (2002) *International taxation: US taxation of foreign persons and foreign income,* New York: Aspen Publishers.

Jensen, M. C. (1986) "Agency costs of free cash flow, corporate finance, and takeovers," *American Economic Review* 76(2): 323–30.

Kane, Edward (1987) "Competitive financial reregulations: an international perspective," in R. Portes and A. Swoboda (eds) *Threats to international financial stability,* London: Cambridge University Press.

Keen, Michael (2004) "Pareto-efficient international taxation," *American Economic Review* 94(1): 259–75.

Krauss, Clifford (1998) "Deaths in Argentina feed a taste for conspiracy", *The New York Times*: October 25.

Levich, Richard M. (1990) "The Euromarkets after 1992," in J. Dermine (ed.), *European banking in the 1990s,* Oxford: Basil Blackwell.

Lowengrub, Paul and Michael Melvin (2002) "Before and after international cross-listing: an intraday examination of volume and volatility," *Journal of International Financial Markets, Institutions, and Money* 12(2): 139–55.

Marino, Anthony and John Matsusaka (2005) "Decision processes, agency problems, and information: an economic analysis of capital budgeting procedures," *Review of Financial Studies* 18(1): 301–25.

Markowitz, Harry (1952) "Portfolio selection", *Journal of Finance* 7(1): 77–91.

Maroney, Neal, Naka Atsuyuki, and Theresia Wansi (2004) "Changing risk, return, and leverage: the 1997 Asian financial crisis," *Journal of Financial and Quantitative Analysis* 39(1): 143–66.

Masson, Dubos Jr (1990) "Planning and forecasting of cash flows for the multinational firm: international cash management," *Advances in Financial Planning and Forecasting* 4(B): 195–202.

Meyers, S. C. (1976) "A framework for evaluating mergers," in S. C. Meyers (ed.), *Modern developments in financial management,* New York: Praeger.

151

Miller, Merton (1977) "Debt and taxes," *Journal of Finance* 32(2): 261–75.

Modigliani, Franco and Merton H. Miller (1958) "The cost of capital, corporation finance, and the theory of investment," *American Economic Review* 48(3): 261–98.

Modigliani, Franco and Merton H. Miller (1963) "Corporate income taxes and the cost of capital: a correction," *American Economic Review* 53(3): 433–43.

Moffett, Michael H. and Arthur Stonehill (1989) "International banking facilities revisited," *Journal of International Financial Management and Accounting* 1(1): 88–103.

Mork, Randall, Andrei Schleifer, and Robert W. Vishney (1990) "Do managerial objectives drive bad acquisitions," Journal of Finance 45(1): 31–48.

OECD (2005) *E-commerce: transfer pricing and business profits taxation,* Paris: Organization for Economic Cooperation and Development.

Ostro-Landau, Nilly (1995) "Avoiding the global tax web," *International Business* 8(9): 12.

Plasschaert, S. R. F. (1985) "Transfer pricing problems in developing countries," in A. M. Rugman and L. Eden (eds), *Multinationals and transfer pricing,* New York: St Martins Press: 247–66.

Roll, Richard. and Stephen A. Ross (1984) "The arbitrage pricing theory approach to strategic portfolio planning," *Financial Analysts Journal* 40(3): 14–26.

Ross, Stephen A. (1974) "Return, risk and arbitrage," in J. Friend and J. Bicksler (eds), *Risk and return in finance,* New York: Heath Lexington.

Ross, Stephen A., Randolph W. Westerfield, and Bradford D. Jordan (1991) *Corporate finance,* 3rd edn, Irwin, IL: McGraw-Hill.

Ross, Stephen A., Randolph W. Westerfield, and Bradford D. Jordan (2005) *Fundamentals of Corporate Finance,* Irwin, IL: McGraw-Hill College.

Salvatore, Dominick (1996) *Managerial economics in a global economy,* 3rd edn, New York: McGraw-Hill.

Sharpe, W. F. (1964) "Capital asset prices: a theory of market equilibirum under risk," *Journal of Finance* 19(3): 425–42.

Shirreff, David (2004) *Dealing with financial risk,* New York: Bloomberg Press.

Soenen, L. A. and Raj Aggarwal (1987) "Corporate foreign exchange and cash management practice," *Journal of Cash Management* 7(2): 62–4.

Solnick Bruno and B. Noetzlin (1982) "Optimal international asset allocation," *Journal of Portfolio Management* 9(1): 11–21.

Srinivsan, VenKat and Yong H. Kim (1986) "Payments netting in internaitonal cash management: a network optimization approach," *Journal of International Business Studies* 17(2): 1–20.

Stillman, R. (1983) "Examining antitrust policy toward horizontal mergers," *Journal of Financial Economics* 11(2): 225–40.

Stultz, Rene M. (1995) "Globalization of capital markets and the cost of capital: the case of Nestlé," *Journal of Applied Corporate Finance* 8(3): 30–8.

Tobin, James (1958) "Liquidity preference as behavior towards risk," *Review of Economic Studies* 26(1): 65–86.

Yunker, Penelope J. (1982) *Transfer pricing and performance evaluation in multinational corporations: a survey study,* New York: Praeger.

Yunker, Penelope J. (1983) "A survey of subsidiary autonomy, performance evaluation and transfer pricing in multinational corporations," *Columbia Journal of World Business* 18(3): 51–64.

PROBLEMS

5.1 The international weighted average cost of capital

Consider the data below of a European IBM subsidiary (in euros; percent per annum). The borrowing rates represent those of the subsidiary in terms of euros. The parent firm has its headquarters in New York.

Cost of debt	10
Cost of equity	15
Capital structure:	
Debt	30
Equity	70
Corporate tax rate:	
United States	35
Europe	45
Expected inflation:	
United States	3
Europe	2

a   Calculate the weighted average cost of capital (WACC) to IBM in euros.
b   Convert the WACC to US dollars.

5.2 Transfer pricing

Consider Figure 5.14, which indicates the marginal costs of production of an inter-mediate good as well as the marginal cost of marketing the final good. The intermediate

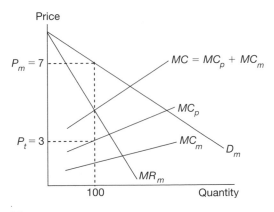

Figure 5.14 *Transfer pricing*

good and the marketing are bundled as a joint product, one-to-one. The demand (average revenue) and the marginal revenue curves are drawn as well.

a   What is the profit maximizing level of sales (units of production)?
b   What will your firm charge the final customer?
c   What is the optimal transfer price that the marketing division will pay for intermediate goods supplied to the marketing division?

5.3 Foreign currency conversion of free-cash flows

Consider the data below on the United States and the UK (percent per annum). Assume the required real rates of return are the same.

US and UK data (percent per annum)

US inflation rate	3
UK inflation rate	2
US Treasury	5
UK Treasury	4
WACC ($)	15
WACC (£)	

a   If the WACC in US dollars is 15 percent, what is the WACC in pounds sterling, given the above data? Recall that the conversion rule for the WACC is:

$$\left(\frac{1+WACC_{£}}{1+WACC_{\$}}\right) = \left(\frac{1+R_{uk}}{1+R_{us}}\right),$$

and the interest rate parity rule for forecasting the exchange rate is:

$$F = S\left[\frac{1+R_{us}}{1+R_{uk}}\right]^{n}.$$

Now consider the estimated free-cash flows in British pounds of a two-year project by a UK subsidiary:

Method A
● Discount foreign currency flows to the present at the foreign currency discount rate, then convert the NPV in FOREX to home currency at the spot rate.

Year	0	1	2
Free-cash flows (£)	−100	60	70
Present value of cash flow (£)	−100		
NPV (£)			
Spot exchange rate ($/£)	1.77		
NPV ($)			

Method B

- Convert foreign currency cash flows to home currency, and discount to the present at the home currency discount rate.

Year	0	1	2
Free-cash flows (£)	−100	60	70
Exchange rate forecast	1.77		
Free-cash flows ($)	−177		
Present value of cash flow ($)			
NPV ($)			

b On the basis of the inflation rate, interest rate, and weighted average cost of capital (WACC), should the US parent firm undertake this project? (That is, compute the net present value (NPV) in dollars using the two methods.)

5.4 Trade finance (I)

You intend to export 100 computers worth $2,000 each from Miami, Florida to Cochabamba, Bolivia. This is the first shipment to a new client, and naturally you hope to be paid in USD for the computers. Essentially, your options are cash-in-advance, an open account, or an L/C. List below the advantages and disadvantages of each, spelling out who bears the counterparty risk in each case:

a cash-in-advance
b an open account
c a letter of credit.

5.5 Trade finance (II)

You have received a confirmed standby L/C indicating that Citibank, Nassau will pay you $1,000,000 (one million Bahamian dollars) every 30 days for one year beginning in 30 days.

a If you need Bahamian dollars now for payments today, what can you do with the L/C immediately?

b What proceeds in Bahamian dollars would you expect?

5.6 International taxation (I)

a The headquarters of your computer company is located in Texas, but you have a branch for assembly and re-export to Europe that is located in Ireland, where the corporate tax rate is 12.5 percent for foreign companies. Fill in the blanks in the data below on international taxation. Explain your result:

> *Irish branch*
>
> | | |
> |---|---|
> | Irish income | $100 |
> | Irish taxes paid | $12.5 |
> | US taxes | [＿＿＿＿＿＿] |
> | Net income | [＿＿＿＿＿＿] |

b The headquarters of your computer company is still located in Texas, but now you export computer parts for assembly to an Irish-incorporated subsidiary that reinvests its profits in Ireland. Fill in the blanks in the data below. Explain your result:

> *Irish branch*
>
> | | |
> |---|---|
> | Irish income | $100 |
> | Irish taxes paid | $12.5 |
> | US taxes | [＿＿＿＿＿＿] |
> | Net income | [＿＿＿＿＿＿] |

5.7 International taxation (II)

As Treasurer of US Exports Inc., you have set up an FSC in the Bahamas for the export to Europe of your US manufactures, and are applying arm's length pricing of your goods "shipped" to the FSC. Your exempt foreign trade income from the sale or lease of export property is indicated below:

Foreign sales corporation

(arm's length pricing)

Foreign trade income	$100
Bahamian taxes paid	[_____]
US taxes	[_____]
Net income	[_____]

a Fill in the blanks above, recalling that the portion of foreign trade income exempt from taxes is 34 percent, and the Bahamas has no income tax.

b In the second case, your FSC is set up according to special administrative rules, which exempt 17/23 of foreign trade income from US taxation. Fill in the blanks below and explain your answer:

Foreign sales corporation

(administrative rules)

Foreign trade income	$100
Bahamian taxes paid	[_____]
US taxes	[_____]
Net income	[_____]

5.8 Mergers and acquisitions

Consider the data below, which indicate the NPV of Firms A and B:

	Firm A	Firm B
Value	$20	$10
Shares outstanding	10	10

a What is the current value of the shares of each firm?

b If Firm A acquires Firm B, and the value of the combined Firm A is $40, what is the value of synergy?

c Suppose that Firm A offers cash of $15 to the shareholders of Firm B; what is the premium A is offering?

d Do you think they will accept (2/3 majority required)?

e If they do, what will be the new value of Firm A?

f Now suppose that Firm A offers $10 in cash and the rest in shares in the new Firm A. How many shares would it have to offer in order to make the equivalent of the cash offer of $15?

5.9 An international business plan

Consider whether or not to acquire a subsidiary that has the cash flow shown below in euros. There is no terminal value. You are given the basic data and the WACC in euros is 10 percent:

Year	0	1	2	3	4	5
Free-cash flows (€)	(50)	10	10.5	11.0	11.6	12.2
Present value (€)	(50.0)					
NPV (€)						
Spot exchange rate (£/€)	0.71					
NPV (£)						

Discount foreign currency cash flows to present at the euro discount rate; and convert the NPV to the home currency, pounds sterling, at the spot exchange rate.

5.10 Offshore banking

You are the head of new accounts in Citybank, New York, when one afternoon Raúl, the brother of the former President of Mexico, appears in your office with your bank's external relations officer in Mexico. Raúl happens to have a big suitcase full of money, $100 million, and wishes to deposit the money in Citybank, NY, an Edge Act bank:

a How much would Citybank stand to make annually on Raúl's $100 million dollars?

b Would you have to report the deposit? If so, to whom?

c Apart from reporting requirements, is it worth it to Citybank to take the deposit?

5.11 Optimal portfolio analysis

Consider the following utility function of an investor:

$$U = E(r_c) - \frac{A\sigma_c^2}{2} = E(r_c) - 2\sigma_c^2,$$

where $E(r_c)$ is the expected rate of return on her complete portfolio (composed of a risky asset and a risk-free asset), σ_c^2 is the variance (the squared standard deviation (volatility) of the complete portfolio), and A is the coefficient of risk aversion:

158

a What is the coefficient of risk aversion, A, of this particular investor? The expected return on the complete portfolio is given by:

$$E(r_c) = r_f + z(E(r_p) - r_f) = 0.05 + z(0.15 - 0.05) = 0.05 + 0.1z,$$

where z is the proportion of the complete portfolio held in the risky asset, which has an expected rate of return, $E(rP)$, of 15 percent, while $(1 - z)$ is the percent held in the risk-free asset, US T-bills. T-bills bear a risk-free rate, r_f, of 5 percent. Furthermore, the variance of the risky asset is given by $\sigma_p^2 = 0.1$, or 10 percent.

b Find the optimal proportion of assets held in the risky asset and the proportion held in the risk-free asset.

c Compute the expected rate of return on the complete portfolio.

d Compute the variance of the complete portfolio.

e Compute the level of utility (happiness!) of this investor.

5.12 Optimal investment analysis

Consider the following data on a complete portfolio composed of 50 percent (that is, $z = 0.50$) risky assets with $\sigma_p^2 = 0.4$ and $E(r_p) = 0.20$. The complete portfolio thus also has 50 percent risk-free assets with certain return of 5 percent (that is 0.05):

a What is the expected rate of return on the complete portfolio?

b What is the variance of the complete portfolio?

c What is the standard deviation of the complete portfolio (its volatility)?

Chapter 6

International financial scams and swindles

PYRAMIDS: AN INTERNATIONAL PERSPECTIVE

Financial history is full of Ponzi schemes, where pyramids of investors invest in notes with no or scant underlying assets. The scheme Carlo Ponzi devised in 1919 is today called a "Ponzi Pyramid." In December, Ponzi initiated an "investment" fund in Boston, establishing his business as The Security Exchange Company. He promised 50 percent interest in 90 days on his notes. Ten thousand initial investors purchased the Ponzi notes. At first, all were redeemed at maturity, and many rolled over. The word got out. New investors beat a path to his door, their cash permitting redemption of his first issues. He had a gimmick that attracted gullible investors, arguing that he could buy international postal reply coupons, then exchange them for US postage stamps of three to four times what he paid. According to Ponzi, the arbitrage opportunity was due to misalignment of postal exchange rates. He claimed to cash in the stamps, thus profiting by up to 400 percent. After fees, he could "plausibly" pay 50 percent semi-annually, yet keep about 200 percent in profits—so he said.

Indeed, he kept a few postal coupons on hand in his office to show to potential investors. With the money he collected from new "investors," he repaid the first ones their principal plus the promised 50 percent return, a classic pyramid scheme with no underlying assets. Naturally, the first investors promoted the scheme by word of mouth. It rapidly mushroomed.

There is always one problem with Ponzi schemes: The last investors who are brought into the scheme ultimately find that there are not enough new investors since the flow of new investment must increase exponentially. The cash flow stops—leaving them holding worthless Ponzi notes. A run to redeem the notes takes place, forcing bankruptcy.

Let's take a simple example of an initial investment in a six-month Ponzi note of $100, which we will roll over in each period. The semi-annual interest rate is 50 percent, equivalent to an annual rate of 125 percent. For the sake of argument, suppose we roll over the Ponzi note for three years, assuming the scheme has not collapsed by then. Table 6.1 illustrates the growth in the liabilities of the Ponzi scheme were the initial $100 rolled over every six months into a new Ponzi note.

Within three years, Ponzi would be liable for $1,139.06 to repay both principal and interest on the initial $100 investment. Since there is no underlying asset yielding a positive return, the rate of growth of new deposits would have to be over 125 percent a year for Ponzi to be able to redeem his notes. That is, new investments would have to more than double yearly. For this reason, Ponzi schemes usually collapse within a year.

In the case of Carlo Ponzi, the cash flow was stopped after nine months by an investigation by the District Attorney of Boston, even though he had not defaulted on a single debt. The scheme broke down in July 1920, when he was ordered not to take new deposits, pending the results of the investigation.

Why would so many people invest in a scheme that ultimately had to collapse? The reason seemed to be that the early investors did see great returns on their money. Those in early on a speculative bubble gain by cashing out early. It was, however, the age-old pyramid scheme. Since investors had their notes redeemed until the investigation, not a single complaint had been filed.

On July 26, 1920, Ponzi's house of cards collapsed. The District Attorney ordered Ponzi to suspend taking in new investments until an auditor examined his books. This was the death knell to the Ponzi game, since there were no underlying investments. The public continued to support Ponzi until August 10, 1920, since he attempted to pay off an investor run from his cash deposits in banks. On August 10, the auditors, banks, and newspapers declared that Ponzi was bankrupt. A final audit of his books concluded that he had taken in enough funds to buy approximately 180,000,000 postal coupons, of which they could only confirm the purchase of two. On the witness stand in his trial, Ponzi discussed locations of various safety deposit boxes in the United States, and deposits overseas, and

Table 6.1 A hypothetical Ponzi scheme

Period	Investment ($)	Principal	Interest
0 months	100	–	–
6 months	150	100	50
12 months	225	150	75
18 months	337.5	225	112.5
24 months	506.25	337.50	168.75
30 months	759.375	506.25	253.13
36 months	1,139.06	759.38	379.69

responded evasively to questions about his solvency. Miss Lucy Mell, his 18-year-old assistant office manager, testified that she only had knowledge of transactions within the office, not of Ponzi's outside dealings. When asked if there were any postal reply coupons in the office, she replied "Yes, one or two for samples" (www.mark-knutson.com). Ponzi's family reported that his attorneys were preparing a defense of "financial dementia."

At the trial, Charles Rittenhouse, an accountant employed by the receivers of Ponzi's estate, testified that $9,582,591 was invested in Ponzi's scheme, reflecting notes with a face value of $14,374,755. When the business shut down, $4,263,652 of investments were outstanding, having a face value of $6,396,353.

Imposing a maximum five-year sentence for a mail fraud count, Judge Hale added these words:

> The defendant conceived a scheme which on his counsel's admission did defraud men and women. It will not do to have the public, the world, understand that such a scheme as his through the United States' instrumentality could be carried out without substantial punishment.
>
> (Ibid.)

The same issue of "substantial punishment" arises in the cases of Enron, Parmalat, Vivendi, BCCI, Barings, WorldCom, and Tyco, to name some of more recent financial abuses. After three and a half years in prison, Ponzi was sentenced to an additional seven to nine years by Massachusetts' authorities. He was released on $14,000 bond pending an appeal. He turned up in Jacksonville, Florida under the assumed name of Charles Borelli and immediately launched a pyramid land scheme. He purchased land at $16 an acre, subdividing it into 23 lots, and sold each lot at $10 apiece. Ponzi promised investors that their initial $10 investment would translate into millions of dollars in just two years. Much of the land was underwater—worthless marsh or swamp land. The land boom in Florida was petering out, too late to rescue Ponzi. In February 1926 the Duval County Grand Jury returned a four-count indictment against Ponzi and his Charpon, Florida Land Syndicate. He was charged with violating Florida regulations for conducting business as a trust, offering securities for sale without filing a declaration of trust, selling units of indebtedness without a permit from the State Controller, and doing real-estate business without paying a $150 license fee. Once again, he jumped bail on June 3, 1926 and ran to Texas. He was captured on June 28 in New Orleans and sent back to Boston to complete his jail term. After seven years, Ponzi was released on good behavior and deported to Italy on October 7, 1934. Back in Rome, Mussolini offered him a position with Italy's new national airline. He served as the Rio de Janeiro branch manager from 1939 to 1942. The airline failed during World War II and Ponzi was unemployed. He passed away on January 15, 1949 in a Rio de Janeiro charity ward at the age of 67 (www.mark-knutson.com).

Parmalat

Parmalat, though having underlying assets and operations, ultimately became a Ponzi scheme.

As Gianfranco Tabasso of the EACT Payment Commission poignantly remarks:

> In situations like Parmalat, it is evident how critically important they [treasurers and CFOs] are in detecting and perpetrating frauds. A serious corporate fraud cannot be carried out without the connivance of the treasurer and the CFO. Put another way, the treasurer and the CFO are more important than internal audit and accounting, in the detection of possible frauds, even when perpetrators are CEOs, board members, or other top brass.
>
> (Tabasso, 2004: 25)

What really defines a Ponzi scheme? Tabasso notes:

> This is the second time in a hundred years that a Parmesan has cheated American investors. In the early 1920s, Carlo Ponzi did it in Boston with the "postal coupon scheme" and became so famous that Ponzi Games and Ponzi Finance are in all university textbooks and Ponzi has his own dedicated web site http://www.mark-knutson.com. Carlo Ponzi's was a pure high-risk financial scheme with no underlying assets. Parmalat is a dairy and food company, with real assets, which produces and sells real goods, in a sector traditionally considered low risk. Carlo Ponzi operated his scheme alone from a central office of two rooms attended by twelve clerks. Parmalat is a multibillion dollar multinational listed on the Milan Stock Exchange which has over 250 companies around the world; its boss, Calisto Tanzi, has had lots of interested helpers, bankers, auditors, family, managers, tax and legal professionals, consultants, etc. Carlo Ponzi's swindle lasted nine months before it was discovered: Parmalat's went on for more than ten years, an unbelievable length of time in a world where listed companies are subject to corporate governance, reporting, anti-money laundering regulations, market abuse legislation, auditing, external regulations and rating companies. Banks place bonds on the market and earn commission, corporations collect the money and don't have to find new shareholders and answer embarrassing questions. Only investors, who lay out capital but remain far away from the game, are at risk.
>
> (Tabasso, 2004: 21–2)

Serious problems started right after the Parmalat stock listing, so Fausto Tonna (Parmalat's CFO, who ran Parmalat Finanziaria, the holding company) created a network of financial companies, all based in fiscal paradises—tax havens. They would be used to issue bonds, channel funds back and forth, create firewalls, and,

163

last but not least, concoct fake balance sheets to shore up the consolidated nearly €8 billion of Parmalat bonds.

Parmalat started in 1962, when Calisto Tanzi inherited from his father a small ham factory near Parma. At 22, he opened a pasteurization plant selling milk for the first time in Tetrapack triangular cartons. The milk cartons were a success: sales grew rapidly from €100,000 in 1962 to 50 million in 1970. It was declared insolvent in December 2003, with Enrico Bondi replacing Calisto Tanzi and later becoming official liquidator. There were:

> Public attorneys pursuing various kinds of crimes and misdemeanors, from money laundering to collusion in fraud, false communication to markets, insider trading, market abuse, obstruction of justice etc. It appears almost all the money went to cover operating losses, particularly in South America, but . . . some of it was diverted to the family's private businesses and to the personal accounts of family members, top managers and various professionals who were privy to and participated in the Parmalat fraud.
>
> (Tabasso, 2004: 23)

"Ponzi finance" is defined by Charles Kindleberger as "a type of financial activity engaged in when interest charges of a business unit exceed cash flows from operations . . . with the repayment of debt with the issuance of new debt" (1989: 86–87).

Clearly, an unintentionally unsuccessful operation could have negative cash flow and thus not be able to pay interest charges. To constitute a pyramid, the payment of old debt from the issue of new debt must be present. This was an aspect common to both the Ponzi game and the Parmalat fraud, though the latter had real operations. WorldCom executives were also involved in borrowing to repurchase stock, but were subject to margin calls they ultimately could not meet. Stocks in WorldCom were collateral for the debt, but triggered the margin calls when they lost value. Lest we think that Ponzi schemes are a thing of the past:

> Investors . . . had allocated at least $115 million to Mr. Wright's hedge-fund firm, International Management Associates LLC. Over the prior seven years, which included the worst bear market since the Great Depression, Mr. Wright had reported average annual returns of more than 27% . . . The Securities and Exchange Commission and International Management investors filed separate lawsuits against Mr. Wright, accusing him of fraud. The SEC estimates that Mr. Wright, who handled International Management's investments, managed somewhere between $115 million and $185 million of client money. After more than two weeks of searching, the hedge fund's court-appointed receiver and the SEC have found only about $150,000 of it . . . in two Ameritrade accounts.
>
> (*The Wall Street Journal*, March 9, 2006: A1, A12)

Kirk S. Wright, an African American, "may have taken advantage of the city's black professionals," including "successful black professionals from Atlanta, and former football players" from the Denver Broncos and the Tennessee Titans American football teams (ibid.). Two Atlanta anesthesiologists turned hedge-fund partners claimed they were also duped out of $1.5 million by Wright. They and others were recruited for the aggressive marketing of the hedge fund, which seems not to have had any underlying investments.

> In 2004, it hired Thomas H. Birk, a Los Angeles-based salesman who had previously raised money for several major brokerage firms. Mr. Birk, who is white, would troll Western golf courses talking up Mr. Wright's investment record . . . Mr. Birk eventually raised more than $10 million.
>
> (Ibid.: A12)

"Mr. Wright is missing," although his lawyer says that "he speaks to him regularly on the phone . . . Regulators believe that virtually all the assets of the funds have been dissipated. Mr. Wright's older brother . . . has urged his brother to turn himself in" (ibid.). Carlo Ponzi must be smiling from his grave.

CORPORATE GOVERNANCE FAILURES

Adam Smith's 1776 observation concerning the principal–agent problem bears repeating:

> The directors of such (joint stock) companies, however, being the managers rather of other people's money than of their own, it cannot well be expected that they should watch over it with the same anxious vigilance with which the partners in a private copartnery frequently watch over their own.
>
> (Smith, 1776: 107)

It is appropriate to begin discussion of corporate governance failures with Smith's perceptive observation.

United Airlines

To set the stage, unsecured creditors and executives at the United Airlines Corporation (UAL) agreed to a deal in which 400 executives will be awarded 10 million shares, 8 percent of the number to be issued in total upon emergence from bankruptcy. UAL stakeholders, including employees, have on the other hand been asked to make great sacrifices, for example to their pension plans. Elizabeth Warren, Professor at Harvard Law School, said on January 12, 2005: "Chapter 11 [of the US Bankruptcy Code] was traditionally about sharing the pain, but now it is more a game of feast and famine—starving the shareholders and creditors while the management team grows fat on big salaries" (Morgenstern, 2006: 3). Annual salaries for the top eight UAL executives will total $3.5 million when UAL exits bankruptcy, rounded up by target bonuses equal to from 55 to 100 percent of salary, depending on the executive. There are also $1.39 million in retention bonuses earmarked for seven top executives. Professor Warren continues:

> The lawyers and management team are running the show. Shareholders are out of the picture and creditors are often unsure about the overall financial stability of the company. That is a perfect set of circumstances for the manage-ment to extract much higher compensation than they would get if other people were competing for those management jobs.
>
> (Ibid.: 4)

As Ms Morgenstern, the *New York Times* journalist, put it: "Got your airsickness bag handy?"

Let's now look back on corporate scandals. Keep your airsickness bag handy.

Enron

Enron filed for bankruptcy on December 2, 2001. Its accountant, Arthur Andersen, LLP, no longer exists. It is a story of one of the largest business fail-ures of its time in the United States. (See www.businessweek.com/magazine/content/01_51/b3762001.htm.) To call it a failure of governance would be an understatement. There are many facets to the story:

1 A fraudulent account, which escaped taxes, booked loans as profits and estimates of future profits as current income from deals, and moved losses off the books, recording them as operational profits.
2 The creation of the Raptors—four private investment partners—managed by Andrew Fastow, the CFO of Enron, a clear conflict of interest. These partnerships drained profits from Enron, and moved losses off the Enron books. The partnerships were an accounting trick to book profits as a hedge. However, they were funded by Enron shares so did not provide the insurance of a hedge.
3 The large-scale shredding and forging of documents, and deletion of e-mails that might compromise Enron in an SEC investigation.
4 Insider trading with the early selling of shares for "estate planning" by CEO Jeffrey K. Skilling, found guilty of insider trading.
5 The misleading of employees and investors as to the true financial condition of Enron.

6 The freezing of the employees' right to sell Enron shares from their pensions in an effort to keep its price from falling further.
7 The payments of large bonuses based on improper accounting reports of earnings.

In May 2006, Kenneth Lay, Enron Chairman, was found guilty of one count of conspiracy, two counts of wire fraud, and three counts of securities fraud. Jeffrey Skilling was found guilty of one count of conspiracy, twelve counts of securities fraud, five counts of falsifying business records, and one count of insider trading. Appeals are in process. Lay died on July 5, 2006, before sentencing. Recovery of his assets is now extremely unlikely.

Accounting and legal firms knowingly approved illegal accounting and business practices, including conflict of interest partnerships (the Raptors). David D. Duncan, head of the Andersen audit team, went along with the deals provided that Enron's board of directors approve them (Behr and Witt, 2002).

In 2000, Enron was burning cash at a rate of $700 million a year. It is difficult to sustain negative cash flow at this rate. It declared bankruptcy in December 2001. In the end, the jury realized that the Raptor partnerships were set up to inflate the earnings at Enron to personally benefit its top executives by moving Enron's losses to the Raptors. When the Raptors' losses and accounting errors (for example a $1.2 billion equity loss) came to light, Enron's shares sank. In a Hyatt ballroom filled with several thousand Enron employees, Kenneth Lay is quoted as saying:

Let me say right up front, I am absolutely heartbroken about what's happened. Many of you were a lot wealthier six to nine months ago, are now concerned about the college education for your kids, maybe the mortgage on your house, maybe your retirement, and for that I am incredibly sorry. But we are going to get it back.

(Witt and Behr, 2002)

The same day, Lay is reported to have taken a $4 million cash advance from the company. Over the next three days, he withdrew an additional $19 million. He immediately repaid $6 million of the amount by transferring his Enron stock to the company. That allowed him to sell stock but avoid an immediate reporting requirement (ibid.).

In a last ditch effort to save Enron, Lay attempted to sell Enron to Dynergy Inc.—a smaller Houston-based company. Enron misled Dynergy before their proposed merger, saying that its European trading operations had a $53 million operating profit in the previous quarter. In its disclosure, Enron reported that its European operations had actually incurred a $21 million loss. Chuck Watson, the founder and CEO of Dynergy, was surprised by the debt disclosure, which he called a "$690 million bullet in the head," killing the merger deal.

167

Ex-Enron Chairman and CEO Kenneth Lay surrendered to FBI authorities on July 8, 2004, after being indicted in the government's crackdown on corporate scandals.

On May 25, 2006 a Federal jury found Lay and Skilling guilty of conspiracy and wire and securities fraud, and Skilling guilty of one count of insider trading in connection with Enron's 2001 collapse (*The Washington Post*, May 25, 2006).

Enron's Chapter 11 business reorganization plan received court approval in 2004. The July 15, 2004 Enron press release stated:

> At the conclusion of the claims reconciliation process, the allowable claims against the company are expected to be approximately $63 billion, Cooper [Stephen F. Cooper, Enron's acting CEO and chief restructuring officer] said. The cash and equity assets available for ultimate distribution are expected to be around $12 billion, he added, not including recoveries from litigation.
>
> (www.enron.com)

Enron was just the first chapter in what was to prove to be a series of corporate scandals of huge proportions.

WorldCom

In July 2005, Bernard J. Ebbers, former CEO of the telecommunications company, WorldCom, was sentenced to 25 years in prison for conspiracy to commit securities fraud, and for false filing of 10Q and 10K income statements with the SEC. In the 31-page indictment, US Attorney David N. Kelley charged:

> Rather than disclose WorldCom's true operating performance and financial condition, in or about April 2002, EBBERS and Sullivan instructed subordinates, in substance and in part, to falsely and fraudulently book certain entries in WorldCom's general ledger, which were designed to increase artificially WorldCom's reported revenue and to decrease artificially WorldCom's reported expenses, resulting in, among other things, artificially inflated figures for WorldCom's EPS, EBITDA, and revenue growth rate. These adjustments included (a) the improper capitalization of line cost expenses, and (b) increases to revenue, which in light of their departure from prior revenue recognition policies, and in light of their aggregate amount, made WorldCom's reported revenue materially misleading. EBBERS and Sullivan instructed others to make these adjustments solely in an effort to report results that would satisfy analysts' expectations, even though EBBERS and Sullivan knew that WorldCom's true results in fact failed to meet those expectations.
>
> (*United States District Court NY, USA* v. *Bernard J. Ebbers*.
> Indictment S3 02 Cr. 1144 (BSJ), p. 15)

WorldCom's CFO, Scott Sullivan, received a five-year sentence, significantly lighter for providing evidence and testifying against Bernard Ebbers. The jury found that Ebbers and Sullivan intentionally defrauded shareholders who owned the company, resulting in the biggest bankruptcy in American history—much larger than the Enron bankruptcy. Accounting fraud was at center stage in the WorldCom bankruptcy, fraudulently reporting high revenues and low costs. Their favorite technique seemed to be moving operation expenses to capital expenditures so that they were not reflected as operating costs, but rather as capital investments. WorldCom operated as MCI, Inc. until it emerged from bankruptcy proceedings in April 2004. It was acquired by Verizon Communications in January 2006.

Adelphia

Adelphia's founder, John Rigas, and his son Timothy, the cable company's former CFO, got 15 years and 20 years, respectively, for their role in fraud that led to the collapse of the US's largest cable company. Prosecutors accused them of conspiring to hide $2.3 billion in Adelphia debt, stealing $100 million, and lying to investors about the company's financial condition.

Tyco International Inc., Bermuda

In September 2002, the SEC indicted former Tyco International Inc. executives, CEO Dennis Kozlowski, CFO Mark Schwartz, and General Counsel Mark Belnick, on charges of civil fraud, theft, tax evasion, and not filing insider sales of the company's stock, as required by the SEC (see www.tycofraudinfocenter.com). They are accused of giving themselves interest-free or low-interest loans for personal purchases of property, jewelry, and other items, which were neither approved by directors nor repaid to the company. Nor did loan forgiveness of $37.5 million appear on Kozlowski's or Schwartz's income returns for 1999.

Kozlowski and Schwartz have also been accused of issuing bonuses to themselves and others without the approval of Tyco's board of directors. It is alleged that these bonuses acted as de facto loan forgiveness for employees who had borrowed company money. They are also being indicted on charges of selling company stock without reporting their insider sales, fraud, and making fraudulent statements. All in all, Kozlowski and Schwartz were accused by the SEC of "looting" Tyco of $600 million. Both Kozlowski and Schwartz were found guilty in June 2005. On September 19, 2005 New York Justice Obus ordered Mr Kozlowski to repay $97 million to Tyco, and an additional $70 million in fines. Mr Schwartz was ordered to pay $38 million to Tyco, and $35 million in fines. In addition, they have been sentenced to serve between 8 years 4 months and 25 years in prison. Under New York State law, each will have to serve at least 6 years, 11 months and 9 days before being eligible for parole (*The Wall Street Journal*, September 20, 2005: C1). They are also liable for civil suits. Both plan to appeal against their convictions.

Hollinger International

A special committee of the publishing company, Hollinger International Inc., concluded in a report that Sir Conrad M. Black and F. David Radler ran a "corporate kleptocracy," diverting to themselves the company's entire earnings of $400 million over seven years. It also ordered certain directors, particularly Richard N. Perle, to return $5.4 million in pay for "putting his own interests above those of Hollinger's shareholders." It criticized the payment of $226 million to Ravelston for management fees from 1996 to 2003—a company controlled by Sir Conrad that, in turn, essentially owned 68 percent of the voting shares of Hollinger. Perle is singled out for "flagrant abdication of duty" in signing bonuses and loans to Sir Conrad at the expense of shareholders. He is also said to have earned a bonus of $3.1 million from Hollinger Digital—his project—even though it lost $49 million. In the report's terms:

> It is hard to imagine a more flagrant abdication of duty than a director rubber-stamping transactions that directly benefit a controlling shareholder without any thought, comprehension, or analysis. In fact, many of the consents that Perle signed as an executive committee member approved related-party transactions that unfairly benefited Black . . . and cost Hollinger millions.
>
> (*The New York Times*, September 1, 2004: C6)

SARBANES-OXLEY ACT OF 2002

The recent scandals in corporate governance spawned new legislation—the US Sarbanes-Oxley Act of 2002. Many companies are complaining about the higher than expected cost of compliance with SOX or Sarbox, as the Act is commonly known. The Act addresses most major issues in corporate governance and disclosure, and has the following main titles:

Title I: Public Company Accounting Oversight Board establishes an independent accounting oversight board with whom public accounting firms, including foreign ones that prepare audits, must register for inspection.

Title II: Auditor Independence prohibits a public accounting firm from providing non-audit services to its client, in particular:

(1) bookkeeping or other services related to the accounting records or financial statements of the audit client;
(2) financial information systems design and implementation;
(3) appraisal or valuation services, fairness opinions, or contribution-in-kind reports;

170

(4) actuarial services;

(5) internal audit outsourcing services;

(6) management functions or human resources;

(7) broker or dealer, investment adviser, or investment banking services;

(8) legal services and expert services unrelated to the audit; and

(9) any other service that the Board determines, by regulation, is impermissible.

(HR 3763-28 Sarbanes-Oxley Act of 2002, Sec. 201)

Title III: Corporate Responsibility requires that CEOs and CFOs certify in annual or quarterly reports that:

(1) the signing officer has reviewed the report;

(2) based on the officer's knowledge, the report does not contain any untrue statement of a material fact or omit to state a material fact . . .

(3) based on such officer's knowledge, the financial statements, and other financial information included in the report, fairly present in all material respects the financial condition and results of operations of the issuer as of, and for, the periods represented in the report.

(HR 3763-28, Sec. 302)

The Act also provides for forfeiture of bonuses and profits as a result of misre-porting (Sec. 304), prohibits insider trades during pension fund blackout periods when the firm suspends the right of more than a majority of participants of pension plans from selling their shares in the company (Sec. 306), and provides for "disgorgement" or fair funds for investors whose rights are violated (Sec. 308).

Title IV: Enhanced Financial Disclosures requires accurate compliance with GAAP principles (Sec. 401) and disclosure of material off-balance sheet transactions, arrangements, and obligations (Sec. 401), prohibits personal loans to executives (Sec. 402), requires greater disclosure of equity transactions involving manage-ment and principal stockholders (Sec. 403), establishes a code of ethics for senior financial officers (Sec. 406), and requires real-time issuer disclosures of material changes in the financial condition or operations of the issuer (Sec. 409).

Title V: Analyst Conflicts of Interest requires disclosure of:

(1) the extent to which the securities analyst has debt or equity investments in the issuer that is the subject of the appearance or research report;

(2) whether any compensation has been received by the registered broker or dealer . . . from the issuer that is the subject of the appearance or research report . . .

171

(3) whether an issuer, the securities of which are recommended in the appearance or research report is, or during the 1-year period preceding the date of appearance or date of distribution of the report has been, a client of the registered broker or dealer, and if so, stating the types of services provided to the issuer.

(Sec. 15D)

Title VI: Commission Resources and Authority appropriates monies for the Commission and its activities.

Title VII: Studies and Reports commissions the study of public accounting firms with the view of increasing competition by studying the factors that have led to industry consolidation (Sec. 701), the study of the role and function of the credit rating agencies in the evaluation of issuers of securities with a view to identifying conflicts of interest (Sec. 702), and a report on the number of securities professions who have violated securities laws, which laws were violated, and what punishments, if any, were meted out (Sec. 703). Sec. 704 mandates a report on enforcement actions, while Sec. 705 requires a study "on whether investment banks and financial advisers assisted public companies in manipulating their earnings and obfuscating their true financial condition."

Title VIII: Corporate and Criminal Fraud Accountability provides for criminal penalties for the destruction, alteration, or falsification of records in Federal investigations and bankruptcy (Par. 1519) and extends the statute of limitations for securities fraud from two to five years after the violation (Sec. 804).

Title IX: White-Collar Crime Penalty Enhancements raises from five to 20 years the possible punishments for mail and wire fraud (Sec. 903) and raises the monetary penalties from $5,000 to $100,000 in one case, and from $100,000 to $500,000 in another, and criminal penalties from one year to ten years for violations of the employee retirement income security act of 1974 (Sec. 904). Sec. 906 establishes corporate responsibility for financial reports, providing criminal penalties of up to $1,000,000 or ten years in prison or both, for certifying a fraudulent report, and up to $5,000,000 or 20 years in prison or both for a corporate officer who "willfully certifies" a fraudulent statement that misrepresents the financial conditions and result of operations of the issuer (Par. 1350).

Title X: Corporate Tax Returns requires that the Federal income tax return of a corporation be signed by the chief executive officer.

Title XI: Corporate Fraud and Accountability proscribes tampering with the records or impeding the carrying out of an investigation (Sec. 1102), and increases criminal penalties of the SEC Act of 1934 substantially—up to ten or 20 years, as well as up to $5 million or $25 million, depending on the violation (Sec. 1106). Finally, it provides for criminal penalties up to ten years and similar fines for retaliating against an employee who provides information on the company to any law enforcement officer (Sec. 1107). The latter is appropriately entitled "Retaliation Against Informants."

To sum up, the Sarbanes-Oxley Act of 2002 means business and severe penalties for knowingly committing securities fraud or false accounting. It also means significantly increased costs of compliance. One prominent accountant gave insight on curatives and SOX:

> If you devote attention to safeguards for minimizing the immense risks of fraud that have happened all too frequently in the last five years especially, my sense of the key preventatives are:
>
> 1 The risks of financial ruin and long jail terms to perpetrators such as Ebbers. (If justice were quicker and harder, we wouldn't have needed SOX, though CEO certifications required by SOX are a positive reminder of the CEO's responsibilities.)
> 2 Independent, competent boards such as SOX supports.
> 3 A strong SEC-type body, perhaps international in scope, to regulate public companies.
> 4 More standardizing accounting rules for the various industries enabling apples-to-apples comparisons.
> 5 More principles-based accounting; today there are in the US too many rules and not enough judgment, even on such issues as revenue recognition.
> 6 SOX rules on auditor independence, including a cooling off period for hiring top level people from the audit firm, are a big step in the right direction.
> (David Lieberman, former CFO, University of Miami)

INSIDER TRADING AND OTHER FINANCIAL ABUSES

Retention bonuses

Retention bonuses are payments that a firm may pay to retain an employee. In principle, the firm should determine the unusually high or unique qualifications of the employee that make it essential to retain an employee. Clearly, they may have the opposite effect. For instance, if an employee is to be awarded a million dollars at the end of the year for staying on one year, he or she has an incentive to seek another job while remaining at his or her post for one year. In many cases, the firm is in financial distress, so the current management awards itself retention bonuses to manage its downfall or cash out its remaining assets. For the same reason, management may make itself personal loans, knowing that the company

173

is headed for bankruptcy. This practice is now prohibited under SOX, but K-Mart managers cashed out a great deal before its bankruptcy through bonuses and personal loans. Retention bonuses are often abused—after all, the managers who took the firm into the ground should not be retained, let alone be awarded a bonus for poor performance. Days before Enron Corp. declared bankruptcy on December 2, 2001, it announced that it would not abide by severance payments to its employees. At the same time, the company gave executives retention bonuses totaling more than $55 million. The generous executive payouts, many of which were made on November 30, were approved by the new Enron management team—Jeff McMahon, Enron president, and Ray Bowen, the CFO. McMahon received a bonus of $1.5 million and Bowen got $750,000. Enron's practices seemed not to change: handsome rewards to executives days before reneging on its employee severance commitment. Enron's planned severance package—subsequently scrapped—cost $120 million and would have provided an average payment to employees of approximately $30,000. That plan was discarded. Instead, at least $105 million was distributed in executive bonuses. To add insult to injury, the Enron blackout of sales of Enron stock by employees, two-thirds of their pension assets, was reported to have been accompanied by un-reported insider sales by management (Witt and Behr, 2002). Once again, this practice would be illegal under SOX, if discovered. Indeed, former CEO Jeffrey Skilling has been found guilty of one count of insider trading.

AMR

Shortly after two of its three unions had ratified $1.8 billion in annual wage and other concessions on April 14, 2003, AMR (parent of American Airlines) filed its annual 10K report with the SEC, revealing a retention bonus plan for the company's top seven executives of about $5 million each for another year of service and a bulletproof $41 million pension trust fund designed to protect executives' retirement monies from possible bankruptcy. AMR stood by its pension trust fund, but the then AMR CEO Donald J. Carty and another six senior AMR executives gave up the retention bonuses on April 18. The remaining stewards union ratified the restructuring plan, despite the considerable anger it provoked among union members. Neither plan was disclosed to shareholders, AMR's labor unions, or the SEC until the April 15, 2003 SEC filing. (See Hoffman, 2003.) In the end, the unions had no better alternative than to approve the restructuring plan. Carty has since been replaced as CEO of American Airlines.

Insider trading

The term "insider trading" can mean the perfectly legal buying and selling of stock by a company's corporate insiders. Insider trading is legal when these corporate insiders trade stock of their own company, but report in advance these trades to the US SEC and their income statements contain all information relevant to the financial standing of the firm. The SEC discloses the intention to sell on the EDGAR database. That way, the insider trading is disclosed and anyone can speculate about the corporate insider's opinion of the fortunes of his or her company. In the past, there have been loopholes that have allowed executives to skirt the disclosure rules, but SOX attempts to close them.

Insider trading is illegal when a person bases their trade of stocks in a public company on information that is not shared with the public. It is also illegal to give someone a tip, so they can trade on the inside information. In Europe, the possibility of insider trading in EADS—the Airbus consortium—is being investigated by the French Finance Commission. Noël Forgeard, co-President of EADS, his three children, and other French and German directors sold their shares in EADS in March 2006, three months before announcing further, lengthy delays in the delivery of the jumbo Airbus 380 jet that triggered a sharp fall in the value EADS shares. Forgeard claims it was not insider trading, and that he had no idea that there would be further delays. Innocent till proven guilty, of course, but the Airbus workers were apparently aware that they were far behind schedule due to extreme "customizing" for each customer. The French press are having a heyday over the affair, saying that Forgeard was either a liar, incompetent, or both! He has since resigned.

The punishment for illegal insider trading depends on the situation. The person can be fined, banned from sitting on the executive or board of directors of a public company, and even jailed. The Securities Exchange Act of 1934 in the United States allows the SEC to give a reward—"a bounty"—to someone who gives the Commission information that results in a fine of insider trading. SOX 2002 makes it illegal to retaliate against whistle-blowers. Yet, it would be wise to think twice before blowing a whistle. The government may not be able to save your job. "Other reasons" might suffice, then you would have to pay lawyers to fight your company—not a pleasant thought.

Abusive tax schemes

Taxes may be evaded by using a foreign jurisdiction. Evasion can be as simple as depositing unreported cash or checks into a bank account in a tax haven. Other methods are more elaborate and involve domestic and foreign trusts and partnerships. Some are perfectly legal; others are not.

A US resident receives checks from customers, and the checks are sent for deposit in the resident's international business corporation (IBC) of an offshore bank. The foreign bank uses its correspondent bank account to process the checks. When the check clears, the taxpayer's IBC account is credited for the payments.

The customer who receives the canceled check does not know that the payment was made offshore. However, the US taxpayer has transferred the unreported income to an offshore tax haven. Some Florida dentists ran foul of the law when they were discovered using credit cards issued by the foreign bank in Nassau in order to transfer the monies back to the United States. UK tax expatriates move to the Bahamas to live from the income transferred or earned there. Or they incorporate in the Bahamas or Bermuda, but avoid staying more than 180 days in the United States over a three-year period to avoid residency issues for the business. False billing scams abroad can also be used to evade taxation.

Undisclosed executive compensation

From January 2006 the SEC required that income statements treat as an expense the value of options granted to executives in order to "improve the value of the firm." The generosity of deferred compensation, bonuses, and options has sometimes only been revealed to shareholders as a result of accidental claims due to divorce proceedings. Jack Welch, former Chairman of General Electric, is retained as a consultant at $86,000 a year after his retirement in 2001; the package includes "lifetime access to company facilities and services comparable to those which are currently made available to him by the company." These benefits are "unconditional and irrevocable" according to a General Electric 2001 proxy statement. The divorce papers filed by his former wife, Jane Welch, detail her husband's use of an $80,000 per month Manhattan apartment owned by the company, in addition to other perks of significant value, such as use of the company airplane. What is surprising is that many of these "retired" executives continue on the payroll, their golden parachutes resembling more golden hammocks. This would be funny were it not for the fact that the owner's wealth is diminished by stock dilution, lower dividends, and self-dealing by managers. It is disingenuous to claim that management does not know how to value options, as they are traded daily in many companies. Further, Black-Scholes and binomial pricing formulas are in place for anyone who wishes to use them. It is amazing that many managers "manage" to protect their pensions and health benefits, while defaulting on those of their employees. Some have the company pay their income taxes, unbeknown to the shareholders. Christopher Cox, the head of the US SEC, won unanimous support from SEC commissioners to overhaul proxy-statement disclosure of top executives in the following ways:

1   Require companies to provide a total compensation figure for executives.
2   Include a dollar value of stock options in the summary compensation table.
3   Disclose any executive perks that are more than $10,000 in value.
4   Provide an actual amount to specify what payments executives would receive should there be a change in control or change in responsibilities.

5 Create a new disclosure table that would cover the details of retirement plans, including what the executive would receive in potential annual payments and benefits.

6 Create a new director compensation table similar to the executive summary compensation table that would disclose payments received by directors in a given year.

(*The Wall Street Journal*, January 10, 2006: A1–2)

At least this is a step in the right direction. The shareholders should know. Adam Smith hit the nail on the head, once again. As Professor Lucian A. Bebchuk, Director, Corporate Governance Program, Harvard University aptly put it:

The positive effect will be that on the margin—and it is an important margin—there will be a new so-called outrage constraint. The caveat is that even though there is an outrage constraint, shareholders have very limited power to do anything about it.

(Labaton, 2006)

In the meantime, average chief executive pay of CEOs of Fortune 500 companies rose from $2.82 million in 1990 to $11.8 million in 2004. Professor Bebchuk also found that, in the S&P 500 companies with pension plans, the median actuarial value given to chief executives is about $15 million (ibid.).

Many of these abusive financial practices are subject to a "Wells letter." The SEC Wells notification letters are mandated under Exchange Rules 17.1 and 17.2, which provide that prior to "submitting its report [to the Business Conduct Committee], the staff shall notify the person(s) who is the subject of the report . . . of the general nature of the allegations" in violations of exchange rules, such as conduct inconsistent with just and equitable principles of trade, failure to provide requested information, and the like. This is to notify the person of the initiation of an investigation into possible exchange violations and to give that person the opportunity to respond to allegations within one year.

Derivative scandals

Barings Bank

Britain's oldest merchant bank had financed the Napoleonic wars, but was brought down by a single rogue trader, Nick Leeson, then 28 years old, in February 1995. His losses were so great that Barings was unable to meet a SIMEX (Singapore International Monetary Exchange) margin call and was declared insolvent. In the British Parliament, on February 27, 1995, the Chancellor of the Exchequer announced somberly:

177

With permission, Madam Speaker, I would like to make a statement about the insolvency of the merchant bank Barings. The Bank of England announced late last night, ahead of the opening of the Far East financial markets, that Barings was unable to continue trading.

At the time of the announcement, Leeson was on the run from the Singapore Branch of Barings, where he was chief trader and settlements officer. Arrested in Frankfurt, Germany on March 3, 1995, he was returned to Singapore where he served four years of a six and a half-year sentence for fraud and forgery. Barings was sold to ING, a Dutch bank, for a symbolic £1 on the same day of his arrest. ING assumed the liabilities of Barings.

Many have raised the twin questions: How did this happen and what are the lessons to be learned? There are two basic versions of how this happened—Nick Leeson's and Barings—but only one set of lessons that everyone seems to agree upon. Let's begin with the problems that led to the debacle with a view of drawing lessons.

First, Nick Leeson was both chief trader and settlements officer, a conflict of interest that left his activity essentially unsupervised. "An internal memo dated in 1993 had warned the London headquarters about allowing Leeson to be both trader and settlement officer . . . 'We are in danger of setting up a system that will prove disastrous'" (BBC, *Crime: Case Closed*; see www.bbc.co.uk/crime/case closed/nickleeson.shtml).

Second, the absence of checks and balances allowed Leeson to set up an error account 88888, which started with £20,000 losses from one of the traders he recruited, but was transferred losses of £827 million, or $1.4 billion in the end. This was done by trading at a loss to other Barings accounts, which profited, showering bonuses on Leeson and his associates.

Third, unauthorized trading for the account of Barings took place. Leeson and his traders were authorized to trade futures and options orders for clients or for other firms within the Barings organization, and were allowed to arbitrage price differences between Nikkei futures traded on the SIMEX and Japan's Osaka exchange. Neither of these activities would risk the assets of Barings, if conducted as authorized. Trading the futures and options for clients only risked the client's monies and margins, while arbitraging according to the law of one price is riskless. Not realizing that Leeson was taking speculative positions, booking his losses in error account 88888, and his profits in other Barings accounts, the management in London did not fully realize the potential danger of his dual role—trader and settler.

Fourth, when the market moved against him, Leeson had the bad habit of doubling his losing position in the hopes of recovering his losses when the market moved in his favor (in this instance, a rise in the Nikkei Index). His long bet might have worked had not the January 17, 1995 Kobe earthquake rocked Japan and the Tokyo Exchange. In the words of authors Stephen J. Brown of the Stern School of Business, NYU and Onno W. Steenbeek of the Erasmus School of Finance, Rotterdam: "The empirical evidence suggests that Leeson followed a doubling strategy: he continuously doubled his position as prices were falling" (2001: 83). Indeed, Leeson confirms that he followed this strategy:

> I was determined to win back the losses. And as the spring wore on, I traded harder and harder, risking more and more. I was well down, but increasingly sure that my doubling up and doubling up would pay off . . . I redoubled my exposure. The risk was that the market could crumble down, but on this occasion it carried on upwards. . . . As the market soared in July [1993] my position translated from a £6 million loss back into glorious profit. I was so happy that night I didn't think I'd ever go through that kind of tension again. I'd pulled back a large position simply by holding my nerve . . . but first thing on Monday morning I found that I had to use the 88888 account again . . . it became an addiction.
>
> (Leeson, 1996: 63–4)

Doubling is disastrous when the market moves systematically against the trader. Yet, there is a temptation to win the money back by doing so. Ironically, ten years later on the SIMEX, Jiulin Chen, the 43-year-old CEO of Singapore-listed China Aviation Oil Corporation (CAOC), kept doubling his bet that oil prices would fall, which they never did. This resulted in another SIMEX scandal. Bear in mind, though, that both companies made margin deposits and margin calls until they could no longer do so. Leeson and Chen tend to fault SIMEX, but the exchange was just doing its business.

Fifth, trading on margin affords a great deal of leverage, which can be your best friend if prices move in your direction, but your worst enemy when they move against you. Consider an asset that you borrow from a broker to sell forward at $100 with a margin deposit of $5. If the market price of the forward falls 5 percent your margin is wiped out and you will get a call to restore your margin from your broker. If you cannot be reached within 24 hours or fail to restore margin, the broker will liquidate your position. The more leveraged you are, the smaller is the price movement against you that triggers a margin call. Leeson had plenty of these from SIMEX, and had to get the cash for margins from London. He argued that large transactions were needed to make small arbitrage profits and that both the SIMEX and Tokyo Exchanges required margin. Also, he stated that there would be intra-day "advance margin calls" that Barings would have to meet due to time differences in the location of the ultimate client. In other cases, he simply traded from account 88888. Leverage was also to play a big role in the downfall of CAOC and Long Term Capital Management (LTCM).

179

Sixth, Leeson was a good liar. In an article ten years later in *The Observer*, he notes:

> Barings people had begun to ask some serious questions at last about the huge amounts of cash that had been disappearing in Singapore. Tony Railton, a senior bank official, had found a hole in the balance sheet—not the sort you plug by putting your finger in the dyke, more like one that threatens to wash the whole dam away. His colleague Tony Hawkes, a London-based director, was on a tour of south east Asia looking at funding requirements, and was due to be in Singapore on my birthday—25 February. But still they allowed me to fob them off with flimsy excuses for my cash-guzzling operation. I believe that they were all so desperate to believe in my success for personal reasons; their bonuses depended on it and there were only a few days before these were due to be signed off . . . By 23 February it all became too much. That day, which will be imprinted on my mind forever, my then-wife Lisa and I packed a couple of small suitcases and made our way to the airport.
>
> (Leeson, 2005)

Since Leeson fled on February 23, leaving his letter of apology and tendering his resignation, it is clear he did not meet with Tony Hawkes when he realized the jig was up. It is disingenuous to tar the very officers who had finally discovered his deceit and were about to take action, albeit too late.

Seventh, Leeson's trades were inherently risky. A short straddle on the Nikkei index is fine if there is low volatility in the Tokyo Exchange, but not when the volatility is high. A short straddle is a combination of a short call and a short put with the same exercise price. Thus, as the seller of both a call and a put on the Nikkei Index, Leeson was betting there would be little movement. In the event, the city of Kobe had a major earthquake and he had to honor the put he had sold. Leveraged long positions in the Nikkei Index ate margin cash when the index fell. Matters became much worse when Leeson doubled his long positions in the Nikkei. Many brokerage houses have stop-loss rules requiring the trader to take the losses, preventing them from growing larger. Options trading, which he also did, is inherently risky since you lose 100 percent of your investment—the option premium—when it expires out of the money.

Eighth, Leeson was, in his own words, "eager to please, eager to succeed" (ibid.). He seemed to have a big ego, anxious to be a star for Barings. He was so anxious to succeed, he falsified documents and trades to generate profits that would generate everyone, including himself, large bonuses. He told a pack of lies. It is also disingenuous to claim, as he does in *The Observer*: "The Bank of England, which a decade ago this weekend was sitting on a powder-keg with a burning fuse, was surely right not to have bailed Barings out. It was a comparatively small bank, poorly run, and an accident waiting to happen" (ibid.); although it is certainly true, as he states: "Open-outcry trading pits are virtually a thing of the past and have been largely replaced with automated systems. Many of the anomalies that existed on the trading floor in my day, often bordering on the illegal, have been removed, and that can only be advantageous in promoting fair and accessible markets for everyone" (ibid.). He is quick to note, however, that the CAOC scandal involving the same type of rogue trading and doubling of losing positions to recover losses happened again in 2005 on the SIMEX. Nick Leeson now lives in Galway, Ireland and is a motivational after-dinner speaker. In April 2005, he was appointed commercial director of Galway Football Club.

China Aviation Oil Company

A Singapore-listed company, China Aviation Oil Company (CAOC)—controlled by a Chinese state-owned enterprise—lost $550 million in 2004 from short sales of oil derivatives on SIMEX. (See www.caijing.com.cn/english/2004/041213/ 041213cover.htm, *The New York Times*, December 2, 2004; *The Wall Street Journal*, December 3, 2004 and December 6, 2004.)

Jiulin Chen, the then 43-year-old CEO, was taken into custody for investigation of Singapore's worst financial scandal in nearly a decade—since Nick Leeson took down Barings in 1995 in unauthorized trading. Chen appears to have pursued the same dogged policy of doubling up his short sales of oil futures in the hopes that oil prices would fall. For example, in April 2004, Chen decided to extend the maturity of the futures sales held by CAOC, as well as dramatically increase the size of their short position. Clearly, he and his risk management team felt that oil prices would fall. In the event, oil prices rose continuously to record highs, now over $76 a barrel.

As oil prices kept rising, the margin requirement on CAOC's futures trading also surged, draining its cash flow. On October 10, 2004 CAOC's books showed losses of $180 million, and it did not have the $80 million necessary to make the margin calls. On October 21, 2004 CAOHC (China Aviation Oil Holding Company), knowing that its Singapore affiliate was in financial distress, sold 15 percent of CAOC's shares to a few fund management companies without revealing its desperate financial condition, in violation of insider trading regulations. The parent CAOHC immediately lent the $108 million in cash from the sale to CAOC in the hope of rescuing it.

Chen's authorized trading purpose was to hedge fuel needs for Chinese aviation companies. In one example of a money-losing trade, CAOC entered into a derivative agreement on September 1, 2004 that involved 100,000 barrels of jet fuel. CAOC sold a call that the average monthly spot price for Singapore-traded jet fuel oil would not rise above $37 a barrel during October. Fuel prices rose

181

to an average price of $61.25. CAOC suffered a loss of $24.25 per barrel, or $2.4 million in total, having to honor the short call that was deep into the money.

CAOC filed for bankruptcy on November 30, 2004, citing losses of some $550 million from oil derivatives trading. Jiulin Chen and CAOC management lost money by doggedly gambling against rising oil prices, increasing the amounts of oil futures it sold. CAOC's short position increased losses from an initial $5.8 million to a staggering $550 million.

Time and again, Chen extended the maturity date of most of the short futures contracts CAOC held to 2005 and 2006, essentially doubling his position. CAOC's trading volume ballooned and oil prices kept rising. By engaging in speculative trading, Chen had violated strict prohibitions by Chinese regulators. He was accordingly jailed for fraud and the violation of security laws.

Some critics suspected that CAOC had no risk-control mechanism in place. But the mechanism did exist. The company's risk-control manuals were developed by the consulting firm Ernst & Young, and were similar to those of other international oil companies. In addition, CAOC had a seven-member risk-control committee, staffed by Singaporean employees. The company also had internal rules that any trader losing more than $200,000 must report the losses to the committee. Losses above $375,000 were to be reported also to the CEO personally. The rules also stipulated mandatory stop-loss sales of the position when they reached $500,000. "The $500,000 must refer to actual losses—all our losses were book-value losses at the time, which didn't count," Chen told *Caijing* magazine on December 7, 2004. In China, airlines were expressing concern that the rescue operation would lead to surging fuel costs, since CAOHC was the country's sole importer of aviation fuel. Chen, the center of the scandal, did not lose his confidence: "If I can get just another US$250 million, I am sure I will turn things around," he said in a mobile phone message to a *Caijing* reporter on December 9, soon after he was freed on bail. Chen also believed that the Chinese government had a responsibility to bail CAOC out, saying: "CAO represents a standard of Chinese enterprises overseas."

The Chinese State Asset Supervision and Administration Commission (SASAC) asked for foreign currency quotas for hundreds of millions of US dollars from the State Administration of Foreign Exchange (SAFE), the exchange control body. SASAC, however, changed its mind. It ruled instead that the state would not go against its own principles, which were against rescuing an insolvent company. It recommended that senior management of the company be punished. In the end, we have a Leeson-like story: unauthorized trading, doubling up of losing positions, and not informing the parent company until the subsidiary could not make its margin calls. In the case of Leeson, he doubled up bets that the Nikkei Index would rise. In the case of Chen, he doubled up bets that the oil price would fall. In both cases, they could no longer make margin calls and their firms went bankrupt.

Long Term Capital Management

Long Term Capital Management (LTCM), a hedge fund company, was founded in 1994 by John Meriwether. Nobel Laureates Myron Scholes of Stanford University and Robert Merton of Harvard University were co-principals. LTCM's reputation afforded them greater leverage than other hedge funds: they reportedly were able to leverage $4.8 billion of investor and principal money into $100 billion of positions. In the end, this leverage was to prove their worst enemy.

In 1996 and 1997, LTCM had paid its investors high yields, nearly 40 percent annually. However, during 1998, the hedge firm engaged in a variety of leveraged bets on the convergence of corporate and sovereign bond yields. Apparently, they also expected sovereign credit spreads to decrease, but once again the spreads increased. LTCM bought Russian short-term sovereign GKOs and sold Japanese bonds. The hedge fund was wrong about the direction of Japanese yields and, worse yet, Russia defaulted (see Wilmott, 2000).

On August 21, 1998 LTCM is reported to have lost $550 million. It was felt that an LTCM bankruptcy was too risky on the grounds of its "systemic" impact on US financial markets. Alan Greenspan, then Governor of the Federal Reserve System, organized a recapitalization of $3.6 billion by 12 investment banks in return for a 90 percent stake in LTCM. In the event, LTCM recovered in the subsequent years, yielding a good return on investment to the banks.

This is a different story from the previous ones, although there are some similarities. The investors were hedge fund participants risking their own and investors' monies, there was far too much leverage in hindsight, and the Russian default left many holding worthless securities.

Backdating of options grants

In a blockbuster article, "The perfect payday," *The Wall Street Journal* has exposed the extremely unlikely dating of options grants to executives at or near the lowest share price of the year. The options are then exercised at or near the high price when vested, or upon leaving the company. Consider the case of Affiliated Computer Services Inc.'s former CEO:

> It was the same through much of Mr. Rich's tenure: In a striking pattern, all six of his stock-option grants from 1995 to 2002 were dated just before a rise in the stock price, often at the bottom of a steep drop . . . Just lucky? A Wall Street Journal analysis suggests the odds of this happening by chance are extraordinarily remote—around one in 300 billion . . . The Securities and Exchange Commission is examining whether some option grants carry favorable grant dates for a different reason: They were backdated.
>
> (Forelle and Bander, 2006)

183

How can this be? Let's say Mr Back Dater, CEO of XYZ Corp., is awarded one million call option grants on July 5, 2005 when the share price is $50 at 4:00 p.m. of that or the previous day. They vest or can be exercised in one year. On July 5, 2006 Mr Back Dater is eligible to buy at $50 and sell, say, at $60, the share price that day, earning $10 million. Fair enough. However, in cahoots with the compensation committee or some board members, the options are back-dated to May 5, 2005, when the stock was at its low point, $20 a share. Bingo, he has hit the jackpot: $40 million in the exercise of the options. Where does the extra $30 million come from? From the shareholders, of course.

The WSJ reports other possible malfeasance:

> On Oct. 13, 1999, William W. McGuire, CEO of giant insurer UnitedHealth Group Inc., got an enormous grant in three parts that . . . came to 14.6 million options. So far, he has exercised about 5% of them, for a profit of about $39 million. As of late February (2006) he had 13.87 million unexercised options left from the October 1999 tranche. His profit on those, if he exercised them today, would be about $717 million more. The 1999 grant was dated the very day UnitedHealth stock hit its low for the year . . . At Mercury Interactive Corp., a Mountain View, Calif., software maker, the chief executive and two others resigned late last year. Mercury said an internal probe found 49 cases where the reported date of options grants differed from the date when the options appeared to have been awarded. The company said it will have to restate financial results . . . Another company, Comverse Technology Inc., said . . . that its board had started a review of its past stock-option practices, including "the accuracy of the stated dates of options grants." Shares of Vitesse Semiconductor Corp. . . . now rest at about the level of a decade ago. But Louis R. Tomasetta, chief executive of the Camarillo, Calif., chip maker, reaped tens of millions of dollars from stock options. In eight of Mr. Tomasetta's nine option grants from 1994 to 2001, the grants were dated just before double-digit price surges in the next 20 trading days. The odds of such a pattern occurring by chance are about one in 26 billion.
>
> (Ibid.)

Following the WSJ story, there have been waves of resignations of top executives, some cashing out to boot, as well as a wave of new SEC investigations into possible backdating.

There are several obvious problems with the backdating of options: first, it is illegal to forge or backdate options grants; second, the shareholders are usually not informed; third, it mocks the supposed link of options grants to the incentives of executives to raise the profitability of the firm; and, finally, it steals wealth from shareholders. While the practice also violates Sarbanes-Oxley's prompt disclosure rules, many corporate executives in the United States are apparently doing so with impunity, so far.

184

LESSONS LEARNED

Many of the financial mishaps and schemes reviewed here resulted from underestimating the risks of leverage. Borrowing to sell short can trigger margin calls as the asset rises in price. Stop losses rather than rolling over losing positions by doubling up are recommended by most internal risk management procedures. When there is too much leverage, a small move in the price of the asset in the wrong direction can initiate large losses and margin calls. That seems to be the lesson to be learnt from Barings, LTCM, and CAOC.

Illegal insider trading, falsification of earnings to ensure gains in options and bonuses, moving losing positions off balance sheets, and other conscious corporate frauds that apparently took place at Enron and WorldCom would seem to merit greater punishments, in addition to the restoration of investor funds and worker pensions. Poor governance and the failure of checks and balances within the firm bring with them the risk of bankruptcy.

Backdating of options grants is outright fraud—direct theft from the shareholders—and should be prosecuted. Retention bonuses seem to be the last refuge of corporate scoundrels. They often seem to fund a year of job-seeking in a troubled company. Debt forgiveness on personal loans to executives is also a bad practice. It is now prohibited since loans to executives are forbidden by SOX.

CONCLUSION

Adam Smith was right in 1776. Managers will usually put their own interest ahead of the interest of the shareholders. The so-called efforts to align the interest of the managers with those of the owners through stock options and grants, bonuses, and other "incentive pay" linked to reported earnings have reaped a harvest of falsified earnings and backdated options grants. Poorly performing firms are rewarding their CEOs at record levels. Indeed, there seems to be little or no relationship between performance and executive reward. Shareholders are not informed of executive compensation, nor are they consulted, as they would surely balk. The Cox ruling attempts to remedy this, but it is unclear what shareholders can do about the issue. Accountants will say what they are told to say in many circumstances, though SOX will punish them severely if they are caught. SOX attempts to eliminate some of the conflicts of interest in auditing firms. There is an ethical crisis in management. At the same time, there will always be pyramid schemes that attract those seeking high short-term gains. Leverage always compounds the risk, and margin calls can rise rapidly when a bad leveraged bet is doubled up. It is difficult to foresee much change, despite the heavy penalties that are now being meted out. There are other scandals about to happen—those involving the backdating of options grants to executives are now unfolding.

REFERENCES AND FURTHER READING

Behr, Peter and April Witt (2002) "Concerns grow amid conflicts—officials seek to limit probe—fallout of deals," *Washington Post*, July 30: A01.

Brown, Stephen J. and O. W. Steenbeek (2001) "Doubling: Nick Leeson's trading strategy," *Pacific-Basin Finance Journal* 9(2): 83–99.

Forelle, Charles and James Bander (2006) "The perfect payday: some CEOs reap millions by landing stock options when they are most valuable. Luck—or something else?," *The Wall Street Journal*, March 18.

Hao, Quing (2004) "Laddering in initial public offerings," Working paper, University of Florida, Gainesville.

Hoffman, William (2003) "Timely disclosure at center of AA flap," *Dallas Business Journal*, April 25.

Jarvis, Christopher (2000) "The rise and fall of Albania's pyramid schemes," *Finance and Development* 37(1): 46–9.

Jorion, Philippe (1995) *Big bets gone bad: derivatives and bankruptcy in Orange county*, San Diego, CA: Academic Press.

Kindleberger, Charles (1989) *Manias, panics and crashes: a history of financial crises*, 2nd edn, New York: Basic Books: 86–87.

Labaton, Stephen (2006) "S.E.C. to tighten reporting rules for executive pay," *The New York Times*, January 18: C2.

Leeson, Nick (1996) *Rogue trader*, London: Little, Brown & Co.

Leeson, Nick (2005) "Bank breaker," *The Observer*, February 20.

Morgenstern, Gretchen (2006) "Gee, bankruptcy never looked so good," *The New York Times*, January 15, Section 3: 3 and 4.

Nimalendran, M., Jay Ritter, and Donghang Zhang (2004) "Are trading commissions a factor in IPO allocation?," Working paper, University of Florida, Gainesville.

Niskanen, W. (ed.) (2005) *After Enron: lessons for public policy*, Lanham, MD: Rowman and Littlefield.

O'Hara, Philip (2001) "Insider trading in financial markets: liquidity, ethics, efficiency," *International Journal of Social Economics* 28(10–12): 1046–62.

Prud'homme, Alex (2004) *The cell game: Sam Waksal's fast money and false promises—and the fate of ImClone's cancer drug*, New York: Harper Business.

Prystay, Chris (2005a) "Five are charged in case involving CAO Singapore," *The Wall Street Journal*, June 10: A6.

Prystay, Chris (2005b) "Singapore Exchange to bolster listing rules," *The Wall Street Journal*, May 31.

Searsey, Dionne and Li Yuan (2005) "Adelphia's John Rigas gets 15 years," *The Wall Street Journal*, June 21: A3.

Tabasso, Gianfranco (2004) "A modern replica of Ponzi finace: the painful lessons of the Parmalat affair," *Treasury Management International* 126: 21–5.

Tapper, Jake (2002) "Enron's last-minute bonus orgy," www.salon.com/politics/feature/2002/02/08/enron_bonuses.

Western, David (2004) *Booms, bubbles, and busts in the US stock market*, London and New York: Routledge.

Wilmott, Paul (2000) *Paul Wilmott on quantitative finance*, New York: John Wiley and Sons.

Witt, April and Peter Behr (2002) "Losses, conflicts threaten survival—CFO Fastow ousted in probe of profits," *Washington Post*, July 31: A01.

www.caijing.com.cn.

www.erisk.com (2004) "Barings case study," www.erisk.com/Learning/CaseStudies/ref_case_barings.asp, February.

www.riskglossary.com (1996) "Nick Leeson and Barings Bank."

www.wikipedia.org.

Zuckoff, Mitchell (2005) "Ponzi's scheme: the true story of a financial legend," New York: Random House.

Solutions to problems

CHAPTER 3

3.1 The time value of money

a   The net present value (NPV) of and internal rate of return (IRR) on the flow of payments and receipts in pounds is given by using the = NPV (values:rate) less initial cost and = IRR (values:guess) formulas in Excel:

Net present value and internal rate of return

Interest rate	10%
Initial investment	−£100
Year 1 income	£50
Year 2 income	£50
Year 3 income	£50
Net present value (NPV)	£24.34
Internal rate of return (IRR)	23.4%

Alternatively, the NPV and return on investment (ROI) can be calculated manually from the formulas:

$$NPV = -100 + \frac{50}{1.1} + \frac{50}{(1.1)^2} + \frac{50}{(1.1)^3},$$

and

$$100 = \frac{50}{1+R} + \frac{50}{(1+R)^2} + \frac{50}{(1+R)^3}.$$

b   If you were to sell this investment at 1.76 dollars per pound, it would be worth £24.34 × 1.76 = $42.84.

3.2 The equilibrium exchange rate

a Setting the quantity supplied equal to the quantity demanded in the foreign exchange market and solving for S yields an equilibrium exchange rate of 20 pesos per dollar. That is:

$90 - 2S = -10 + 3S$ yields $5S = 100$

or

$$S = \frac{100}{5} = 20$$

b If the central bank maintained a fixed exchange rate of 15 pesos per dollar, there would be an excess demand for dollars equal to $25. That is:

$Q_D - Q_S = 90 - 2(15) + 10 - 3(15) = 100 - 75 = 25.$

c If the central bank had only $15 million left in foreign reserves, it could devalue to 20 to reach equilibrium without selling reserves, or partially devalue and sell some reserves. It could borrow additional reserves and sell them on the exchange market. To maintain its reserves for a rainy day, it could float the currency, letting supply and demand equilibrate at 20. The imposition of exchange controls would only create a parallel market—an implicitly floating exchange rate.

d If the central bank instead wanted to add $10 million to its holdings of foreign reserves, it could depreciate the exchange rate to 22 pesos per dollar. Adding 10 to the demand curve, solve for S by setting supply equal to demand. That is:

$100 - 2S = -10 + 3S$ yields $5S = 110$

or

$$S = \frac{100}{5} = 22.$$

3.3 Intervention in the foreign exchange market

a With a floating exchange rate, the equilibrium rate is determined by the supply equals demand equilibrium. Looking at Figure 3.28 (p. 80), the equilibrium exchange rate would be 1.2 pesos per dollar.

b To maintain a one-to-one exchange rate the central bank must supply an additional $10 million to the foreign exchange market, just enough to satisfy total demand at that price. Essentially, the central bank adds horizontally $10 million to the supply curve, shifting total supply to the right by that amount.

c The sale of dollars by the central bank to the foreign exchange market reduces the money supply held by commercial banks and the public. As the money market in Argentina becomes less liquid, interest rates in pesos rise and the rate of inflation falls. This reduces the demand for dollars and simultaneously increases their supply in the foreign exchange market. The graphic illustrates the flows of funds from foreign exchange market purchases and sales of foreign exchange.

189

3.4 The bid–ask spread (I)

a   The bid–ask spreads are indicated in the table below. Recall the rule that 1/bid in one quotation equals the ask in the other. Similarly, 1/ask in one quotation equals the bid in the other:

Quotations	European (£/$)		American ($/£)	
	Bid	Ask	Bid	Ask
Spot	0.5658	0.5660	1.7669	1.7675
Spread	0.0002		0.0006	
Mid-point	0.5659		1.7672	

b   The spreads are simply the difference between the ask and the bid.
c   The mid-point equals the sum of the bid and the ask divided by two.
d   In both cases, the bid–ask spread as a percent of the mid-point is 0.03395, or about 3 percent.

3.5 The bid–ask spread (II)

a   Recalling the rule that 1/bid in one quotation equals the ask in the other and 1/ask in one quotation equals the bid in the other, we have the results shown below:

Quotations	European (£/$)		American ($/£)	
Blank	Bid	Ask	Bid	Ask
Spot	0.5658	0.5660	1.7668	1.7675
Spread	0.0002		0.0007	
Mid-point	0.5659		1.7671	
Spread/ Mid-point (%)	0.00040492		0.00040492	

b   The bid–ask spread is 0.0002 in pounds and 0.0007 in dollars.
c   The mid-points are 0.5659 pounds per dollar and 1.7671 dollars per pound respectively.
d   The bid–ask spread is 0.04 percent in terms of each quotation.

3.6 Points quotations

Since the points quotation is lower than the offer, add 0.0214 to the one-month spot outright bid and 0.0220 to the outright offer. Similarly, add the points of the two and three months divided by 10,000 to obtain the two- and three-month forward outright quotations in American terms.

Quotations ($/£)	Bid	Ask
Spot	1.7669	1.7675
Points	Bid	Ask
1 month	214	220
2 months	283	298
3 months	388	416

Quotations	Bid	Ask
1 month	1.7883	1.7889
2 months	1.7952	1.7967
3 months	1.8057	1.8085

3.7 Interest rate parity

a By inspection, the forward premium on the pound is 2 percent, while US T-bills are 1 percent higher than UK T-bills at point Z. Consequently, the gain on forward cover in selling the pound will more than offset the loss on investing in UK T-bills.

b Ignoring transactions costs, the steps taken in this riskless arbitrage opportunity are:

1 Sell US T-bills (R_{us} rises).
2 Buy pounds spot (sell dollars spot) (S rises).
3 Buy US T-bills (R_{uk} falls).
4 Sell pounds forward (buy dollars forward) (F falls).

The net gain for the individual arbitrageur would be 1 percent, a 2 percent gain on forward cover and a 1 percent loss on the interest rate differential. As a result of

191

many arbitrageurs taking advantage of this profit opportunity, $F/S - 1$, the premium on the pound falls, and $R_{us} - R_{uk}$ the interest rate difference in favor of US T-bills rises.

3.8 Purchasing power parity

a The absolute version of PPP predicts that the exchange rate will reflect the different costs of purchasing the same bundle of goods (the inverse of the absolute purchasing power of each currency in terms of goods). Consequently, the PPP rates are indicated in the table:

	Cost of basket	PPP rates
United States	$60	1.666667 dollars per pound
England	£36	0.6 pounds per dollar
Mexico	N$540	9 pesos per dollar

b No, because the market exchange rates do not accurately predict the true purchasing powers of different currencies. Those countries that are relatively cheap with regard to labor-intensive goods such as haircuts, a non-traded good, will find that the equilibrium rate does not fully reflect the purchasing power of the currency. There is little arbitrage in non-traded goods such as haircuts.

c Therefore, it is not a surprise to find that the PPP prediction for the pound is fairly accurate, but the equilibrium rate of 11 pesos per dollar "overvalues" the dollar in terms of the PPP rate of 9 pesos per dollar.

d Taking the current equilibrium rates as given, the PPP predictions are:

Currency	Initial equilibrium rates	Relative PPP	PPP forecast
Pounds per $	0.566	1.5	0.849
Pesos per $	11	1.5	16.5

Essentially, take the initial equilibrium rates as the base rates for the forecast, then multiply by 3/2, the expected inflation differential relative to the United States. While the absolute PPP forecast may be significantly off, the relative PPP is still the best forecast of the movement in future exchange rates. It is embodied in the nominal interest rate on risk-free T-bills, which do not exist in Mexico due to previous default. For this reason, the relative PPP forecast may be the most accurate.

e   Mexico and England are both net oil exporters, while the United States is a net oil importer. A rise in the price of oil would appreciate the pound and the peso relative to the PPP forecast. It would cause a real appreciation of the pound and the peso. However, a rise in the price of wheat would be likely to cause a real appreciation of the dollar.

CHAPTER 4

4.1 Hedging (I)

a   "I never hedge, since it reduces my bottom line!"

This CFO has reckoned the costs of hedging foreign exchange risk against the benefits, and concluded that the costs exceed the benefits. This is likely to be a firm that does not face significant losses due to being exposed to foreign exchange risk in operations and contracts. This firm has a low probability of bankruptcy costs. As a result, it does not perceive any benefits in lowered borrowing costs due to risks of financial distress from foreign exchange losses. The cost of the hedges clearly outweighs the benefits in lowered risk of financial distress. Put simply, the foreign exchange exposure of this firm may be minimal.

b   "I always hedge, since I cannot take the risk of exchange rate losses bankrupting my firm."

This firm is likely to have significant foreign exchange exposure, so that its value at risk from unanticipated changes in the exchange rate is high. Higher earnings in foreign exchange must be volatile and/or the exchange rate volatile. The high risk of financial distress from going unhedged would significantly increase its borrowing costs. Investing in the hedges provides the benefit of significantly lowering the chances of financial distress and bankruptcy costs. In this situation, the CFO chooses to hedge. This may even increase the net present value of the firm due to lowered borrowing costs. Put simply the foreign exchange exposure of this firm is large.

4.2 Default risk

a   The Brady Bond's yield to maturity (that is, its IRR), R, is solved for by:

$$\$80 = \frac{\$100}{1 + R} \quad \text{or} \quad R = \frac{\$100}{\$80} - 1 = 0.25 = 25\%.$$

b Its risk premium, ρ, is approximately 25–5 percent, or 20 percent. More precisely, it is solved by:

$$(1.05)(1 + \rho) = 1.25 \quad \text{or} \quad \rho = \frac{1.25}{1.05} - 1 = 19.05\%.$$

4.3 Stock options as executive compensation

a Your options expire today out of the money. You would never buy at £80 when the spot price is £50. Consequently, your total annual compensation is £12,000.
b Zero percent of your compensation was in the form of stock options since they are out of the money.
c Your options are now in the money—profitable if exercised. Since you buy at £80 and sell at £100 you make £20 in profits on each share. Buying 1,000 shares at £80 and selling them at £100 earns you £20,000 today. Your total compensation is thus £32,000.
d Consequently the percent of your total compensation in the form of stock options is:

$$\frac{20,000}{32,000} - 1 = 62.5\%.$$

4.4 Foreign exchange options

a She made two cents per option upon exercise, but paid one cent for each one. Her profit per option was one penny. She thus made only one dollar in net profits.
b (i) The put was in the money—the buyer bought at $1.20 and sold at $1.25, making five cents per option.
  (ii) Tomas lost 4.5 cents per option or $40.50 in total. His gain from the sale of the option of half a cent was outweighed by losses of five cents per option.
  (iii) Yes, the writer or seller of the option is contractually obligated to honor the option if it is presented for exercise. If it expires out of the money, the writer keeps the premium.

4.5 Hedging (II)

a This is an example of transactions exposure.
  (i) Martha might sell £100,000 for delivery in 90 days. She would lock in the bid price of the pound now, $1.78, for settlement in 90 days. This would be a forward market hedge.

(ii) She might purchase a put option to sell pounds sterling at a strike price of $1.78 and a cost per option of $0.0028 per £, or $280 for a notional amount of £100,000. This would be an options hedge.

(iii) She might borrow £100/1.02 = £98.04 thousand today for three months, and sell the pounds spot, having no further pound exposure. With the proceeds from accounts receivable, she would pay the principal, £98.04, and interest, £1.96, in pounds, exactly equaling her expected receipts in pounds. This would be a money market hedge.

b British Baking can similarly buy dollars forward, purchase an option to buy dollars at a strike price, or make today a money market loan in USD that matures in 90 days with principal and interest of $178,000.

4.6 Balance sheet hedging

a The translation of these assets into US dollars on the consolidated balance sheet of the US parent firm would have a favorable effect on this portion of the balance sheet:

Assets	Original value	New value
€200	$200	$240
(thousands)		

b Some alternative balance sheet hedges would be:

(i) Acquire short-term debt, an equal liability, of 200 thousand euros.

(ii) Sell the 200 thousand euros spot (i.e. buy dollars spot), thus removing the exposure from the balance sheet.

(iii) Acquire accounts payable of 200 thousand euros.

4.7 Operating exposure (I)

a As a French company, I am exposed to operating exposure next year. If the dollar falls below 0.8 euros, I will lose, while if it rises above 0.8 euros I gain. My exposure equals $10 × 110 = $1,100.

b Operating exposure can be hedged in a number of ways: some involve financing; others involve operations. First, I can borrow in dollars so that my revenues from the sale of widgets in dollars are offset by payments of interest and principal on a matching basis. If my comparative advantage is borrowing in euros, I could do so then swap the euro loan for a dollar loan. These would be financial hedges. In terms of operations, I could move production from France to the United States, thereby acquiring a "natural hedge" involving payroll, rent, and other expenses in US dollars. These are just two techniques for hedging my operating exposure. A risk-sharing currency contingency clause or invoicing in euros would also be techniques for managing exchange rate exposure. All these techniques of hedging involve some costs.

195

4.8 Operating exposure (II)

a If the exchange rate unexpectedly changes to $0.25 per peso, "operating losses" due to not hedging would equal 25 cents per peso, or $2,500.

b Since this is ongoing operating exposure, Tiny Tots could seek a loan in pesos and use the earnings from accounts receivables in pesos to service the loan. Any loss on the peso would be offset by an equal gain on its peso loan. To obtain the loan on favorable terms, Tiny Tots could borrow in USD, its currency of comparative advantage, then swap the USD loan for an Argentine peso loan. Indirect financing could also be done by back-to-back parallel loans, whereby Tiny Tots makes a dollar loan to an Argentine subsidiary in the United States, and Argentine headquarters makes a similar loan to Tiny Tots in pesos. Relocating production to Argentina would also give Tiny Tots a "natural hedge,"—matching expenditures in pesos.

c If Tiny Tots relocates production to Argentina and expects second-quarter costs of production and distribution to be 5,000 pesos, the net exposure would only be 5,000 pesos. Only that amount would need to be hedged to be "perfectly" hedged.

d Theoretically, profitability could go either way. The costs of the hedges might be offset by lowered borrowing costs. In this case the NPV of Tiny Tots would rise. The more likely case is that the cost of the hedges would reduce the NPV of the firm.

4.9 Accounting exposure

a Headquarters gains because euro denominated assets are 400, while liabilities are 300. There is a net 100 long position in euros on the balance sheet.

b The gains of $0.10 \times 100 = \$10$ would be added to the cumulative translation adjustment line in the balance sheet.

c Some alternative ways of acquiring a perfect balance sheet hedge would be to pay off 100 euros of accounts payable or debt in advance, sell the 100 euros in cash for dollars, or increase short-term debt in euros by 100.

CHAPTER 5

5.1 The international weighted average cost of capital

a The weighted average cost of capital (WACC) in euros would be, using the European marginal income tax rate of 45 percent:

$$WACC = 0.3[10(1 - 0.45)] + 0.7(15) = 12.15\% \text{ in euros.}$$

If IBM is able to apply the higher tax as credits against other income, it would imply an effective marginal income tax rate of 35 percent. In this case, the WACC in euros would be:

$$WACC = 0.3[10(1 - 0.35)] + 0.7(15) = 12.45\% \text{ in euros.}$$

b In terms of USD, the weighted average cost of capital would be:

$$1.1215\left(\frac{1.03}{1.02}\right) - 1 = 0.1325 = 13.25\% \text{ in USD,}$$

using the European marginal income tax rate; or

$$1.1245\left(\frac{1.03}{1.02}\right) - 1 = 0.13552 = 13.552\% \text{ in USD,}$$

using the US marginal income tax rate.

5.2 Transfer pricing

a The profit-maximizing level of sales is 100, since the marginal cost of the bundled product equals its marginal revenue at that level of output.
b The firm will charge the final customer $7.00 per unit, found by the demand for that quantity of output (its average revenue).
c To guarantee that the production unit provides exactly the optimum amount to the marketing division, the latter will pay the production unit a transfer price of $3.00. The production unit in turn maximizes its profits by setting marginal production cost equal to the fixed transfer price.

5.3 Foreign currency conversion of free-cash flows

a The WACC in pounds sterling is indicated below as 13.9 percent:

US and UK data (percent per annum)

US inflation rate	3
UK inflation rate	2
US Treasury	5
UK Treasury	4
$WACC_{us}$	15
$WACC_{uk}$	13.9

which is solved for either by using PPP or IRP, that is:

$$WACC_£ = (1.15)\left(\frac{1.02}{1.03}\right) - 1 = 0.139 = 13.9\%,$$

or

$$WACC_£ = (1.15)\left(\frac{1.03}{1.04}\right) - 1 = 0.139 = 13.9\%.$$

b The NPV in USD differs only by rounding down by both methods:

Method A

Discount foreign currency flows to the present at the foreign currency discount rate, then convert the NPV in FOREX to home currency at the spot rate:

Year	0	1	2
Free-cash flows (£)	−100	60	70
Present value of cash flow (£)	−100	52.68	53.96
NPV (£)	6.64		
Spot exchange rate ($/£)	1.77		
NPV ($)	11.74		

Method B

Convert foreign currency cash flows to home currency, and discount to the present at the home currency discount rate:

Year	0	1	2
Free-cash flows (£)	−100	60	70
Exchange rate forecast	1.77	1.787	1.8042
Free-cash flows ($)	−177	107.22	126.29
Present value of cash flow ($)	−177	93.24	95.50
NPV ($)	11.73		

5.4 Trade finance (I)

Your shipment of 100 computers worth $2,000 each amounts to $200,000 in export revenues. Here are some of the international means of payment and who bears the counterparty risk:

a Cash in advance guarantees the exporter of payment, but does not guarantee the importer of shipment. The importer bears the counterpary risk.

b An open account into which the importer pays upon delivery of the shipment puts the counterparty risk on the exporter. The exporter could ship coincidentally with the payment, the bank invoicing the importer, receiving the funds at the same time the exporter delivers the bill of lading to the bank.

c   A documentary L/C is a guaranteed means of payment for goods, which, when confirmed, substitutes the bank's credit for that of the importer. The bank bears the counterparty risk. In return, it collects fees for issuing the L/C.

5.5 Trade finance (II)

a   CitiBank, Nassau has issued an irrevocable standby L/C confirming payment to you for the sum of $1,000,000 US payable to you monthly for one year beginning in 30 days. If you need Bahamian dollars today, you can sell (discount) the L/C today since it is confirmed and irrevocable. The L/C is a negotiable instrument.

b   The L/C is virtually riskless, so you might use the Bahamian Treasury rate of 6 percent per annum, representing nearly half a percent per month (0.486755 per cent per month). The discounted value of the L/C would therefore be worth 11,628,800 Bahamian dollars at a compound monthly rate of 0.49 percent and 11,618,932 at a simple monthly rate of 0.5 percent.

Month	1	2	3	4	5	6
L/C payment	1,000,000	1,000,000	1,000,000	1,000,000	1,000,000	1,000,000
PV at 0.487%	995,156	990,336	985,538	980,764	976,014	971,286
Month	7	8	9	10	11	12
L/C payment	1,000,000	1,000,000	1,000,000	1,000,000	1,000,000	1,000,000
PV at 0.487%	966,581	961,899	957,239	952,603	947,988	943,396
Sum of PV	11,628,800					

Month	1	2	3	4	5	6
L/C payment	1,000,000	1,000,000	1,000,000	1,000,000	1,000,000	1,000,000
PV at 0.5%	995,025	990,075	985,149	980,248	975,371	970,518
Month	7	8	9	10	11	12
L/C payment	1,000,000	1,000,000	1,000,000	1,000,000	1,000,000	1,000,000
PV at 0.5%	965,690	960,885	956,105	951,348	946,615	941,905
Sum of PV	11,618,932					

5.6 International taxation (I)

a   In the first case, repatriation of earnings gets the firm a tax credit of 12.5 percent, but 22.5 percent is added to make the effective corporate tax rate on Texas headquarters of 35 percent. Thus we have $65 in net income:

Irish branch

Irish income	$100
Irish taxes paid	$12.5
US taxes	$22.5
Net income	$65

b   In the second case, the earnings are not repatriated but instead reinvested in Ireland. Consequently, the firm has $87.5 in net earnings, or:

Irish branch

Irish income	$100
Irish taxes paid	$12.5
US taxes	0
Net income	$87.5

5.7 International taxation (II)

a   The portion of foreign trade income exempt from taxes is 34 percent, meaning taxable income from the FSC in the Bahamas is $66. Applying a corporate income tax rate of 35 percent to taxable income yields taxes of $23.10, leaving $76.9 as net income under arm's length pricing:

Foreign sales corporation (arm's length pricing)

Foreign trade income	$100
Bahamian taxes paid	0
US taxes	23.1
Net income	76.9

b   In the second case of an FSC set up according to special administrative rules exempting 17/23 of foreign income taxation, the result would be:

Foreign sales corporation (special administrative rules)

Foreign trade income	$100
Bahamian taxes paid	$0
US taxes	9.13
Net income	90.87

since only $26.08 is taxable at the 35 percent rate.

200

5.8 Mergers and acquisitions

a By inspection, the value of Firm A is $20 and of Firm B is $10.
b If the value of the consolidated firm is $40, "synergy" is $10 since the separate firms only have a combined value of $30.
c If Firm A offers cash of $15 a share to the owners of Firm B, they are offering a "premium" of 50 percent, that is, a premium of $5 per share.
d It is likely that two-thirds of the shareholders will accept the premium, unless management of Firm B activate an extremely effective poison pill defense. The basic idea of a poison pill is to make a hostile takeover less attractive, by diluting the value of the shares of the takeover firm.
e Using the formula $a = 15/40$, and solving:

$$n_w = \frac{an}{(1-a)} = \frac{\frac{15}{40}(20)}{\left(1 - \frac{15}{40}\right)} = 12 \text{ Shares.}$$

f If Firm A offered $10 in cash and the rest in shares, it would have to offer:

$$n_w = \frac{an}{(1-a)} = \frac{\frac{5}{30}(20)}{\left(1 - \frac{5}{30}\right)} = 4 \text{ Shares.}$$

This is because, after the $10 cash offer, Firm A would be worth $30 and the new shares would have to be 5/30 of the new firm's value.

5.9 An international business plan

At a 10 percent cost of borrowing in euros, this investment would have a negative net present value. It should not be undertaken.

Year	0	1	2	3	4	5
Free-cash flows (€)	(50)	10	10.5	11	11.6	12.2
Present value (€)	(50)	9.1	8.7	8.3	7.9	7.5
NPV (€)	(8.5)					
Spot exchange rate (£/€)	0.71					
NPV (£)	−6					

5.10 Offshore banking

a   If fees are about 4 percent, Citybank would stand to earn annually about $40,00, hardly worth the money laundering.

b   Yes, the cash deposit is over $40,000 so would have to be reported to the US Treasury.

c   The transfer would also constitute money laundering and thus be in violation of anti-money laundering laws and conventions. The fees are certainly not worth the reputational risk.

5.11 Optimal portfolio analysis

a   The coefficient of risk aversion is 4, since $A/2 = 2$, $A = 4$.

b   The optimal fraction of the complete portfolio held in the form of risky assets is given by:

$$z = \frac{E(r_p) - r_f}{A\sigma_p^2} = \frac{0.15 - 0.05}{4(0.1)} = \frac{0.1}{0.4} = 25\%.$$

Consequently, 75 percent is held in the risk-free asset.

c   The expected rate of return on the complete portfolio is given by:

$$E(r_C) = 0.05 + 0.25(0.15 - 0.05) = 0.075 = 7.5\%.$$

d   The variance of the complete portfolio is:

$$\sigma_p^2 = z^2\sigma_p^2 = (0.25)^2).1 = 0.00625.$$

e   The level of utility of this investor is indicated by:

$$U = E(r_C) - 2\sigma_C^2 = 0.0725 - 2(0.0065) = 0.0595.$$

5.12 Optimal investment analysis

a   The expected rate of return on the complete portfolio is a weighted average of returns on the risky and the risk-free assets:

$$E(r_C) = 0.5(0.20) + 0.5(0.05) = 0.125 = 12.5\%.$$

b   The variance of the complete portfolio is:

$$(0.5)^2 \, 0.4 = 0.1 = 10\%.$$

202

c   The standard deviation or volatility of the complete portfolio is the square root of its variance, or:

$$\sqrt{0.10} = 0.3162,$$

or about 32%.

Index

Page references in *italic* indicate figures and tables.

204